The Ethics of Multiple Citizenship

Citizenship is no longer an exclusive relationship. Many people today are citizens of multiple countries, whether by birth, naturalization, or even through monetary means, with schemes fast-tracking citizenship applications from foreigners making large investments in the state. Moral problems surround each of those ways of acquiring a second citizenship, while retaining one's original citizenship. Multiple citizenship can also have morally problematic consequences for the coherence of collective decisions, for the constitution of the demos, and for global inequality. The phenomenon of multiple citizenship and its ramifications remains understudied, despite its magnitude and political importance. In this innovative book, Ana Tanasoca explores these issues and shows how they could be avoided by unbundling the rights that currently come with citizenship and allocating them separately. It will appeal to scholars and students of normative political theory, citizenship, global justice, and migration in political science, law, and sociology.

ANA TANASOCA is a postdoctoral research fellow at the Centre for Deliberative Democracy and Global Governance, University of Canberra. Broadly interested in analytic normative political theory, her principal current research project explores the moral and epistemic dimensions of deliberation. Her work has been published in the *European Journal of Sociology*, the *Australasian Journal of Philosophy*, and *Moral Philosophy and Politics*.

Contemporary Political Theory

Series Editor

Ian Shapiro

Editorial Board

Russell Hardin†   Stephen Holmes   Jeffrey Isaac

John Keane   Elizabeth Kiss   Susan Okin†

Phillipe Van Parijs   Philip Pettit

As the twenty-first century begins, major new political challenges have arisen at the same time as some of the most enduring dilemmas of political association remain unresolved. The collapse of communism and the end of the Cold War reflect a victory for democratic and liberal values, yet in many of the Western countries that nurtured those values there are severe problems of urban decay, class and racial conflict, and failing political legitimacy. Enduring global injustice and inequality seem compounded by environmental problems, disease, the oppression of women and racial, ethnic, and religious minorities and the relentless growth of the world's population. In such circumstances, the need for creative thinking about the fundamentals of human political association is manifest. This new series in contemporary political theory is needed to foster such systematic normative reflection.

The series proceeds in the belief that the time is ripe for a reassertion of the importance of problem-driven political theory. It is concerned, that is, with works that are motivated by the impulse to understand, think critically about, and address the problems in the world, rather than issues that are thrown up primarily in academic debate. Books in the series may be interdisciplinary in character, ranging over issues conventionally dealt with in philosophy, law, history, and the human sciences. The range of materials and the methods of proceeding should be dictated by the problem at hand, not the conventional debates or disciplinary divisions of academia.

Other books in the series

Ian Shapiro and Casiano Hacker-Cordón (eds.)
Democracy's Value

Ian Shapiro and Casiano Hacker-Cordón (eds.)
Democracy's Edges

Brooke A. Ackerly
Political Theory and Feminist Social Criticism

Clarissa Rile Hayward
De-Facing Power

John Kane
The Politics of Moral Capital

Ayelet Shachar
Multicultural Jurisdictions

John Keane
Global Civil Society?

Rogers M. Smith
Stories of Peoplehood

Gerry Mackie
Democracy Defended

John Keane
Violence and Democracy

Kok-Chor Tan
Justice without Borders

Peter J. Steinberger
The Idea of the State

Michael Taylor
Rationality and the Ideology of Disconnection

Sarah Song
Justice, Gender, and the Politics of Multiculturalism

Georgia Warnke
After Identity

Courtney Jung
The Moral Force of Indigenous Politics

Sonu Bedi
Rejecting Rights

Richard Vernon
Cosmopolitan Regard

Lawrence Hamilton
Freedom is Power

Jonathan Floyd
Is Political Philosophy Impossible?

The Ethics of Multiple Citizenship

Ana Tanasoca
University of Canberra

CAMBRIDGE
UNIVERSITY PRESS

University Printing House, Cambridge CB2 8BS, United Kingdom

One Liberty Plaza, 20th Floor, New York, NY 10006, USA

477 Williamstown Road, Port Melbourne, VIC 3207, Australia

314–321, 3rd Floor, Plot 3, Splendor Forum, Jasola District Centre,
New Delhi – 110025, India

79 Anson Road, #06–04/06, Singapore 079906

Cambridge University Press is part of the University of Cambridge.

It furthers the University's mission by disseminating knowledge in the pursuit of education, learning, and research at the highest international levels of excellence.

www.cambridge.org
Information on this title: www.cambridge.org/9781108429153
DOI: 10.1017/9781108554176

© Ana Tanasoca 2018

This publication is in copyright. Subject to statutory exception
and to the provisions of relevant collective licensing agreements,
no reproduction of any part may take place without the written
permission of Cambridge University Press.

First published 2018

Printed and bound in Great Britain by Clays Ltd, Elcograf S.p.A.

A catalogue record for this publication is available from the British Library.

Library of Congress Cataloging-in-Publication Data
Names: Tanasoca, Ana, 1986- author.
Title: The ethics of multiple citizenship / Ana Tanasoca.
Description: Cambridge [UK] ; New York, NY : Cambridge University Press, 2018. | Series: Contemporary political theory | Originally presented as the author's thesis (doctoral)–University of Essex, 2015. | Includes bibliographical references and index.
Identifiers: LCCN 2018009352 | ISBN 9781108429153 (hardback)
Subjects: LCSH: Dual nationality. | Citizenship. | Conflict of laws–Citizenship.
Classification: LCC K7128.D8 T36 2018 | DDC 172/.1–dc23
LC record available at https://lccn.loc.gov/2018009352

ISBN 978-1-108-42915-3 Hardback

Cambridge University Press has no responsibility for the persistence or accuracy of URLs for external or third-party internet websites referred to in this publication and does not guarantee that any content on such websites is, or will remain, accurate or appropriate.

To my parents, Doina and Sandu Tanasoca

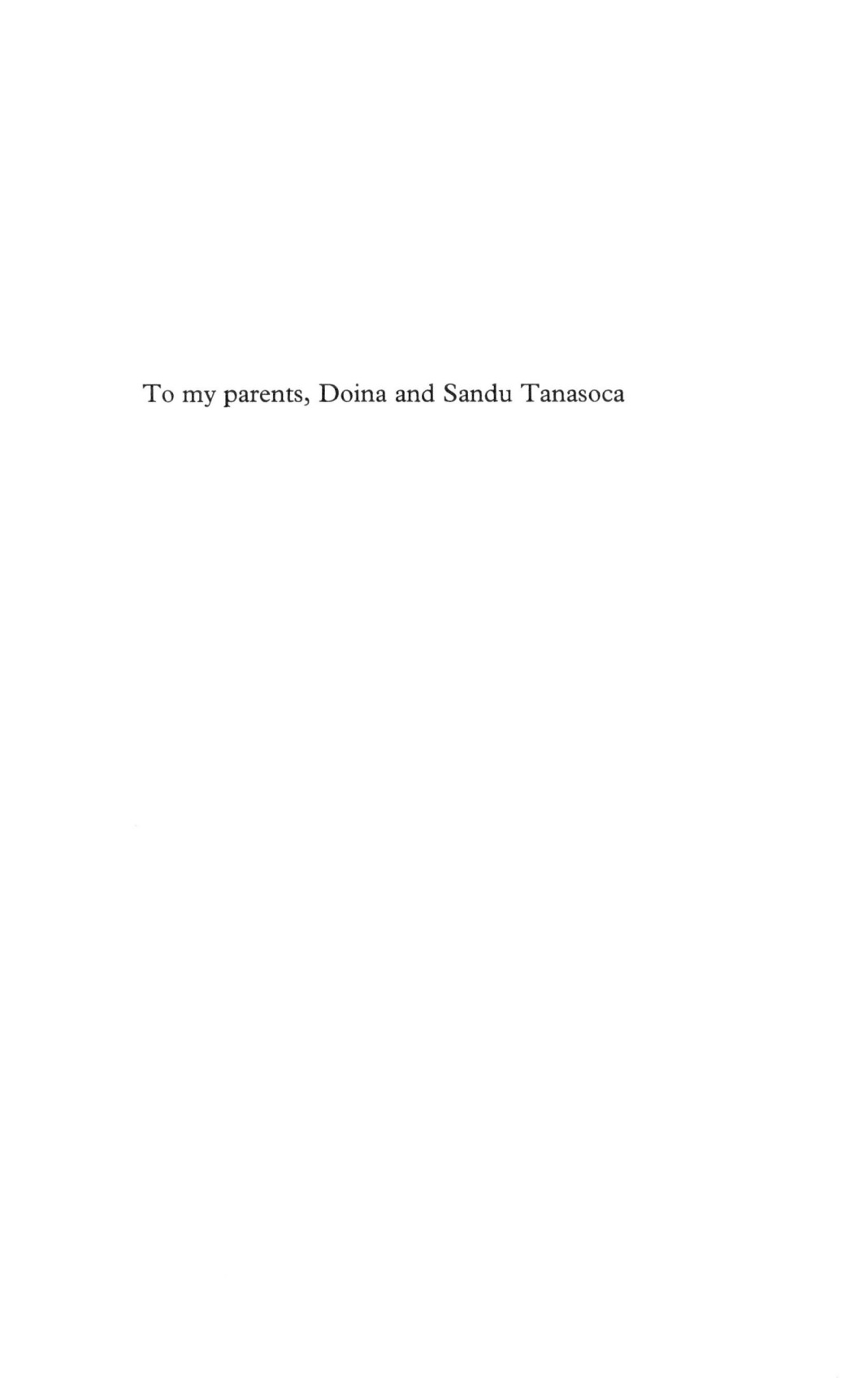

Contents

List of Figures		*page* xii
List of Tables		xiii
Acknowledgements		xiv

1 Introduction 1
   I   The Legal History of Multiple Citizenship   2
   II   Academic Reception and Debates   3
      A What Will Be Said   4
      B What Has Been Said   5
   III   The Arguments to Come   10

Part I Acquisition   15

2 Multiple Citizenship by Birthright   17
   I   The Efficiency Argument behind Birthright   20
   II   What, If Not Efficiency, Could Justify Birthright Multiple Nationality?   22
      A *Jus Soli*   23
      B *Jus Sanguinis*   28
      C Reform   34
   III   Conclusion   35

3 Multiple Citizenship by Naturalization   36
   I   Legal Framework   38
   II   Against the Citizenship Renunciation Requirement   38
   III   In Defence of the Citizenship Renunciation Requirement   41
      A The Demands of Consistency   41
      B No Different from Other Conditions   43
      C Not like the Other Conditions: What Is Permissible and What Is Not   43
      D Acting against One's Interest   45
      E Loss Aversion   46
   IV   Default Rules and Dual Citizenship   47
      A What Are Default Rules?   48
      B Dual Citizenship by Default   49
      C Reform   52

Contents

4	**Multiple Citizenship by Investment**	**55**
I	The Rise of Economic Citizenship	56
II	Selling Honours: The Historical Record	58
III	Lessons from the Sale of Honours	60
	A Merit and Reciprocity	60
	B Fairness	66
	C Signalling	68
	D Social Values and Meanings	72
	E Political Consequences	75
IV	A Clarification	79
V	Conclusion	80

Part II Consequences 83

5	**Multiple Citizenship and Collective Decision Making**	**85**
I	Multiple Citizens as Political Agents	86
II	Voting, Deliberation, and Collective Rationality	89
	A The Condorcet Paradox: How Majority Rule Can Yield Inconsistent Collective Decisions	89
	B From Aggregating Preferences to Aggregating Judgements	90
	C Why Consistency Matters	92
	D Avoiding Inconsistency: Single-Peaked Preferences, Unidimensionally Aligned Judgements	92
	E The Need for Structured Disagreement or Meta-Agreement	94
	F Structuring Disagreement through Deliberation	96
	G Recap and the Role of Citizenship	97
III	How Multiple Citizenship Could Undermine Collective Rationality	99
	A Deciding in Two Countries	99
	B A Perceptual Analogy	106
IV	Conclusion	110
6	**Multiple Citizenship and the Boundary Problem**	**112**
I	Three Boundary-Drawing Principles: Affectedness, Subjection to Law, and Unaffectedness	114
	A The Affected Interests Principle	114
	B The Legally Subjected Principle	116
	C The Unaffected Interests Principle	117
II	Multiple Citizenship and Boundaries: An Assessment	119
	A The Affected Interests Principle	119
	B The Legally Subjected Principle	124
	C The Unaffected Interests Principle	126
III	Untying the Gordian Knot: Citizenship-*sine*-Political Rights, Political Rights-*sine*-Citizenship	129
7	**Taxing Multiple Citizens and Global Inequality**	**134**
I	Citizenship and Global Inequality	135
II	Multiple Citizenship, Inequality, and the Birthright Levy	136
III	Interactive Effects, Extra-Benefits, and Double Taxation Agreements	138
	A What Do Double Taxation Agreements Entail for Dual Citizens?	140

	IV	Impact on Global Inequality	142
		A The Poor Do Not Move	143
		B Dual Citizens Reside in and Pay Taxes to the Richer of Their Countries	144
	V	Solutions	146
		A A Levy on Multiple Citizenship	147
		B Alter Double Taxation Agreements	148
	VI	Objections to the Proposed Solutions	149
		A People Would Renounce Their Additional Citizenships	149
		B Countries Would Close Borders to Immigrants from Poor Countries	150
		C The Money Will End Up in the Wrong Hands	151
	VII	An Implementation Strategy	153
	VIII	Conclusion	157
8	Conclusion	158
	I	The Promises	158
	II	Debunking the Myth: Broken Promises	159
	III	A Reprise of Policy Proposals	162
	IV	Unbundling Citizenship	163
		A Institutional Design Options	165
		B Advantages and Disadvantages	167
	V	Conclusion to the Conclusion	177

Bibliography 178
Index 197

Figures

5.1 K's single-peaked preference profile in A *page* 102
5.2 K's non-single-peaked preference profile in B 102
5.3 'Kaninchen und Ente' ('Rabbit and Duck'), the earliest known version of the duck–rabbit illusion, from the October 23, 1892, issue of *Fliegende Blätter*   107

Tables

5.1 Aggregating judgements   *page* 91
6.1 What gets distributed to whom in the unbundling   132

Acknowledgements

This book stems from a 2015 PhD dissertation in normative political theory, written during the three years I spent as a PhD student in the Department of Government, at the University of Essex. I thank the department for its support during those years and for allowing me to be surrounded by great minds.

The introductory and concluding chapters of this book were written during my completion year that I spent as a visitor at the Philosophy Department, Australian National University. I thank the members of the department for their hospitality, which allowed me to complete this manuscript.

My greatest gratitude goes to those who guided my steps through my PhD. I thank the members of my supervisory board, Paul Bou-Habib, Avia Pasternak, and Jeffrey Howard, for the very generous and helpful comments and suggestions they offered during my PhD. While they did not always agree with everything that I wrote, they always provided important feedback. But this book would not have been possible without one person in particular: my supervisor Bob Goodin. My greatest thanks go to him for his invaluable advice, patience, and reassurance and for believing in me. His sharp comments and objections constantly challenged me and helped improve each chapter. Thank you for cultivating my mind – the way I think, the way I write – but also for putting up with my constant worries (rightly dismissed as wasted time!) and innumerable questions about academic life. Thanks are also due to Christian Barry and Todd Landman, who served as examiners and who offered advice on how to best transform the thesis into a book. Many thanks also to John Dryzek, who encouraged me to publish my dissertation and allowed me the time to do so. I am also grateful to Joseph Carens, who was very kind to share with me his draft chapters of *The Ethics of Immigration.*

I am also very grateful to the anonymous referees for Cambridge University Press. Their comments and suggestions proved extremely useful while doing the final revisions to the book manuscript. Thanks also to John Haslam and Toby Ginsberg at Cambridge University Press for guidance through the publication process and to their team for their help in making ready the manuscript for publication.

Two chapters of this book are based on articles that have been previously published: Chapter 4 is based on an article entitled 'Citizenship for sale: neomedieval, not just neoliberal?', published in *Archives Européennes de Sociologie/European Journal of Sociology*, vol. 57 (April 2016), 169–95. Chapter 6 is based on an article entitled 'Double taxation, multiple citizenship and global inequality', published in *Moral Philosophy and Politics*, vol. 1 (2014), 147–69. I thank the publishers and editors of these journals for allowing me to reproduce these articles in revised form.

Drafts of some chapters were presented to audiences at the University of Essex, Sciences Po Paris, University of Luzern, Sorbonne-Paris I, Social and Political Sciences at the University of Sydney, and the Sydney Law School. I thank the organizers of these conferences for giving me the opportunity to present my work and the audiences for their questions and comments.

Last, I thank my mother for letting me make my own decisions from a very young age. Her encouraging me to always pursue what makes me happy made this book possible in no small part.

1 Introduction

Increasingly many people today are 'multiple citizens'[1] – individuals who belong to, and have membership rights in, more than one state. Their exact number is not known. Few states have gathered or published data.[2] But from what is already known, these numbers are likely to be substantial. Furthermore, given the increasing acceptance of multiple citizenship in the citizenship laws of many states,[3] it is highly likely that their number increased rapidly over the past dozen years.

Some estimates are so rough as to be virtually worthless. For example, estimates of the number of US citizens with additional citizenships elsewhere vary wildly, between half a million and 5.7 million.[4] And it is said – once again, ever so roughly – that Western Europe harbours a total of 'several million and rising' dual citizens.[5] But in some places there are more precise estimates. For example, in 2009 the Netherlands had more than 1.1 million dual citizens (out of 16.5 million total population), three times the number in 1995.[6] And according to a Parliamentary Library brief, fully 23 per cent (4.4 million out of 19 million) of Australia's population were estimated to be dual citizens at the turn the twenty-first century.[7]

Even if precise numbers are not easy to come by, the phenomenon of multiple citizenship is clearly common, and increasingly so. As such, it is a phenomenon fully worthy of academic inquiry, at both theoretical and empirical levels. Yet despite significantly influencing the political and

---

[1] For convenience and clarity, throughout this book I will use 'dual citizens' and 'multiple citizens' – as well as 'dual citizenship', 'multiple citizenship', and 'plural citizenship' – interchangeably.
[2] The Australian Bureau of Statistics, for example, explicitly declined to gather data about Australian dual citizens. See Millbank 2000–1.
[3] De Groot 2003; Sejersen 2008.
[4] Faist and Gerdes 2008.
[5] Feldblum 2000.
[6] Nicolaas 2009.
[7] Millbank 2000–1.

economic life of states, multiple citizenship remains 'among the most understudied incidents of globalization'.[8]

I The Legal History of Multiple Citizenship

Prior to the liberalization of multiple citizenship, mono-nationality was the universal standard: everyone had to be citizen of one state only. Moreover, for a long time, state membership was considered to be an unbreakable tie. According to the doctrine of 'perpetual allegiance' – a remnant of the feudal system – one was supposed to belong to one state once and for all time. Blackstone's eighteenth-century *Commentaries on the Laws of England*, for example, holds that obligations to one's state are 'a debt of gratitude, which cannot be forfeited, cancelled, or altered by any change in time, place and circumstance ... An Englishman who removes to France, or to China, owes the same allegiance to the king of England there as at home, and twenty years hence as well as now.'[9]

The doctrine of perpetual allegiance was one of the *casus belli* of the 1812 war between the United Kingdom and the United States. The United Kingdom refused to recognize the US naturalization of its subjects and impressed some of its expatriates (whom the United States insisted were UK ex-citizens) sailing under the US flag in order to make up for a shortage of sailors in its own fleet. Also, during the 1860s, some Western states (France, Prussia, and the Scandinavian countries) tried, upon their return home, to conscript some of their natives who had in the meantime become American citizens.[10] Moreover, in 1868, the United Kingdom prosecuted a group of naturalized Americans, members of the Fenian Brotherhood, treating them as natives despite their request to be tried by a special procedure reserved for aliens. The United States objected on the grounds that upon naturalization they were no longer British subjects but American citizens. In response, the American Congress also adopted the Expatriation Act in 1868, reasserting an individual's right to change allegiance from one country to another.

Across the second half of the nineteenth century, states gradually came to acknowledge a right to expatriation, thus ending the doctrine of perpetual allegiance. Yet expatriation was understood as only a swap of allegiance from one state to another (a trade, that is), not as involving a multiplication of the bonds of allegiance (as with multiple citizenship). Allegiance to the state was still supposed to be exclusive and

---

[8] Spiro 2008b, p. 189.
[9] Blackstone [1753] 1893, book I, ch. X, p. 369.
[10] Roche 1951, p. 282.

absolute.[11] International efforts aimed to reduce cases of multiple nationality,[12] first through bilateral agreements such as the Bancroft treaties,[13] and later through international treaties under the patronage of the League of Nations, such as the 1930 *Convention on Certain Questions Relating to the Conflict of Nationality Laws*.[14]

The proliferation of multiple citizenship in more recent times was facilitated by several shifts in international and domestic law in the post-war era. One was that, after 1945, with the growing professionalization of the military (fuelled subsequently by post-materialism and pacifist movements in the 1960s), citizenship was increasingly decoupled from military duties. In consequence, states increasingly started turning a blind eye toward the 1963 *Strasbourg Convention on the Reduction of Cases of Multiple Nationality and Military Obligations in Cases of Multiple Nationality*. Another important factor in the evolution of multiple citizenship was a set of decisions made by some law courts in Germany and France during the 1970s, recognizing a right to permanent residence for long-term immigrants.[15] Gender equality was a third factor spurring the expanding acceptance of multiple citizenship. From the 1980s onward, states began recognizing the right of women (as well as of men) to pass on their citizenship to their offspring (*jus sanguinis a patre et a matre*).

In consequence of all of those influences, under the 1993 *Second Protocol* amending the 1963 Convention and the 1997 *European Convention on Nationality*, dual citizenship was no longer banned. On the contrary, states now see dual citizenship as a powerful instrument incentivizing naturalization and promoting integration.

II Academic Reception and Debates

How did academics react to these developments? Unsurprisingly, the first academics to notice and discuss multiple citizenship were legal scholars. And as pointed out below, today's literature on multiple citizenship remains largely dominated by the legalistic perspective. But while

---

[11] Aleinikoff 1986.
[12] Throughout this book I will use 'nationality' and 'citizenship' interchangeably.
[13] The first treaties were conventions signed in 1868 between the United States and the German states (negotiated by diplomat and historian George Bancroft, hence the name), prior to German unification, relating to expatriation, military service, naturalization, and resumption of nationality. (The Bancroft treaties are available at https://archive.org/details/cu31924005227503.) Later, however, the United States signed similar conventions with other states as well (e.g., Mexico, China, Sweden, and Norway). See Boll 2007, p. 185, n. 40.
[14] Available at www.refworld.org/docid/3ae6b3b00.html.
[15] Weil 2002, p. 16.

rich in legal detail, such studies are theoretically remarkably thin, especially at the normative level. The rich normative and political implications of the phenomenon have thus so far passed with little comment.

A   What Will Be Said

This book aims to fill precisely this gap. Its goal is to shed light on the ethical and political aspects of multiple citizenship, integrating this phenomenon with mainstream normative political theory. I will be thus less interested in the legal and empirical details of multiple citizenship as such, and more in how the phenomenon resonates with some of the burgeoning debates in political theory: debates concerning immigration and the boundaries of the demos, domestic and global equality and justice, public justification and deliberation, and commodification. Such a holistic and eclectic approach to the topic might, of course, leave narrower specialists on the topic of citizenship dissatisfied. Yet this book targets precisely that wider audience of mainstream political theorists, rather than the smaller set of citizenship specialists.

The main argument of this book is that, in its present form, multiple citizenship should not be embraced and defended indiscriminately. There are numerous reasons for that, which I discuss at length throughout the book: multiple citizenship may undermine the democratic consensus legitimizing collective decisions (Chapter 5). It sustains global inequality (Chapter 7). It may even compromise more ambitious cosmopolitan projects that are more morally justifiable and politically efficient (Chapter 8). Hence I discuss alternatives to multiple citizenship, as well as reforms that can improve its practice. These alternatives and reforms (Chapters 2, 3, and 8) capture all the advantages of multiple citizenship and more, while at the same time avoiding the problems it poses. The main alternative is an *unbundling* of citizenship rights and the granting of only a subset of full citizenship rights in the case of a second or third citizenship. Awarding people less than the full current bundle of citizenship rights in those circumstances would circumvent the overinclusiveness that granting multiple citizenship can currently cause (see Chapters 6 and 8).

As will be clear by the end of this book, I do not propose any grand theory of citizenship. The main point of my constructive critique of multiple citizenship is, after all, that the category of citizenship as we know it should, at least in certain cases, be abandoned in favour of a more flexible separate allocation of the different rights and duties usually associated with it. One should not have to go through the burdensome process of becoming a citizen (potentially a multiple citizen as well) just to have access to particular rights we have good reason to believe one should be entitled to on other grounds (residence, contributions, social ties, affected interests, and so on). Indeed, as the phenomenon of 'denizenship' shows, some states (in particular, Western liberal democracies) have already started decoupling some rights from citizenship, the most prominent example being that of foreign residents being entitled to vote in regional elections.[16] What I argue for is, if you will, a more extensive, systematic, and radical decoupling of rights from citizenship – an extension of denizenship rather than a proliferation of multiple citizenships. Instead of making people citizens, granting them all the rights of citizenship once and for all, states could grant particular categories of rights to people according to different criteria, for limited periods of time. Different rights could be allocated according to different principles in order to maximize democratic legitimacy, (global) equality, and efficiency. I will give some examples of different grounds we can envisage for the allocation of some categories of rights. Yet my basic point is simple: instead of granting people a second or third citizenship – instead of turning people into multiple citizens – we should grant them particular categories of rights without making them (much less requiring that they become) citizens.

Before elaborating the structure of the book and summarizing the themes of its component chapters, I will offer a brief overview of what scholars have already said about multiple citizenship. I will engage with, rely on, and offer challenges to many of these claims in the chapters to come. But that is for later. The aim of the summary that follows is merely to situate the book in the ongoing discussion, showing how its foci fit with, and differ from, those of the existing literature.

B   *What Has Been Said*

Two different strands can be identified in the literature on multiple citizenship. In one camp are found the legal scholars (for example, Martin, Bosniak, Spiro, Schuck, Aleinikoff, Klusmeyer, and Hailbronner)[17] examining, with a light theoretical touch, the growing acceptance of multiple citizenship in both domestic and international law. In the other camp are found the social theorists and political scholars focusing on the effects of globalization (such as Soysal, Sassen, Castles and Davidson, Hansen, and Weil).[18] These two camps are by no means isolated from

---

[16] Hammar 1990.
[17] See Aleinikoff and Klusmeyer 2001; Bosniak 2001–2; Martin 1999, 2014; Martin and Hailbronner 2003; Schuck 1998; Spiro 1997, 2010, 2016.
[18] Castles and Davidson 2000; Hansen and Weil 2002; Sassen 2002b; Soysal 1994.

one another. Quite the contrary, they definitely *do* speak to one another. For example, after social theorists couched multiple citizenship as the epitome of postnationalism, legal theorists seized upon that thought and developed it further.[19]

Still, the literature on multiple citizenship is limited. It consists primarily of a few notable legal treatises[20] and various articles and chapters focusing specifically on this phenomenon mostly (with some exceptions[21]) from a purely legal standpoint.[22] Then there are several edited volumes combining legal perspectives with single country case studies.[23] Finally, there are some scattered references to multiple citizenship in works on postnationalism and globalization,[24] as well as in works on immigration and citizenship more generally.[25]

What general claims about multiple citizenship can be found in that scholarship? The first and perhaps most important claim concerns the *postnational* character of multiple nationality. Multiple citizenship is above all – and *wrongly* I shall argue (see Chapters 7 and 8) – embraced by the social theorists of postnationalism (from Soysal to Sassen) as an eminently postnational form of membership. 'Postnational citizenship' is an umbrella term capturing various global developments, such as

> the membership of the long-term noncitizen immigrants in western countries, who hold various rights and privileges without a formal nationality status; ... the increasing instances of *dual citizenship*, which breaches the traditional notions of political membership and loyalty in a single state; ... European Union citizenship, which represents a multitiered form of membership; and ... subnational citizenships in culturally or administratively autonomous regions of Europe.[26]

Postnationalists point out the fact that states are no longer the sole locus of democracy, identity, and solidarity or the sole depository of rights. Spurred by globalization, such developments (multiple citizenship included) signal the waning of state sovereignty, the denationalization of citizenship, and the advent of a new cosmopolitan order.[27] Most

---

[19] Bosniak 2001–2; Spiro 2008b.
[20] See Aghahosseini 2007; Boll 2007; Vonk 2012.
[21] Political theoretical approaches can be found in Blatter (2011) and Weinstock (2010).
[22] See, for example, Bloemraad 2004; Cook-Martin 2013; Faist 2001; Hammar 1985; Jones-Correa 2001; Kruger and Verhellen 2011; Martin 1999, 2014; Spiro 1997, 2010, 2016.
[23] E.g., Faist and Kivisto 2008; Hansen and Weil 2002; Kalekin-Fishman and Pitkänen 2007; Martin and Hailbronner 2003; Pitkänen and Kalekin-Fishman 2007.
[24] E.g., Castles and Davidson 2000; Jacobson 1996, 1998–9; Mathias, Jacobson, and Lapid 2001; Sassen 1999, 2002a, 2002b; Soysal 1996.
[25] See Aleinikoff and Klusmeyer 2001; Bosniak 2006; Schuck 1998.
[26] Soysal 2004, p. 335.
[27] Sassen 2002b, p. 279.

importantly, postnationalists have high hopes for postnational forms of membership like multiple citizenship to be more inclusive and global-egalitarian than standard membership, and thus better able to support an extension of the scope of justice from the domestic to the global level.

I debunk some of these claims in Chapter 7, where I focus on the global justice consequences of multiple citizenship. There I emphasize how it amplifies original inequalities and injustices in the allocation and exercise of state membership. Contrary to postnationalists, I argue that multiple citizenship is by no means globally egalitarian or more all-inclusive than regular state membership. On the contrary: it is accessible mostly to the global financial elites (see Chapter 4 on dual citizenship by investment) and considerably less to the global poor.[28] It is avant-garde all right, but in its elitist and exclusivist form! More importantly, multiple citizenship is far from being a brand-new cosmopolitan (or postnational), hence, *progressive* form of membership. Its distribution is still uniquely controlled by states; the rights and duties it enables are exercised inside these states; and, moreover, these states still claim that citizenship speaks to national identity, one way or another (note well the 'nationalism' inside 'trans*nationalism*', for example). In short, multiple citizenship is a very poor proxy for far more ambitious projects such as global citizenship (Chapter 8).

Legal theorists agree with social theorists when it comes to the postnational character of multiple citizenship, although they typically see it as more of a mixed blessing.[29] 'Plural citizenship both reflects and accelerates postnationalism', they agree, warning that the 'acceptance of plural citizenship is likely to lower the intensity of the citizen-state affiliation, and in turn, the intensity of bonds among citizens'.[30] Whether those developments are good or bad is, however, an open question. Some worry that multiple citizenship marks a devaluation of state citizenship, that it undermines exclusive attachment to a community and encourages strategic behaviour on the part of the individuals, and that it erodes the distinctiveness of national communities.[31] Even if they do not stem from sheer blind nationalism, such complaints reflect an obsolete understanding of state functioning. Setting aside any initial suspicion they might have had about it, in the end legal theorists accept that realistically

---

[28] Calhoun 2002.
[29] Spiro (2008b) was initially sceptical but in a later article is more favourable to a liberalization of multiple citizenship, seeing it as a way of lowering naturalization costs and boosting individual autonomy (Spiro 2010). The same can be said about other scholars as well. (See, e.g., Martin's other works cited above.)
[30] Spiro 2008b, p. 189.
[31] See Schuck 1998; Spiro 2008b.

states can no longer resist multiple citizenship. The best thing states can do in order to avoid becoming irrelevant is to *adapt* – with multiple citizenship being precisely one of the main adaptations that will permit states (and *state* citizenships as such) to survive, and perhaps even thrive.

A second important claim concerns the relationship between multiple citizenship and *democracy*. A major principle in democratic theory is that a *democratic* state cannot deprive a segment of its population of the right to participate in decision making. Multiple citizenship allowed states to integrate more efficiently large numbers of long-term immigrants. One reason for the latter's reluctance to naturalize was precisely the cost they had to bear upon doing so, namely, renouncing their citizenship in their state of origin. By accepting multiple citizenship, receiving states decreased the costs of naturalizing and thus encouraged naturalizations. Some claim there is a direct causal relationship between the increase in the number of naturalizations and this liberalization of multiple nationality.[32] That might well be the case.

But while dual citizenship may solve problems of political *under-inclusiveness* in immigration states, it stokes problems of political *over-inclusiveness* in emigration states. (It does so at least according to some democratic principles for constituting the demos, like the legally subjected principle.) In Chapter 6, I point out how this problem could have been easily solved: instead of keeping citizenship unitary but allowing for its duplication (that is, dual citizenship), states could have insisted on *unbundling* citizenship rights and allocating component rights separately. A disaggregation of citizenship rights would permit immigration states to integrate migrants politically without naturalizing them – by granting them political rights *only*. It would also permit emigration states to solve their *over*inclusiveness without losing their citizens (if another state requires them to renounce their previous citizenship upon naturalizing there) or denaturalizing their citizens (if this is the state's policy in cases where its citizens acquire another citizenship). The proposal would achieve that by allowing emigrants to keep, in their state of origin, the rest of the rights of citizenship, just not political rights as well.

The relationship between dual citizenship and *political participation* is less straightforward. It is not really known, for example, whether dual citizenship makes a difference for people's electoral behaviour, and if so what the difference is. Are dual citizens more or less likely to vote in elections? That is not known. The existing studies are ill-designed and too limited to give a clear answer (see my critique in Chapter 5).[33]

---

[32] Vink 2013.
[33] See, e.g., Escobar 2004; Roikanen 2011; Staton, Jackson, and Canache 2007b.

Introduction 9

In this book, however, I set aside claims about the electoral behaviour of dual citizens and focus instead on other aspects of political participation, like public deliberation and collective rationality, which could well be affected by dual citizenship. In Chapter 5, I examine the ways in which dual citizenship disrupts one type of democratic consensus – meta-agreement – which serves the important function of legitimizing collective decisions.

Another common discussion concerning multiple citizens revolves around *jurisdictional conflicts* that can occur between the states of citizenship.[34] One main argument against multiple membership has, for a long time, been the potential conflict between a multiple citizen's military duties toward each of his different countries. As I have already noted, this was historically a major obstacle in the way of dual citizenship, but it is one that gradually disappeared as states professionalized their armies and abandoned compulsory military service. Still, other types of legal conflicts between states remain possible, since in addition to territorial jurisdiction states exercise personal jurisdiction over their citizens as well. The latter means that a state has an internationally recognized right to prosecute its own nationals for what it considers as crimes even if they are perpetrated on another state's territory, and perhaps even to prosecute nationals of other states for what it regards as crimes perpetrated against its own nationals, as well as to offer diplomatic protection to its own nationals wherever these might be.[35] Multiple citizenship makes it possible for several states to exercise jurisdiction, under one heading or another, over the same individual – thus making conflicts of jurisdiction between states more likely.

It has long been legally the case that dual citizens could not invoke the protection of one of their states of citizenship against their other state of citizenship. Such interventions were deemed to be unwelcome by the community of states insofar as they breached the principle of sovereign equality among states. This norm was repudiated, however, in the cases of the US-Iran claims tribunal, and it has come into question from then onward.[36] Dual citizens have come to enjoy extensive opportunities for jurisdiction shopping. The more countries persons are citizens of, the larger their set of options as to where to settle their legal affairs (with respect to various issues ranging from family matters to business dealings).

---

[34] See Oeter 2003; Orfield 1949.
[35] The passive personality principle is, however, often overruled in favour of other legal principles (e.g., the territorial principle). For a discussion, see Dickinson 1935 and Doyle 2012.
[36] See Aghahosseini 2007.

These legal and political consequences of multiple citizenship are certainly pertinent from the point of view of democratic theory, as I shall observe at various points in this book. Yet jurisdictional conflicts are only incidentally rather than uniquely associated with multiple citizenship. Accordingly, they figure in this book only occasionally and in passing.

III   The Arguments to Come

This book consists of two parts. Part I examines the legitimacy of various *grounds of acquisition* of multiple citizenship and their justification. The chapters in Part I aim to answer several questions: Is multiple citizenship more or less legitimate depending on how it was acquired? And if so, why? I consider three modes of acquisition: birth, naturalization, and investment, each the subject of a dedicated chapter.

Chapter 2 focuses on *birthright* multiple citizenship. In an era of increased global mobility, more children are born into mixed multinational families, and hence more individuals become multiple citizens on the basis of their birth circumstances. *Jus sanguinis*, on its own or in combination with *jus soli*, can create a legal entitlement to multiple nationality. Some states, like Norway or Germany, have imposed restrictions on birthright dual citizenship, but not without stirring social protest. This chapter discusses whether such restrictions are legitimate and whether birth circumstances alone (blood ties to another citizen or birth on the state's territory) ought normatively give individuals moral entitlements to multiple nationality. I maintain that such arguments in favour of multiple citizenship – grounded in the special relationship between children and their parents or in the parents' 'right' to transmit citizenship to their children and the children's 'right' to take on this citizenship – are misguided and reflect a grave misunderstanding of the nature and particularity of citizenship as such. I conclude by introducing a policy proposal – a system of citizenship renewal – that would reform birthright (multiple) citizenship.

Chapter 3 explores multiple citizenship by *naturalization*. Naturalization rules and citizenship tests – citizenship conditionality, more generally – have been much-discussed among immigration theorists. Yet little has been said about the legitimacy of each and every naturalization requirement, taken separately. In this chapter I address two issues related to naturalization and multiple membership. First, I analyze the legitimacy of one naturalization requirement that makes a crucial difference to dual citizenship: the renunciation of previous citizenship requirement. I conclude that that requirement is morally problematic only if it is made by the state of residence instead of by the state of origin. Second, drawing on the literature on choice architecture and nudging,[37] I develop a novel objection to dual citizenship via naturalization. I argue that what is morally problematic in such cases is that dual citizenship arises by default, rather than through an explicit individual choice. The reforms of naturalization procedures proposed in this chapter emphasize the importance of actively choosing one's citizenship (a concern found in Chapter 2 as well).

Chapter 4 focuses on multiple citizenship via *investment*. Although not all states grant citizenship upon investment, increasingly many do so. States (for example, Austria) that standardly require renunciation of previous citizenship upon naturalization tend especially to waive this requirement for investors, thereby allowing investors but not other individuals to become dual citizens. In truth, investor citizenship allows people virtually to 'buy' citizenship. Citizenship was not the first status historically to be put on the market, however. In this chapter, I put forward arguments against multiple citizenship-by-investment drawing on the analogy between the sale of citizenship and of noble titles. I explore the historical objections to the sale of honours and show how similar ones can be raised against investor dual citizenship as well. The aim of the chapter's central analogy is merely to reveal the ways in which markets undermine values that commonly are (and arguably ideally should be) associated with both systems of citizenship and systems of honours. Through this analogy, this chapter offers a broader than usual account of citizenship, bridging normative and historical perspectives on the topic.

Having discussed the modes of acquisition of multiple citizenship I move on to discuss, in Part II, its *consequences* at both domestic and global levels. At the *domestic* level, I study two mechanisms of decision making, voting and deliberation, to show how multiple citizenship can affect the legitimacy of decisions made by majority rule by undermining collective rationality. At the *global* level, I analyze the implications of multiple citizenship for global justice, and in particular its impact on global inequality, by focusing on its interplay with international taxation rules.

Chapter 5 explores the implications of multiple citizenship for *collective decision making* drawing on insights from social choice theory and psychology. An important source of legitimacy of collective decisions is their capacity to embody the coherent collective judgements and preferences of a political community – the collective will of a people. If they do not, they risk being meaningless. An important precondition for a coherent collective decision to be reached through majority rule is the existence of

---

[37] See Sunstein 2013a and 2013b; Thaler and Sunstein 2009.

a common frame of reference to guide collective decision making. I point out how dual citizenship could undermine collective rationality inside a community by exposing its citizens to alternative frames of reference guiding the decisions of another political community. Drawing on the psychology of perception, I then cast doubt on whether dual citizens will be able to systematically and reliably reformulate their preferences and reconstitute their judgements in line with their two different communities' frames of reference.

Chapter 6 studies multiple citizenship by reference to one of the hottest debates in democratic theory, the problem of *constituting the demos* (commonly known as the 'boundary problem'). It thus addresses a second aspect of collective decision making – the distribution of voting rights. Various principles have been proposed as a solution to the boundary problem. In this chapter I have in view three of them: the affected interests principle (Arrhenius, Goodin), the legally subjected principle (Miller, López-Guerra), and the unaffected interests principle (Frazer).[38] I start by noticing that migration constitutes a challenge for each of these three principles. What I am interested in, here, is whether or not multiple citizenship brings demos boundaries more nearly in line with those that are ideally prescribed by any of these principles. My argument is that it does not, and that other policies would do a better job in this respect. I argue that the problem lies in what is standardly seen as the inextricable tie between citizenship status and political rights. Breaking this tie – *unbundling* citizenship rights, and allocating political rights separately from the rest – can make demos boundaries congruent with those ideally prescribed by any of the aforementioned principles. I come back to one of these policy proposals in Chapter 8, the concluding chapter.

Chapter 7 focuses on the consequences of multiple state membership for *global distributive justice*. Is multiple citizenship more likely to serve the cause of global equality than mono-nationality? I argue that multiple citizenship accentuates global inequalities in virtue of two factors. One is the present regime for allocating multiple citizenship, which advantages the global rich. The second is the international norms regulating taxation, which favour the (typically more prosperous) states of residence over the (typically less prosperous) states of source. As regards the first factor, I note that citizenship acts like a gatekeeper of good or bad life opportunities and, by its exclusive character, locks people in what are advantageous or disadvantageous environments. This gives us a reason to neutralize the effects of citizenship *tout court*, whether mono-national

---

[38] See Arrhenius 2005; Frazer 2014; Goodin 2007; López-Guerra 2005; Miller 2009.

or multiple and whatever its mode of acquisition. But *multiple* citizenship magnifies those objectionable advantages. To address them, I propose that a separate tax be imposed on multiple citizenship. As regards the second factor, I argue that global inequality is aggravated by multiple citizenship coupled with an international double taxation regime favouring states of residence. Very briefly, this happens as a result of several things: first, double taxation regimes favour the state of residence over the state of source; second, dual nationals will typically prefer to reside in the richer of their states of citizenship, paying thereby their taxes to the richer state; third, dual citizenship will make individuals more likely to take advantage of double tax agreements and to do so in the longer term; and fourth, the global rich will have greater access to dual nationality, in turn allowing them to maximize their resources through double tax agreements. I propose two solutions to address the global inequalities aggravated by multiple citizenship. The first is a tax on multiple citizenship. The second is the introduction of a prioritarian clause in the OECD Model Tax Convention that would avoid double taxation but do so by always giving priority, for taxation purposes, to the most economically disadvantaged state having a potential tax claim on the same revenue.

In concluding, Chapter 8 begins with a short recap of the major claims found in the literature on multiple citizenship, closing the circle opened by this introduction. There I argue that those claims are misguided, by reference to the arguments developed in the substantive chapters of the book. But the concluding chapter does more than offer a mere recap. In the conclusion, I also return to elaborate upon one particular policy proposal offered in Chapter 6 as alternative to multiple citizenship: the unbundling of citizenship rights. I argue that many of the pitfalls of multiple citizenship discussed in all the previous chapters could be solved by that unbundling proposal. I then offer some fine-tuning of the proposal, identifying different variants of it and discussing implementation strategies for them. I argue in favour of one in particular: a *partial* unbundling, to be applied only to a second (or third or more) citizenship. In this way the conclusion lays the foundations for new theoretical work that would form a natural successor to this project.

Part I

Acquisition

Upon what basis should a political theorist assess the moral justifiability of multiple citizenship? It should be acknowledged from the beginning (as I have done) that such inquiry would fall short of establishing analytic truths, logically necessary, as are most sought after by normative political theorists. The reason for that is simple: citizenship is a *socially constructed* legal category whose content *varies greatly* depending on the decisions of those who construct the category and define its content. So, political theorists cannot aspire to any timeless truths about the concept of citizenship, or hence multiple citizenship. One cannot expect to be able to put forward arguments that multiple citizenship is logically and necessarily justifiable or unjustifiable. Instead, one can only inquire into the phenomenon of 'real existing' multiple citizenship (i.e., as it is found in the world) or any realistically likely variation of it (multiple citizenship as it could be in worlds not *too* far from our own). In this book I aspire to doing exactly that, looking at how multiple citizenship emerges (Part I) and what its consequences are (Part II).

In Part I, I will look at the way(s) multiple citizenship is distributed. Again, its distribution, as well as all other details of multiple citizenship, is a purely contingent matter, without any logical necessity about it. Hence, I will focus on the present *grounds of acquisition* of citizenship that might give rise to multiple citizenship, paying attention also, as appropriate, to various state-related peculiarities. Is there anything morally objectionable about the way multiple citizenship emerges in the first place? Depending on the circumstances of its emergence, is multiple citizenship more or less morally justifiable? Finally, are state measures restricting (the emergence or retention of) multiple citizenship legitimate? To answer these questions, I will examine three modes of acquisition: *birth*, *naturalization*, and *investment*, in Chapters 2, 3, and 4, respectively.[1]

---

[1] I do not discuss here citizenship *restoration*, which can also give rise to dual citizenship. Different categories of people can benefit from citizenship restoration – from political exiles stripped of their citizenship by a hostile regime to external kin minorities inhabiting territories that were once part of their 'homeland'. In such cases, citizenship restoration may be used as a compensatory measure of reparative justice. One could, of course, wonder whether citizenship is the right currency for such policies. (For a discussion, see Bauböck 2009, p. 481.)

2 Multiple Citizenship by Birthright

One can become a multiple citizen by virtue of one's birth circumstances, being born either to the right parents (*jus sanguinis*) or in the right place (*jus soli*). For example, a child born to a Spanish father and a French mother who was born and raised in the United Kingdom might simultaneously be a citizen of Spain, France, and the United Kingdom. The Spanish and French citizenships would be granted on the ground of a birth tie to his parents (*jus sanguinis*), the UK citizenship on the ground of a birth tie to the state territory (*jus soli*).

Both grounds of citizenship allocation based on birthright, *jus sanguinis* and *jus soli*, were widely adopted by states quite late, typically in the nineteenth century.[1] Before that the main ground for citizenship ascription was *jus domicili*, or the principle of residence.[2] Urban citizenship – one of the main types of membership before the introduction of nationality in the late eighteenth century – was distributed largely (but not exclusively) according to residence in the city (*jus domicili*). Urban citizenship served an important social welfare function, rewarding those who contributed to the public good of the city while at the same time keeping at bay those who would be a drain on it, such as the migrant foreign poor. In the Netherlands, for example, one could be treated in a local hospital only after ten years of residence and could have access to municipal welfare institutions only after fifteen years of residence.[3] Urban citizenship unlocked other opportunities as well: membership in guilds with monopolies on trade, representation in local government, and protection of and accountability to the legal courts.

Nowadays states commonly recognize *birthright* as a legitimate ground for citizenship allocation. And, as intercultural marriages are becoming

---

[1] Although we find proto elements of *jus soli* in ancient Athenian law as well as in Calvin's Case (1608), a legal decision according to which children born in Scotland after the Union of the Crowns in 1603 were considered British subjects.
[2] Brubaker 1992.
[3] Prak 1997.

more frequent thanks to global migration, it is increasingly the case that ever larger numbers of newborns will be *multiple* citizens by birthright. Yet some states refuse to grant citizenship on the basis of birthright, in some circumstances, or impose further conditionality on its grant or on its preservation.[4] One such circumstance is when the recognition of a birthright claim would entail multiple citizenship. Such limitations imposed by states have provoked strong emotional reactions, but so far there has been very little cool-headed reflection on their legitimacy. Hence the question at the heart of this chapter: Is the limitation of *birthright* multiple citizenship (a limitation on the accumulation of citizenships on the basis of birthright) fair or not?

To get a flavour of what these state limitations entail and what reactions they provoke, take a case that made the headlines some years ago. It had as main protagonists an Australian-Norwegian couple fighting for their children's dual citizenship.[5] Their story is the following. The couple's twins were born in Norway. They were issued Norwegian passports, which means they were acknowledged as citizens by the Norwegian state (in virtue of both *jus sanguinis* on their mother's side, and *jus soli* given the location of their birth). Their father subsequently completed the 'Australian Citizenship by Descent Application' (form 118) in order for the twins to become Australian citizens as well. The surprise came, however, when the couple tried to renew the twins' passports. They were informed that their children had forfeited their Norwegian citizenships when acquiring the Australian ones, and thus that they were no longer Norwegian citizens.[6]

Now, the legal aspects of the whole affair are quite complex (as pointed out in a footnote below). However, I will not inquire into whether the Norwegian authorities' decision was right from the *legal* point of view.

---

[4] Take, for example, restrictions on *jus soli*. In many countries only children of citizens or permanent residents born on the state territory are entitled to citizenship.

[5] See Sandelson 2013. The parents even dedicated a Facebook page (www.facebook.com/NorwegianChildrensRights) to their legal battle, where everyone was invited to express support for dual citizenship. Their plea received 'likes' from various politicians and political parties.

[6] As a norm, Norway accepts dual citizenship in a limited number of cases. Norwegian citizens acquiring the citizenship of another state lose their Norwegian citizenship, for example. Although Norway allows its citizens to legally hold two citizenships when these are *acquired at birth*, the Norwegian Directorate of Immigration took the father's application not as a registration of birth but as an application for a new citizenship, subsequent to birth. Had the twins been born on Australian soil, they could have received Australian citizenship at birth and subsequently the parents could have applied for them to become Norwegian citizens as well on the basis of birthright without problem, making their children thereby dual citizens. See Brochmann 2013. On the distinction between *ex lege* acquisition and option acquisition, see de Groot 2002.

Instead, I will examine the normative justification of such decision and similar attempts by other states. It is clear, for now, that the aforementioned story sparked strong reactions in defence of dual citizenship and against the Norwegian authorities' decision. Moreover, the language used by both parents and their supporters is quite telling, offering us a glimpse of people's moral intuitions on the matter. For example, one Facebook post of the parents reads:

> We know many of you are afraid to post about this situation or even like this page for fear of reprisal from UDI [Norwegian Directorate of Immigration] – either on yourselves or your children. Taking a stance on this issue is not an admission of anything. Many here are not personally affected and some are not even parents yet. *It is a matter of principle* for everybody who has, wishes to, or may *want to start a multicultural family* involving a Norwegian, or simply cares about *what is right and wrong*.[7]

One reader of an article narrating the couple's story urges: 'Perhaps it is time for all the Aussies and others affected by these *draconian, oppressive and clearly discriminative rules* to just pack our bags, take our kids and go home.' Another reader goes even further: 'Take it to court. If you lose in Norway (which you will not) take it to the *European Court of Human Right*s. These officials do not know what they are talking about!'[8]

As the words in italics show, the language used is normatively loaded. There is talk of principles and (human) rights, of discrimination and oppression. People's intuitions run in favour of expansive concepts of citizenship, including multiple citizenship, and against all state attempts of restricting it. But are these intuitions well grounded? It is worth asking, especially as Norway is by no means the sole country to limit the propagation of dual citizenship. Germany, for example, until very recently[9] required those born to immigrant parents to choose, by their twenty-third birthday, between German citizenship and all other citizenship(s) they held.

Are such restrictions on *birthright* dual citizenship justified or not?[10] To answer that question one needs to explore what could be a good moral justification underlying birthright dual citizenship – or indeed birthright *mono*-nationality, come to that. How and why can birth ties ground a

---

[7] Taken from the parents' Facebook page campaign (www.facebook.com/Norwegian ChildrensRights), emphasis added.
[8] Posted comments to the article cited earlier (Sandelson 2013). Emphasis added.
[9] Note that the 2014 reform does not, however, allow those born of foreign parents to become dual citizens *automatically*. Dual citizenship status is still conditional on the satisfaction of a list of criteria (proof of residence in Germany for at least eight years, proof of attending a German school for six years, etc.) See Conrad 2014.
[10] In Chapter 3 I will turn to restrictions of dual citizenship arising from *naturalization*.

moral claim to the citizenship of a particular state? And to what extent do those grounds extend to claims to the citizenship of *multiple* states *simultaneously*?

Let us first notice one obvious, but not unimportant, detail. As practiced, restrictions on birthright dual citizenship, as the one just discussed, do not render (or even risk rendering) the targeted individuals *stateless*. In that respect, at least, they are innocuous. That also means that the classic 'violation of human rights' allegations raised against such measures may be misguided. The right to citizenship (that is, 'the right to have rights') is indeed a human right. (Article 15 of the Universal Declaration of Human Rights states that 'everyone has the right to a nationality'.) Yet the human right to citizenship is only a right to *one* citizenship.[11] Insofar as statelessness is not at stake in the restrictions, there is no potential for a violation of the human right to citizenship.

Yet some might still think that if one automatically acquires *one* citizenship at birth, on the basis of either *jus sanguinis* or *jus soli*, then one should also acquire *more than one* if the same grounds (*jus sanguinis* or *jus soli*) support it. If birthright is a good enough ground for receiving citizenship at all, then surely it is also a good ground for being granted as *many* citizenships as one can genuinely claim under that same principle. Thus, first, one needs to clarify why birthright (*just sanguinis* or *jus soli*) should have become a universal ground for the allocation of *one* citizenship.

I will argue that allocating citizenship at birth, whether on the basis of *jus sanguinis* or *jus soli*, was historically not meant to be – and morally is not justified as – recognition by states of an entitlement created by birth circumstances. Instead, states have rightly relied on *jus sanguinis* and *jus soli* essentially for efficiency reasons – as the best way to satisfy *everyone's human right to a citizenship*. Yet, in its abstract form, this human right to citizenship does not entail a right to the citizenship of any *particular* state, or a right *to more than one citizenship*. Hence my argument against *birthright dual* citizenship below is also one against the more common and general claim that *birth alone* creates an entitlement to the citizenship of a *particular* state for a *particular* person. To claim otherwise obviously conflicts with the spirit of human rights, interpreted in efficiency terms.

I   The Efficiency Argument behind Birthright

Let us begin with a logical reconstruction of the best reason why states might have adopted birthright in the first place. Some legal scholars have

---

[11] *Perez v. Brownell*, 356 US 44 (1958); Arendt 1968, p. 177; Benhabib 2005.

already noticed that birthright was introduced as universal ground for citizenship allocation on account of its efficiency in matching each and every individual to a state. They say it is 'the *main allocation mechanism* to ensure that everybody is a citizen of at least one state'.[12] The main priority, on this view, in adopting birthright was to avoid statelessness – to make sure that nobody is denied the right to a citizenship, hence that everyone's human rights will be protected by *some* state. As every individual is inevitably born on some state's territory (the world being partitioned into mutually exclusive and jointly exhaustive state jurisdictions), and every individual is born of two other individuals who are (almost invariably) already citizens of some state,[13] distributing citizenship on the basis of birthright grounds (whether *jus sanguinis* or *jus soli*) virtually guarantees that nobody is left out. And if one ground fails, for some reason or another, to match an individual to a state (because, for example, she was born on an unregistered ship on the high seas), the other ground will surely not.[14] And while birthright citizenship 'is not without significant anomalies', one being 'multiple citizenship (two or more citizenships)',[15] this allocation mechanism, among all other possible ones, legal scholars argue, comes closest to guaranteeing the satisfaction of Article 15 of the Universal Declaration of Human Rights.

Thus, most justifiably, birthright would have been introduced purely out of a concern with efficiency in linking people to states and *not* for *satisfying merit or desert claims* by giving an individual born in state *X* what she is *entitled* to, or to an individual born to person *Y* what is *rightfully* hers. And if the goal of birthright is to ensure *only* that everyone is a citizen of *some* state, then limitations on birthright *multiple* citizenship are at least prima facie legitimate, as they do not undermine this goal. By

---

[12] Vink and de Groot 2010, p. 3, emphasis added.
[13] The desideratum of gender equality pushed states to recognize *jus sanguinis a patre et a matre*.
[14] To be sure, statelessness still affects at least 10 million people worldwide. Notice, however, that this cannot be blamed on the birthright principle, as such. It is rather caused by a poor implementation of the principle by states, or simply the states' refusal to implement the principle altogether. For example, statelessness is caused by exclusionary policies including gender discriminatory legislation, lack of clarity of nationality provisions, denationalization (withdrawal of citizenship), refusal of state authorities to register births, or refusal of individuals to declare births. State dissolution, such as that of the USSR and Yugoslavia, also caused statelessness. The problem is mainly a bureaucratic one and has to do with the issuance of new nationality documents. Sometimes, however, it is the result of deliberate state policies (for example, in some Baltic states the ethnic Russians had to regain their citizenship after state independence). Nowadays, statelessness is a widespread phenomenon across Nepal, Bangladesh, the Caribbean, the Middle East, and Africa. See UN Refugee Agency n.d.
[15] Vink and de Groot 2010.

restricting birthright multiple citizenship, states are just remedying anomalies that have no reason to exist, given this rationale for ascribing citizenship to people in the first place.

Yet birthright citizenship does more than prevent statelessness. It serves to underwrite a *minimal form of global equality*. According to legal doctrine, everyone has an equal human right to citizenship somewhere. Conferring citizenship as a birthright honours this requirement by guaranteeing that all people be citizens of some state, in a world otherwise ravaged by inequalities of all sorts.[16] If one cares about this minimal, albeit formal, equality, then it is imperative to remedy all deviation from the norm 'one individual, one state'.[17] One should do so for this simple reason: while there is an allocation mechanism (birthright citizenship) to ensure that every individual will be member of one state, there is no such mechanism to ensure that every individual will be equally a multiple citizen, much less be a member of the same number of states.

Multiple citizenship largely comes to one as a privilege, from the chance event of one's being born in the right place or in the right family (or, often, both).[18] Insofar as multiple citizenship cannot be distributed equally, equality would dictate that everybody should be content with a more modest version of formal global equality: mono-nationality.

II What, If Not Efficiency, Could Justify Birthright Multiple Nationality?

The moral and legal justification of birthright offered above is thus not supportive of dual citizenship. What, then, could morally justify birthright dual citizenship?

Citizenship is commonly regarded as an entitlement *outside* the human rights framework discussed above.[19] The rules of *jus sanguinis* and *jus soli*

---

[16] Of course, a more substantive version of this equality would further require that states be similar in various other respects (from natural resources to political systems). This would enable a uniform *fulfilment* of human rights across states.

[17] Some might rightly object that this minimal form of global equality is not worth much anyway, precisely because of the gross substantive inequalities between states. Hence, they may say, we should not be bothered too much by deviations from it. To those, I point out that formal inequalities can easily translate into substantive advantages that would aggravate existing substantive inequalities. See Chapter 7 for a discussion of the substantive negative consequences multiple citizenship can have for global equality.

[18] The acquisition of multiple citizenship is thus contingent on being born in a multinational family and on the territory of a state that accepts dual citizenship, for example.

[19] Indeed, the bulk of the literature on migration refers to citizenship as entitlement, especially when discussing the migrants and their progeny's right to citizenship, for example. See Carens 2013 and Rubio-Marin 2000; cf. Schuck and Smith 1985; Shachar 2009. Carens (2016) argues that, as a matter of *justice*, the children of both

are often thought (mistakenly, I shall argue) to reflect the fact that sheer birth circumstances (location of birth or parentage) create an *entitlement* to citizenship – one, two, or more.

When discussing birthright citizenship, things often get quite personal and go beyond abstract notions like human rights. We are, after all, implicitly talking about children, their parents, and families. Seen through that emotive lens, it is all too easy to forget that 'legal citizenship is *not* a natural category, and acquiring citizenship is *not* a natural outcome of being born. People acquire citizenship as a result of some chosen set of legal rules, some political practice that states have established.'[20] It is equally easy to forget that citizenship remains a democratically deficient,[21] if not obscurantist institution: an important gatekeeper of life opportunities, but also one of the few sources of opportunities that is essentially a birth privilege.

Despite having come to terms with birthright citizenship in his more recent writings, Carens accurately pointed out, years ago, how present-day democracies and medieval communities are similar with respect to their membership practices: 'Citizenship in Western liberal democracies is the modern equivalent of feudal privilege – an inherited status that greatly enhances one's life chances. Like feudal birthright privileges, restrictive citizenship is hard to justify when one thinks about it closely.'[22]

But what makes people think of citizenship in terms of a personal entitlement acquired at birth? Below I will critically examine some arguments in favour of birthright citizenship that might be thought, by extension, to serve as arguments in favour of multiple citizenship arising from birthright as well.

A   Jus Soli

Some might be tempted to think that the children of the Norwegian-Australian couple mentioned earlier had *a right to dual citizenship* that was violated by Norway. They might think the twins had a right to Norwegian citizenship *simply because they were born there*. On this view, one does not have simply a right to *a* citizenship; under *jus soli*, one has a right to the citizenship of the state on the territory of which one was born. As Carens

---

immigrants and émigrés should be granted citizenship, even when this results in multiple citizenship, and that the distribution of citizenship is governed by *moral principles*.

[20] Carens 2013, p. 21. I will refer extensively to Carens's book, which provides one of the most important defences of birthright (dual) citizenship.
[21] For Schuck and Smith (1985), this deficit stems from the lack of consent.
[22] Carens 1987.

notices, the need for a child to have citizenship in *some* state 'does not explain why a *particular state* ought to grant citizenship to a *particular child* ... So, we are back at the question of why states confer citizenship at birth on particular infants and why we should do so.'[23] He continues: 'The answer to that question has to lie in our sense of the *moral relevance* of the connections that are *established at birth* between a particular baby and a particular political community.'[24]

This view is not new, however; quite the contrary. That those born in a certain land have the right to the protection of that land's lord or sovereign was, after all, a deeply entrenched doctrine of the feudal system (see Blackstone's writings).[25] True, in that period one is not talking of citizens but merely of subjects. Yet the fact that birth on the lord's territory made one subject to that lord's dominion draws attention to the fact that both a state's relationship to its citizens and a lord's relationship to his subjects are justified in the same way. Granting citizenship on the basis of birth in a particular territory implies that, by birth, people are somewhat 'tied' to that territory in a way reminiscent of how serfs were 'tied' to their lord's lands, being born on his seigniorial estate. People do not think that way anymore.

My own view, mooted above, is that *particular* states grant citizenship to *particular* infants not because of any deeply moralized connections established by birth but purely out of *efficiency*. First, if one recognizes a duty to protect newborns, then one must set up a system that can ensure, at the lowest possible cost, that all the babies get saved from the pond (to use Singer's image),[26] that is, that all children are granted citizenship. We are less concerned about any connections to a particular land (often created by chance) that an individual may have, and more about avoiding a situation where, in principle, all states are liable to granting citizenship to any individual, and hence no particular state has any special responsibility of doing so – which may result in *none* of the states fulfilling their duty toward individuals and granting them citizenship.[27] *Jus soli* is just a way of guaranteeing that everybody's right to one citizenship, *somewhere*, is satisfied in the most efficient way before any coordination problems among states even arise.

---

[23] Carens 2013, pp. 21–2, emphasis in original.
[24] Ibid., p. 22, emphasis added.
[25] Blackstone [1753] 1893, bk. 1, ch. X, p. 370.
[26] Singer 1972.
[27] This is akin to the 'bystander effect' (or 'bystander apathy') in socio-psychology, where people do not help someone in need when others are in the position to help as well. The probability of providing help decreases with the number of bystanders. (For discussion, see Elster 2007, ch. 23.)

Here is another possible rationale for *jus soli*, building on the previous one: basic needs have to be satisfied *immediately* or the soonest possible. States ought to discharge the duties entailed by human rights as soon as possible toward each bearer of these rights – particularly so in the case of highly vulnerable infants with urgent care needs. Here is where *proximity* plays a role. Indeed, it seems the state on the territory of which one is born can ordinarily satisfy these needs most promptly. At least in theory that seems generally right, although in practice failed or struggling states (like South Sudan, Somalia, or Timor-Leste) may not be in a position to protect the human rights of those born on their territory in the most efficient or prompt way.

Second, Carens argues that it makes sense for a state to grant citizenship to those born on its territory because that state *matters* a lot to them (much more so than to others born elsewhere, I presume he means to imply). He claims that 'the state where she [the baby] lives matters a lot to her life ... Beyond that, the state where she lives inevitably structures, secures and promotes, her relationship with other human beings, including her family in various ways.'[28] (Notice that Carens here presupposes that one's family inevitably lives, or will live, on the same territory on which one was born – which is, of course, not always true, especially with the rise of migration, the increasing number of multinational couples, and the separation of such couples, sometimes leaving members of the same family residing in different countries or even on different continents.)

In my view, Carens gets things backward. By granting citizenship to individuals *at birth*, rather than later on in life, a state *ensures* that those born on their territory are more likely to have their entire lives structured by its rules.[29] States are making it happen, precisely by granting them birthright citizenship. In the absence of their holding that state's citizenship, that would not automatically happen immediately upon birth. So, by granting citizenship at birth, states are nudging people (and in some cases, constraining them) to spending their entire lives there. It is not that, immediately upon birth, the state where one is born matters a lot to the individual's life; rather, that state wishes to ensure that it will matter a lot to that individual's life by granting him its citizenship and making him an official member of the state. States are just being proactive.

---

[28] Carens 2013, p. 23. Of course, in defence of Norway's decision we can say that the application for Australian citizenship could have been interpreted as a sign that the children *will not* spend their lives in Norway.

[29] On the other hand, we could argue that states affect individuals *in utero* as well, taking into account how important prenatal care is to their subsequent development.

What is more, if basic human rights can be indeed protected by means other than citizenship (for example, by the granting of legal rights *tout court*[30]), then that means that states' granting citizenship upon birth is a step beyond what is required. It is perfectly possible that states are *actually* pursuing *their own interests* when granting citizenship upon birth to infants born on their territory. They could, after all, very well provide newborns with legal protection in the first instance, and only grant them citizenship later on, when the child's connections to the state will be more salient. One can doubt, however, whether state interests are morally – politically maybe, but not morally – a good ground for citizenship allocation.[31]

Now let us think of it differently. Instead of rejecting Carens's view, one can endorse it and still make a point against *jus soli* citizenship allocation. Let us bite Carens's bullet and accept, for the sake of argument, that states structure the life of infants born on their territory immediately upon birth, and that this justifies the granting of citizenship to those infants. Then one can easily turn Carens's argument on its head, by noticing that states can have the same effect in structuring the life of infants born *outside* their borders as well. Just by choosing *not* to grant them its citizenship, a state can do much to structure the lives of infants born *outside* its borders. Not being granted citizenship means that those infants born elsewhere will not have the same rights and life opportunities as those born on the state's territory. So, both by granting citizenship and by not granting it, states are in fact structuring people's life opportunities. If structuring their life opportunities is what gives rise to a right to citizenship (or rights *tout court*) for those born on the state's territory, that same consideration should, by the same token, give rise to a right to citizenship (or rights *tout court*) for many others across the world as well. My argument here against *jus soli* is structurally similar to the refutation of the classic argument that being subjected to a state's coercion is what grounds an entitlement to citizenship rights in that state; those coerced include, after all, not only insiders but also outsiders who are, for example, coerced by the states' immigration controls and other state laws that apply extra-territorially to non-citizens as well.[32]

---

[30] If citizenship is valued for giving access to other rights, those rights could in principle be granted without granting citizenship (see Carens 2013, p. 22).

[31] Carens rejects state interests as a morally legitimate ground for citizenship allocation, too. Yet his discussion of how states relate to infants born on their territory seems to actually support the claim that state interests are indeed at stake in birthright citizenship. See Carens 2013, pp. 22–3.

[32] See Abizadeh 2008; Anonymous 2011; Beckman 2014; Goodin 2016.

It would also be mistaken to think that states are recognizing the *relationship* they *have* with the infants born on their territory by granting them citizenship upon birth. After all, what they are doing can hardly be recognizing any *preexisting*, ongoing relationship with them. Rather, by granting them citizenship, states *create the bases* of a relationship with these newborns. There is simply no relationship with the state to recognize, at the moment of birth. The relationship is not created by the fact of birth, but emerges directly from the state's action to make them citizens – and from the facts, following from that, that they will likely grow up in that state and interact with its institutions and other members of that community.[33]

Residence, rather than citizenship per se, will more likely play the central role in determining a child's relationship to a state. As previously remarked, granting citizenship at birth makes long-term residence on that state's territory more likely – which can thus be considered an entrapment strategy, and seen in that way may be morally problematic. But a state can also shape the upbringing of a child even if that child was not born there and is not one of its citizens, but merely *resides* there for a long enough period of time. (Consider, for example, the case of the United States and the DACA children – undocumented immigrant children having arrived in the United States under the Deferred Action for Childhood Arrivals program.[34]) If citizenship is indeed about recognizing some sort of special relationship or deep connection to the state, then on that basis states should grant citizenship only some years after birth to those born on their territory and, as well, after some years of residence on state territory to those born elsewhere.[35] The point is simply that birth alone does not create relationships.

Even if it did, one should ask whether relationships created by 'accident', not voluntarily endorsed, and having a very thin content (location of birth and parentage) should create moral entitlements to the citizenship of *particular* states. That would be to say that children born on Swiss soil deserve or are morally entitled to *Swiss* citizenship, while children born in Sudan deserve or are morally entitled to *Sudanese* citizenship.

---

[33] Indeed the relationship develops later on, as Carens himself acknowledges. But it is a *direct consequence* of the state's decision to grant citizenship at birth: 'A young citizen will automatically acquire all of the rights and face all the duties of an adult citizen once she reaches the age of maturity. She does not have to pass any tests or meet any standards to qualify for full citizenship' (Carens 2013, p. 24). In Chapter 6, I focus on a particular subset of such rights automatically acquired upon reaching adulthood in virtue of birthright citizenship: political rights.

[34] See Somin 2017.

[35] Carens 2013, p. 25.

But it is a matter of pure chance, and hence should be irrelevant from a moral point of view,[36] on which state's territory one is born. All have the right to one citizenship, yet the accident ('lottery' as Shachar calls it[37]) of birth cannot entitle one to the citizenship of any *particular* state. Indeed, one can reasonably doubt that the Norwegian-Australian couple would have insisted on their twins acquiring the citizenship of the state where they were born, had they been born in Togo or a less economically developed part of the world instead. It is normal for parents (and one might even expect them) to try to give their progeny an advantage over others, in the form of an additional citizenship or otherwise. But it is equally legitimate for states to say 'no' to granting such advantages, when it is only fair and within their power for them to do so.

B   Jus Sanguinis

What other objections can there be to restricting birthright dual citizenship? I will next set out several other objections based on *jus sanguinis* claims and examine their soundness.

In the case presented in the beginning of the chapter, some people might think the twins in question were entitled to Norwegian citizenship not merely by virtue of being born on Norwegian soil but also (or instead) by virtue of *being born to a Norwegian citizen*.[38] Insofar as Norway ordinarily recognizes *jus sanguinis*,[39] its decision to deny the twins Norwegian citizenship creates a double standard. Why should these children be denied, just because of their *nationally diverse* blood ties, what is *rightfully* theirs – something that other children born to Norwegian citizens are granted as a rule?[40] (Of course, one reason why other children born to

---

[36] Arneson 2001; Cohen 1989; Dworkin 2000; Roemer 1996.
[37] Shachar 2009.
[38] Bauböck argues that by virtue of the right of return, first-generation émigrés should be allowed to be dual citizens. The same, however, does not apply to second-generation émigrés. Return being less likely, such émigrés could – under the stakeholder principle he advocates, for example – be denied dual citizenship (Bauböck 2009, p. 485). But otherwise, as I suggest in the next chapter, states might just impose *additional conditionality* on the acquisition or retention of dual citizenship. For example, states might assess the strength of stakes of second-generation émigrés, and condition citizenship preservation on a declaration of intent or on repeated returns and residence in the state.
[39] Countries may recognize only *jus sanguinis*, only *jus soli*, or both birthright criteria.
[40] Take also the case of children born to Norwegian émigrés. These children could easily become dual citizens by a combination of *jus sanguinis* (applied their Norwegian citizenship) and *jus soli* (applied to the citizenship of the state where they are born). Norway permits dual citizenship in this situation (perhaps as a safeguard against statelessness), and that can be considered an unfortunate double standard that flies in the face of fairness.

Norwegian citizens are granted Norwegian citizenship is that – unlike the twins who could claim Australian citizenship – such children might otherwise be stateless.) A second worry would be that granting these children the citizenship of their father but not also that of their mother (where the legislation of both Australia and Norway ordinarily recognizes *jus sanguinis a patre et a matre*) flies in the face of gender or parental equality. In this case, it represents the children's *relationship* with their father as more important or deserving than that with their mother. Of course, in principle things could be the other way around, and privilege the mother's relationship to the child over the father's. But either way, it constitutes a violation of parental equality.

To build on that thought, another objection to Norway's decision might proceed by emphasizing that citizenship acquisition rules should be sensitive to the importance of *special relationships* and of *goods* distributed inside those relationships. Insofar as children are in a special relationship with both their parents, they ought to enjoy the goods associated with and distributed within *each* of those relationships. And that is so, even when the children in question would thereby receive *more* in virtue of their relationships to their parents than would other children in virtue of their relationship to theirs.[41] After all, some children will always get more love and care than others. Yet it would be unconscionable to suppose that the former should be deprived of a part of this care just because their parents are more caring than other children's parents. Goods distributed inside special relationships are not the ordinary target of distributive justice.[42] From that, there is only one small step to thinking that the twins in question are entitled to both citizenships on the ground that they happen to be in a special relationship with *nationally different* individuals (their parents), just as they are entitled to all the love and care their parents offer them even if this exceeds the amount of love and care other children receive on the average. Why should they get less, just because other children are not in a similar position to their own?

The problem with this type of reasoning is that it is based on a grave misunderstanding of citizenship. First, citizenship marks the relationship of an individual to a state, and not the biological or affective relationship between two individuals (parent and child, or husband and wife).[43]

---

[41] Fishkin 1983.
[42] For an inquiry, see Cordelli 2015; Lister 2013.
[43] Of course, parents may *prefer* to share with their children membership in the same organization. But this alone does not provide a sufficient reason for their children's inclusion in the same organization. A refusal to include their children would be entirely legitimate insofar as the purpose of these associative organizations goes beyond the satisfaction of the parents' narrow preferences.

Second, citizenship is not on a par with the other goods of a non-legal and apolitical kind, mentioned above (love and care). The distribution of love and care is primarily, and almost exclusively, the prerogative of parents; the distribution of citizenship is not. While the main providers of love and care for a child are her parents, the main (indeed, only) provider of citizenship remains the state. Citizenship is not a relational good or resource tied to the relationship between a child and her parents, and should not be treated like one.[44]

The same misunderstanding of citizenship could lead one to thinking that a proscription of dual citizenship is a violation of the *parents' right to pass on citizenship to their children*. The parents' request of dual citizenship for their progeny could, after all, be regarded as just another case of 'legitimate parental partiality' that ought to be satisfied by the state.[45] A couple of parents of different nationalities should, on this view, be able to transmit both nationalities to their offspring. Just as states should not prevent people from bequeathing all their property to their children,[46] states should not prevent children from 'inheriting' their parents' citizenships or prevent their parents from transmitting these citizenships to their offspring (insofar as they recognize *jus sanguinis* at all).[47]

But forget property.[48] Why not think that parents should be able to share their citizenship with their children just as they share inherited physical features or other *identity* features with them? Such a reason might be lurking in people's minds when defending *jus sanguinis*. Carens, for example, admits in his book that one reason why he wanted American citizenship for his children was, at root, *common identity*: 'We [Carens and his wife] still

---

[44] See Brighouse and Swift 2009; Kolodny 2010. Another question would be whether the parents' action in the above case is *just* or not. They are trying to give their children more than what is legally, and perhaps even morally, permissible. While many people would agree that parents have a duty to offer their offspring the best possible start in life, few people would agree that this duty makes permissible the robbing of banks or bribing of teachers to give good marks to do so.

[45] Surely there are limits to parental partiality, and the passing on of citizenship may just be *im*permissible partiality. Parental partiality should, after all, be weighed against other considerations such as equality and fairness.

[46] For a discussion of this claim, see Halliday 2013. Of course, just because they recognize *property rights* does not necessarily mean that states must recognize also a *right to pass on* these rights to others. The right to own property could simply be enjoyed during one's lifetime and be extinguished upon death.

[47] While defending birthright citizenship (even in the case of children of émigrés or even their grandchildren), Carens (2013, p. 30, emphasis added) nonetheless recognizes – as quoted before – that '[i]t would be wrong to regard citizenship in a democracy as a sort of *feudal title* or *property right* that could be passed on from one generation to the next regardless of where the heirs actually lived their lives.'

[48] Surely some rights, which are purely personal, are extinguished upon death and cannot be passed on. They include those related to civil personality and discharge of office.

saw ourselves then primarily as Americans rather than Canadians, and we wanted our children to have an American identity as well as a Canadian one.'[49] On this view, the transmission of citizenship would be analogous to the transmission of genetic features, like good immunity or eye colour. Parents may want to share an identity with their children, if not necessarily in every respect, anyway in certain central respects, citizenship included. Sharing particular features with their children might figure high on their agenda. True, some 'inherited' genetic endowments, like talents, constitute important competitive advantages over others.[50] And equally true, such advantages can easily challenge equality and fairness.[51] Yet parents *are* free to pass on valuable genetic material by letting nature take its course or by intervening to the margins (for example, with piano lessons).[52] Citizenship might be considered to be just another identity feature from the same repertoire that parents may wish[53] – and if they so wish, should be allowed – to share with their offspring.[54]

I leave aside the discussion of whether or not such practices – of shaping or determining a child's identity in the end – are morally acceptable. Just briefly however, consider that such practices can constitute an attack on the children's *right to identity*. This right would entail the freedom to be as one wishes to be on reflection. Attribution of name, religion, or citizenship at or shortly after birth all limit one's identity choices and restrict one's freedom of making identity decisions. Some imposed identity decisions can be reversed. But sometimes, shedding one's identity imposed at birth is hard if not impossible. For example, apostasy and reconversion are not

---

[49] Carens 2013, p. 28.
[50] See Rawls's (1971, pp. 65–75) discussion of whether these advantages are fair or not, and should be mitigated.
[51] In Chapter 7, I will discuss at length global fairness and equality in relation to dual citizenship. It is quite obvious, however, that global equality of opportunity and birthright citizenship cannot be easily squared. For this view, see Shachar 2009. Cf. Miller 2005.
[52] I leave aside whether genetic manipulation is wrong or unfair (see Bostrom and Savulescu 2009; Buchanan 1995; Sandel 2009).
[53] This argument proceeds from the parents' perspective, but a similar story could be told from the child's perspective, if the child wants to share some features with its parents, and might for that reason claim the citizenship that its parents enjoy. Notice, however, that the child would be able to make such a judgement only after a number of years into her life and not immediately after being born, which means that such an argument cannot justify birthright citizenship, which is typically allocated immediately upon one being born.
[54] A child is often seen by its parents as their 'mini-me' – an individual who will 'take their place in the world' when they are gone. While parenting is not *only* about ego drives and identity relations, for many, identity still represents an important aspect of the parent–child relationship. This could in part explain why so many couples are fiercely trying fertility treatments and IVF sessions, while so few consider adoption as an option. For a moral argument for adoption, see Friedrich 2013.

accepted in all religions. Similarly, some states do not accept citizenship renunciation, and until having the opportunity to take on another citizenship (which many might never have), one is literally stuck with one's birth citizenship. We should thus strive to afford people with as many choices as possible when it comes to their identity. This would in itself be another argument for limiting the scope of birthright citizenship.

Furthermore, citizenship and its allocation are different in important respects from genetic features, such as eye colour, talents, and so on and their allocation, as well as from material goods that may be transmitted from parent to child. First, *jus sanguinis* does not actually regulate the *transmission* of a good – citizenship – from one individual (parent) to another (child). Birthright provisions, unlike wills, for example, regulate the allocation *de novo* of a good, *not* its transmission. A new citizenship gets distributed to every newborn. The base for this allocation may be parentage, but that is not akin to saying that citizenship is 'passed on' from parent to child just like family furniture or the family peerage or a blood-borne disease contracted *in utero*.

Second, parents cannot dispose of citizenship just like they can dispose of their car or house. Citizenship is *not their property* to begin with. Insofar as the whole citizen community decides on its distribution and on the benefits attached to this membership, citizenship and its benefits may be rightly regarded as public property. Furthermore, citizenship is a good conferring power over other people's lives, and creating duties toward those others as well.[55] Citizenship is not a *private* good. While physical individuals are the *bearers* of citizenship, this does not make them its *owners* in any real sense.

Think of an analogy here: noble titles are the property of the Crown. Only the Crown can distribute or revoke them. Likewise, only the state can distribute or revoke citizenship.[56] Think of what is commonly the physical proof of one's citizenship: one's passport. Carrying one's passport does not make one its 'owner'. Somewhere on the passport's cover there is invariably a note reminding one that that document is actually the property of the issuing authority. So, even the passport is not *quite* one's property; it was rather entrusted to them by the state. The same goes for citizenship. Citizenship is not a private good that can be transmitted from one person to another just like property, even if *jus sanguinis* regulations might trade on an analogy that makes it wrongly seem so.[57]

---

[55] I discuss what implications this has for the sale of citizenship in Chapter 4.
[56] On citizenship withdrawal, see Barry and Ferracioli 2016; Gibney 2013a, 2013b.
[57] Otherwise parents would not have to bother registering the birth of their children. It is up to the state to issue these children birth certificates and acknowledge them as citizens.

Even more worrisome, birthright dual citizenship puts forward a very ethnic, indeed tribal, conception of the *political community* (the demos) that cannot be easily squared with democratic values.[58] Talking of citizenship as a *blood* tie to a *political* community, talking of an essentially *political* relationship as if it were a *personal* one, harks back centuries to a time where society was based on purely ascriptive, inherited status.[59]

What constitute the heart and soul of citizenship are, after all, political *rights*. It would seem natural thus for the ties among members of a *political* community to be purely *political* as well. These ties should derive from the reality of government, not blood. They are ties uniting individuals whose lives depend on the same political institutions, individuals who are at the mercy of the same political powers. 'We the People' should not be confused with 'We the Family or extended Tribe'.[60] To be sure, family ties also demand recognition and state protection, but citizenship as a political relationship *par excellence* should simply relate to different kinds of ties – political, not biological.

Last but not least, there is one more thing to be said in favour of restrictions on birthright dual citizenship. Ascribing even a single citizenship upon birth – potentially *different* from one person to the next – is more than enough to endow people with very dissimilar life opportunities and to create inequalities that can be hard to overcome. An accumulation of these *birth* citizenships can easily increase the advantages some people get from being born in the right place or into the right family. These advantages are not purely symbolic. Citizenship unlocks, fast-tracks, or at least facilitates access to precious benefits ranging from suffrage to health and wealth and education. According to some theorists like Rawls, the main function of state institutions is to redress 'deep' inequalities like those created by arbitrary birth circumstances. The effects of such circumstances have the potential of being profound and long term.[61] It is difficult to overcome such birthright inequalities, globally. Yet inside each polity, states have concentrated their efforts to neutralizing, or at least minimizing, their impact, more or less successfully.

Broad domestic equality among members of the same polity remains an ideal at least formally embraced by a great many states. The decisions of states like Norway or Germany to prevent their members from accumulating birthright citizenships can be justified by that same concern

---

[58] Again, acknowledged by Carens (2013, p. 28).
[59] Maine 1901.
[60] Goodin 1998.
[61] Rawls 2000, p. 7. Equality of fair opportunity entails that competitive advantages born out of favourable circumstances should be reduced or neutralized (see Rawls 2000, esp. §§12 and 13).

with domestic equality. These states may be simply pursuing legitimate state purposes in trying to make sure that all Norwegian and all German citizens get more nearly equal or equivalent life opportunities. That can be a morally good reason for Norway not to allow its birth citizens to retain Norwegian citizenship upon naturalizing elsewhere. Hence the decision of a state like Norway not to allow the accumulation of birthright citizenships could be considered fair on the following ground: it ensures that Norwegian citizens who acquire another citizenship through *naturalization* and Norwegian citizens who acquire another citizenship via *birthright* are treated the same. Neither category is allowed to retain Norwegian citizenships and thus enjoy dual citizenship. On egalitarian premises, at least, that is just as it should be.

C   Reform

Above, I have discussed and expressed doubts about the arguments raised in favour of birthright multiple citizenship. These arguments give rise, however, to some reasonable concerns. I will here point out how a reform of birthright multiple citizenship could accommodate these concerns, while at the same time avoiding the flaws of birthright multiple citizenship I discussed earlier.

One common argument for a state granting citizenship to those born on its territory or born to its citizens is that there is a high probability that those people will spend their lives there and thus have a complex future relationship to that state's community. As I have pointed out, such a claim is dubious insofar as birthright citizenship works as a *self-fulfilling prophecy*[62] – people tend to spend their entire life in their birth state *in no small part because* they are granted citizenship of it at birth. Birth citizenship creates the incentive and conditions for people to develop these relationships in one state rather than another. It has an anchoring effect, rooting individuals in a particular institutional setting and in a particular political community.

The second, subsidiary reason would point to a feasibility constraint. Perhaps it might be said that there is no plausible way to construct birthright citizenship rules in a way that responds to individual variations – to the variety of cases where birth citizens will not spend their entire life or have a meaningful relationship to their state of origin.[63] Once again, however, as pointed out above, what is the rule and what are the exceptions are largely the consequences of the principle of birthright itself.

---

[62] Aleinikoff and Rumbaut 1998–9.
[63] Carens 2013, p. 29.

But leaving all of that aside, there are ways of reforming birthright. Think of a system of *renewal* of citizenship, where birthright citizenship has to be renewed every ten years, as to express an individual's choice to retain it. Alternatively, retention of birthright citizenship might be automatic but only when certain conditions are fulfilled (for example, there is proof of repeated previous residence on that state territory in the last seven years, no acquisition of second citizenship involved, and so on). States could also ask for such renewals up to a certain age, say sixty-five, after which citizenship could persist until death.[64]

III Conclusion

In this chapter I have argued that there is no good moral justification for multiple citizenship arising from birthright, and that limitations of birthright multiple citizenship are hence permissible.

Over the course of my discussion of multiple citizenship, I made some more general, and perhaps more generally useful, points about the distribution of citizenship and the rights comprised by it. At various points in the chapter I found the need for a *more inclusive* or diverse ground for citizenship allocation emerging surprisingly enough from the various justifications offered for birthright itself. I argued that, while the fact of birth alone does not create any moral entitlement to these rights, residence might. So too might other factors, such as the fact of being affected by the state's institutions, decisions, or environment; one can be affected in all those ways without residing on the state's territory. I also hinted at the possibility of allocating the rights of citizenship separately and gradually over time, instead of the way states presently do. I will return to these ideas and discuss them more extensively in Chapters 6 and 8.

---

[64] One rationale for that might be simply that elderly people ought not be bothered with such bureaucratic hassles. Another might be that – on the assumption that if people have always renewed their birthright citizenship up to that age, they will be likely to want to do so evermore – it is unlikely that they will have any major life changes at that age to alter that (such as relocation in another state and naturalization there).

3 Multiple Citizenship by Naturalization

Having discussed birthright multiple citizenship in the previous chapter, I now turn to *multiple citizenship acquired by naturalization*.

Naturalization requirements have attracted a fair amount of academic attention of late. Some theorists have bemoaned the unfair or illiberal character of such regulations.[1] They have argued, more positively, in favour of making naturalization a means of political integration of both long-term legal and illegal immigrants.[2]

Some of them focused on the *duties* that receiving states have toward these people. First, naturalizing long-term legal immigrants and thereby granting them political rights is, arguably, an essential requirement of democracy. A state cannot be fully democratic if a part of its population is prevented from participating in its government. For government to be legitimate, there must (ideally) be a perfect match between law-takers and law-makers. Second, states also have a duty to protect the vulnerable. That entails that they should naturalize immigrants (especially, but not exclusively asylum-seekers or stateless individuals) if this is the best way of protecting them. They should also grant citizenship to immigrants, whether legal or illegal, if they have been long living on the state territory and have developed harmonious social and economic relationships with that community. That merely amounts to formally recognizing the equal social standing that these people already have within the community.[3]

But integrating immigrants is not just a matter of duty: it is to the *advantage* of receiving states as well. Another part of the conversation, both political and academic, emphasizes the ways in which states can benefit from immigration. Immigrants enrich their host communities both culturally and economically,[4] and they would do even more so as

---

[1] Bauböck and Joppke 2010; Carens 1998, 2010, 2013, ch. 3; Etzioni 2007; Hansen 2008; Joppke 2010; Orgad 2010; Spiro 1998–9.
[2] See Carens 1998.
[3] Carens 2010.
[4] Borjas 1995; Goodin 2006.

citizens. There are thus multiple reasons why immigrants should be offered and should take up[5] the citizenship of their new receiving states.

Yet the reasons given above do not necessarily provide a defence of *dual citizenship* as such. Just because immigrants should become citizens of their receiving state does not *necessarily* mean that they should *also* remain citizens of their sending states as well. From this, an important question arises: Is it legitimate for the receiving state to grant its citizenship only conditional on immigrants shedding their previous citizenships, in effect denying immigrants the option of becoming dual citizens upon naturalization?

That will be my concern in this chapter. I will be interested here in the fairness of one particular condition for naturalization: *renunciation of previous citizenship*.[6] Such a requirement, which precludes dual citizenship, is currently contained in the citizenship laws of several countries.[7] In the first part of this chapter I will discuss various arguments for and against this requirement. In discussing its legitimacy, I will also compare it with an analogous requirement that can be imposed by the *sending* state with the same effect – loss of citizenship *ex lege*.[8] My conclusion will be that the legitimacy of requiring immigrants to give up their previous citizenships depends upon the *source* of that requirement. It is most morally problematic if that request comes from the *receiving* rather than the *sending* state.

In the second part of the chapter, I will discuss the converse case, in which the sending state's laws provide for *automatic retention of citizenship* upon naturalization elsewhere (and the receiving state does not demand renunciation of previous citizenship upon naturalization, either). When the citizenship laws of the receiving and sending state are arranged in that way, a migrant will automatically become a dual citizen upon naturalization, by default. Emphasizing the downside of having such default rules, I will argue that the dual citizenship emerging from such a legal arrangement may be problematic in a different way. I conclude with a proposal to reshape *the structure of choice* available to naturalization applicants, and

---

[5] For a discussion, see De Schutter and Ypi (2015), who argue that immigrants have a duty to take on the citizenship of their states of residence.
[6] Where that is an option; it is not, if the sending state does not allow its citizens to renounce its citizenship.
[7] That is true (at the time of writing) in, e.g., Denmark, Norway, Germany, Austria, and the Netherlands.
[8] By 'loss of citizenship *ex lege*' I refer to the 'loss of nationality by an act of law that requires neither explicit expression of intent (application, declaration, making use of an option or similar modalities) by the target person or his or her legal agent to renounce nationality, nor a decision or act by a public authority. Used synonymously with lapse of nationality.' See EUDO Glossary on Citizenship and Nationality n.d.

hence potential dual citizens. The reform I propose would likely decrease the number of dual citizens but, at the same time, enhance the meaningfulness of dual citizenship, lifting it from the status of 'citizenship of convenience'[9] to a *citizenship of choice*.

I   Legal Framework

The naturalization requirement in view in the first part of this chapter is mandatory renunciation of other citizenships upon acquiring the new one. That requirement avoids dual citizenship, but it should be distinguished from other legal measures that could have the same effect.

One would be *denaturalization* or *denationalization* (withdrawal of citizenship), where state A revokes citizen K's citizenship (without K's consent).[10] A second would be *loss of citizenship ex lege* upon naturalization elsewhere, where K, a citizen of state A, loses citizenship in A *automatically* upon becoming citizen of state B under state A's citizenship law.[11]

What I shall here be discussing is different from the citizenship provisions above. It is what may be called 'expatriation-conditioned naturalization'. Under that type of citizenship law, state B conditions K's naturalization on his renunciation of citizenship in state A, thus precluding K from becoming a dual citizen of both states A and B. While both denaturalization and loss of citizenship *ex lege* may also thwart multiple nationality, those policies differ both empirically and normatively (as I will point out below) from the policy of making renunciation of citizenship a condition for naturalization.

II   Against the Citizenship Renunciation Requirement

Should receiving states condition naturalization on renunciation of previous citizenships? According to Carens the answer is 'no'. He argues that the citizenship renunciation requirement is unjust.[12] Insofar as dual citizenship does not cause any problems, states should not use their coercive power to force immigrants into choosing, for no good reason,

---

[9] The phrase 'citizenship of convenience' is borrowed from Spiro (2008a).
[10] States may withdraw citizenship for reason of fraud, disloyalty, treason, violation of 'duties as a national', or other criminal offences. See de Groot and Vink 2010. For a normative analysis of citizenship withdrawal, see Gibney 2013a, 2013b.
[11] Until recently, the Czech Republic and Denmark relied on such provisions, but those were repealed in the last few years. At the time of writing, Austria, Estonia, Germany, Ireland, Latvia, Lithuania, the Netherlands, Norway, Slovakia, Spain, and Ukraine still had such provisions in place, with the scope of the exceptions to the rule varying across the states. See de Groot, Vink, and Honohan 2010; see also GLOBALCIT 2016.
[12] Carens 2013, ch. 3.

between two citizenships. A dual citizen can be loyal to both her countries, just as one can love both of one's parents. Divided loyalties to two different countries are not an issue insofar as there is no potential conflict between military duties or complications related to diplomatic protection (as argued in Chapter 1); various international treaties prevent potential state conflicts related to dual nationality in those respects.[13] A renunciation requirement is harmful insofar as it does not respect the immigrant's *interests* or *identity*. Immigrants might still be attached in various ways to their country of origin. They might still want to pursue certain economic opportunities they have there as citizens. They might want to retain the right to travel easily to and, perhaps, even resettle in those states. 'Vital' interests, such as inheriting property or running a business there, might also be at stake.[14]

Perhaps the most important argument against erecting barriers (such as the renunciation requirement) to residents acquiring citizenship is the following. As I shall argue at greater length in Chapter 6, democracy demands that those *subjected to the laws* should participate in the making of those laws. This means that all those subjected to the law (including settled immigrants) should receive the citizenship of their receiving state (at least if they want it) – and they should do so, if not *unconditionally*, anyway only on conditions that can be squared with the democratic ideal (literacy in the language of the country, enabling one to vote in an informed way, for example). This is a powerful argument against imposing democratically irrelevant conditions on the receipt of citizenship in the receiving state.[15]

Yet, as I will argue below, this does not necessarily also constitute an argument in support of dual citizenship. Just because the *receiving* state should not ask the immigrant to give up previous citizenship does not

---

[13] As I have pointed out elsewhere (Chapters 1 and 8), this is not entirely accurate. While conflicts of military duties are no longer an issue, conflicts of jurisdiction are still possible and increasingly common thanks also to multiple citizenship.

[14] In truth, however, few states restrict the right to inherit to citizens. The barriers were lifted at the beginning of twentieth century through state reciprocity statutes. See Anonymous 1963, 1969; Murphy 1967.

[15] In Chapter 5, I will argue that, when a dual citizen exercises political rights in two states, that can undermine democratic decision making by disrupting meta-agreement (which is a prerequisite for reaching coherent collective decisions by majority rule) in one or both of those countries. This argues against allowing someone who is already a citizen-voter in one country to become a citizen-voter in a second country as well. Naturalization conditioned on renunciation of prior citizenships does not necessarily solve this problem, however. It neither guarantees that the persons lose the frame of reference formed through deliberations in their previous country not does it guarantee that the persons will acquire the frame of reference appropriate to deliberations in their new country.

mean that the immigrant should, all things considered, remain a citizen of the sending state. It may well be that the sending state would be within its moral rights to block dual citizenship by refusing to allow its émigrés to retain their citizenship upon naturalizing in another state.

Democratic principles requiring that all those subjected to the law have a say in the law means that immigrants should, prima facie at least, be entitled to political rights in the state of which they are long-term residents. That means that it would be illegitimate for a *state of residence* to impose arbitrary conditions on granting them political rights, such as demanding they renounce their previous citizenship as a condition of naturalization and of acquiring voting rights there. Yet according to the same democratic principle, it would be perfectly legitimate for the *sending* state to ask its long-term émigrés to give up their citizenships or to make legal arrangements so that they automatically lose their citizenships upon naturalization elsewhere (loss of citizenship *ex lege*). If what grounds the moral right to citizenship is 'social membership and the fact of ongoing subjection to the laws', then such a moral claim to citizenship is lost when these conditions are no longer fulfilled, as may well be the case with long-term émigrés.[16]

Notice, however, that in democracy-based arguments over naturalization or loss of citizenship, *political rights* are really what is at stake. *They* are the reason why the state of residence *cannot* legitimately impose conditions on naturalization, from a democratic point of view, while the sending state *can* legitimately impose loss of citizenship *ex lege*. Thus, perhaps what troubles us the most, at least on this view, is that the state of residence restricts *the exercise of political rights* when it conditions naturalization on citizenship renunciation, thus imposing conditions on the grant of something that should be given as a matter of right in virtue of subjection to the state's laws.

But suppose we separated out political rights and allocated them separately. It might be perfectly legitimate for the state of residence to impose conditions on the grant of *other* citizenship benefits or on the grant of citizenship solely as a *formal non-voting membership status*. (The thought here would be that subjection to the state's laws entitles one to political rights, but *not* to other collective goods, the latter of which could be extended, for example, on a contributory basis.) Analogously, if what makes external citizenship problematic is the exercise of political rights by people who have no legitimate claim to exercise such rights there, then the sending state could just expunge its émigrés from its electoral rolls

---

[16] See López-Guerra 2005.

instead of stripping them of citizenship *tout court*. Unbundling citizenship rights and allocating political rights separately – a solution I will discuss extensively in Chapters 6 and 8 – could thus render a certain sort of (partial) renunciation requirement less problematic.

Once that unbundling has been effected, the revised renunciation requirement would apply only to political rights. On this model, the receiving state would ask immigrants *only* to give up their political rights in the sending state but not other benefits or formal membership there. The sending state would impose *only* the *ex lege* loss of *political rights* and not of the full bundle of rights as currently entailed by unitary citizenship. I will come back to the unbundling proposal in Chapter 6.

III   In Defence of the Citizenship Renunciation Requirement

What can nonetheless be said *in favour* of the citizenship renunciation requirement in its current form?

A   The Demands of Consistency

One justification for requiring new citizens to trade in their former citizenships could be that states want to preserve *equality among fellow countrymen* (as discussed in Chapter 2). Equality could be a legitimate reason for conditioning naturalization this way. A state whose community is composed of mono-nationals cannot accept outsiders into citizenship without requiring them to become mono-nationals as well, if the equality requirement is to be respected. If Germany's community is made up of individuals who are citizens of Germany *alone*, then all foreigners wishing to join the German community should share this status of mono-citizenship with their new fellow countrymen. On this view, the citizenship renunciation requirement is just a requirement of *consistency* within the community.

Yet for this argument to really stick, egalitarian concerns must permeate *all* citizenship provisions. For example, if naturalization in state A is conditioned on expatriation in the case of immigrants, then for the sake of symmetry, A's citizenship laws should also provide for the automatic loss of citizenship for its birthright citizens naturalizing in another state. That is to say, the state should ensure that, just like its naturalized citizens, its birthright citizens could not become dual nationals – whether through the application of another state's birthright regulations, through the application of its own birthright regulations, or as a consequence of those citizens naturalizing in another country. The requirement of citizenship renunciation thus seems legitimate only when coupled with other legal provisions against dual citizenship. If states choose to restrict dual citizenship on egalitarian grounds, they should do so all the way, ensuring equal treatment for birthright and naturalized citizens alike with respect to their access to dual citizenship. This is not always the case, however.

Take, for example, the instance of Germany, prior to the most recent revisions in its citizenship laws. Although it required first-generation immigrants to shed their citizenship when naturalizing, it allowed second-generation immigrants born on its territory to be dual citizens only up to the age of twenty-three, at which point it required them to make a choice between their citizenships.[17] Thus, the later could enjoy multiple citizenship for a number of years, whereas the former were not allowed this privilege. If Germany wished to pursue equal treatment in its dual citizenship policy, it might have, for example, adopted a system that also allowed first-generation immigrants to keep their citizenships of origin *for a number of years* after naturalizing, thus allowing them to enjoy the status of dual citizen just as some of their fellow Germans did, under the same citizenship law. Another double standard concerns how EU immigrants are treated in comparison to immigrants from non-EU states: while Germany requires the latter to give up their citizenships of origin upon naturalization, it does not in the case of the former, thus allowing them privileged access to dual citizenship and reducing the cost of naturalization for them.

It would, of course, be possible for a state to want to ensure equality among citizens along other lines, not in terms of mono-nationality but (why not?) in terms of multiple citizenship. If all the state's birth citizens were multiple citizens, then consistency would require the state not to impose a citizenship renunciation requirement on those who wish to naturalize. In realistic terms, it is of course unlikely for a state's population to be made up entirely of mono-nationals or entirely of multiple citizens. But there is no need for a state's *entire* population to be made up of multiple citizens for that state to lose its claim to consistency-based legitimacy when requesting citizenship renunciation. It would be enough for some of its birth citizens to be – or to be allowed to be – multiple citizens in order for the state to lose any consistency-based legitimacy claim when demanding renunciation of citizenship elsewhere from those wishing to naturalize.

---

[17] Germany changed its law recently, and starting with December 2014 that choice is no longer required. Instead, second-generation immigrants are able to retain both citizenships upon fulfilling certain criteria. Yet, those not qualifying under these criteria will have to make a choice between their citizenships, as before.

B No Different from Other Conditions

But can the citizenship renunciation requirement be justified even when the receiving state adopts a double standard with respect to dual nationality, that is, when naturalized and birth citizens are not treated alike? In truth, non-members and members of a group are treated differently all the time. Such differences are what makes group membership valuable in the first place. In order to protect group identity and other group benefits, group members restrict the access of other individuals to membership in their group as they please. This is an instance of discrimination, to be sure, but one that is generally considered to be legitimate.[18]

Renouncing one's citizenship is just one requirement of naturalization among many. Some claim that *all* naturalization requirements should be removed or, at least, be made easier to satisfy.[19] That may be so. It is worth wondering, however, whether renunciation of citizenship is indeed more problematic than other naturalization requirements, such as tests of knowledge of language, history, and social culture; proof of economic integration; or penal clearance. And if indeed it is more problematic, what makes it so?

Renouncing citizenship undoubtedly represents a personal cost. Yet other naturalization requirements are costly as well, in terms of the applicant's time, money, and energy. Immigrants must take various courses to prepare for the tests. They must also obtain the necessary documents to go with their applications. All these constitute costs an immigrant assumes when deciding to become a full member of the receiving state. Hence a citizenship renunciation requirement might not seem to be different in *kind* from the various other requirements.[20]

C Not like the Other Conditions: What Is Permissible and What Is Not

Some might think that there should, however, be a limit to the *magnitude* of costs or sacrifices required for naturalization. Citizenship renunciation, they may say, is beyond the acceptable limit. But in order to say that

---

[18] Freedom of association would grant associations (states included) the right to refuse or withdraw membership to some people. See Wellman 2008, p. 112.

[19] According to Carens (1998, p. 143), for example, 'as a matter of fundamental justice, anyone who has resided lawfully in a liberal democratic state for an extended period of time (e.g., five years or more) ought to be entitled to become a citizen if he or she wishes to do so'.

[20] Think also that naturalization was introduced as recognition of the right to expatriate oneself – to end allegiance to one's birth state. This could be done only by a rejection of dual citizenship. The right to choose one's citizenship was commonly understood as the right to *change* one's citizenship. Naturalization entailed *one citizenship being exchanged for another*. See Martin 2014.

citizenship renunciation is beyond such a limit, one would need to know where that limit is. I shall discuss the magnitude of costs issue below. First, let us consider the possibility that the requirement to renounce one's previous citizenships is *different in kind* from other conditions that may properly be imposed on naturalization.

What conditions can the state impose on the grant of citizenship, and what conditions can it not? It could well be thought that, because a state has the power to naturalize or not, it can impose *any* condition it likes upon naturalization – citizenship renunciation included. Following Grotius and Locke, it might be supposed that any greater power subsumes lesser powers.[21] For example, if in war one can kill one's enemy, then one can also enslave, beat, or torture him – in short, do anything short of killing him. Similarly, one might think that if the state has discretionary power to grant or deny citizenship to foreigners to begin with, then it can also impose whatever conditions it wishes upon the granting of that citizenship.

Other philosophers have argued, however, that any greater power *does not* subsume lesser powers, *unless* the powers are of the *same kind* – that is, unless they are used *for the same purpose*.[22] That means, for example, that if it is permissible to kill one's enemy in war in order to defend oneself, it is *im*permissible to enslave him after he has been captured and disarmed, insofar as one's survival is no longer at stake.

Seen in that light, whether or not the citizenship renunciation is legitimate depends ultimately on what one thinks is the *purpose* for which states are granted the power to naturalize foreigners. If one thinks its purpose is to formally recognize as members those who already act like members of the community, then it seems that the citizenship renunciation condition is impermissible.[23] One might, on the other hand, think of the citizenship renunciation condition as precisely the kind of test that is meant to show who acts like a member and who not: if one is ready to shed one's prior citizenship in order to acquire ours, the state might think, then that individual may be regarded as acting 'like a true member', showing just how much she values our community. Thus, we can easily imagine arguments both for and against the legitimacy of the requirement to renounce prior citizenship, depending upon what we take to be purpose for which states have the power to naturalize foreigners, and on whether the citizenship renunciation requirement serves that purpose or not.

---

[21] Grotius [1625] 2012, vol. III, ch. 4, §10; Locke [1690] 1764, ch. 4, §23 and ch. 7, §85.
[22] Goodin 2004.
[23] On the same ground, imposing language conditions on naturalization is clearly permissible.

D Acting against One's Interest

A big worry about the citizenship renunciation requirement – perhaps the primary one for most advocates of dual citizenship – is that the receiving states are thereby asking immigrants to *act too much against their interests*. Retaining the citizenship of their sending state might be valuable to them for various purposes, ranging from facilitated travel to their sense of identity[24] to the expressive exercise of political rights.[25] Thus asking immigrants to give up such advantages in order to become citizens of the new community may be asking a lot of them – perhaps so much as to constitute an abuse of power on the part of the receiving state.

But becoming citizens of the receiving state is presumably in their interest as well – perhaps even more so than continuing being citizens of their sending states. Conditionalizing naturalization on citizenship renunciation will indeed prompt immigrants to weigh their interest in being citizens of their sending states against their interest in being citizens of their receiving ones. But such requirement does not necessarily *prevent* immigrants from acting in their interest. If the sending state's citizenship is more valuable to them, they can retain that and simply not naturalize in the receiving state. If they do naturalize in the receiving state on condition that they renounce their original citizenship, the interests they have in remaining a citizen of that state could suffer a setback. But acting against some of their interests could ultimately be in their *best* interest when faced with the choice. All that the citizenship renunciation requirement does is to force them to weigh and rank their interests, before deciding whether to apply for naturalization. But that applies to any big decision involving both benefits and costs. As long as naturalization is *voluntary*, one can reasonably think that, whenever long-term immigrants choose to naturalize on condition of renouncing their prior citizenship, the interests they have in the receiving state exceed whatever interests they may have in their sending state. Otherwise, they would surely not proceed with the naturalization procedure.

Maybe, from the receiving state's point of view, there is a good reason to ask immigrants to rank their interests and choose among them. If the immigrant's interest in being a citizen of the receiving state does indeed

---

[24] This is a common objection. Yet it would be exaggerated to say that one loses one's identity with one's passport. Cultural features or attachments do not disappear with the passport, and may not depend on the passport to begin with (e.g., I can have a cultural attachment to France – speak French, read French novels, listen to French music, drink French wines – without being a French citizen). Someone's identity naturally consists of more than his or her passport. For a related view, see Waldron 2000.

[25] Of course, such advantages on the part of the immigrants may have negative externalities for others, as discussed in Chapters 6 and 7.

outweigh that of being a citizen of the sending state, that may constitute proof in itself that that individual is indeed part of that community in such a way that deserves the formal recognition from the receiving state. It sends an important signal to the state: individual K is ready to commit to being member of the community. It may also ensure that membership in the group is not taken lightly by potential newcomers. If the interest in being a citizen of the sending state is indeed stronger, it should mean that the immigrant is indeed ready to join the new community.

Also, asking people to commit to one community or another might be just one way of testing who is more reliable and trustworthy in the long term and not just in the short run. (In this connection, see also my critique of citizenship-by-investment on the same grounds in Chapter 4.) 'Burning bridges' by giving up citizenship means that returning to the sending state is not such an easy option. From the receiving state's point of view, this might be seen as good news: in a democracy, exercising voice should, after all, be encouraged, and exiting (in any form) should be discouraged.[26] A second citizenship would be bad news insofar as, for those who have it, exit would be readily available at a relatively low cost.

E   Loss Aversion

There is, however, another important difference between the citizenship renunciation requirement and other naturalization requirements. This difference best explains, I think, people's initial outright rejection of the citizenship renunciation condition. While meeting the other requirements involves people *acquiring* something they did not have before (whether it is language skills and other knowledge, employment and bank accounts, medical insurance, and so on), the citizenship renunciation requirement is, par excellence, a requirement to give up something one has, and has long had, typically since birth. The requirement of citizenship renunciation will likely trigger a *loss aversion bias*[27] like no other requirement would.[28]

---

[26] Hirschman 1970.
[27] On loss aversion bias (or the endowment effect), see Ariely, Huber, and Wertenbroch 2005; Kahneman, Knetsch, and Thaler 2000; McGraw, Larsen, Kahneman, and Schkade 2010.
[28] True, one might object that the other naturalization requirements also entail a loss – of time and money in particular. I doubt, however, that the loss of time and money would be conceived in the same way or would trigger a loss aversion bias. This is mainly because time and money achieve their value only when they are spent or consumed, that is, get their value through their 'loss'. E.g., time is valuable to us for how we can spend it doing other activities, rather than as such; money is valuable to us for what it can buy us.

What is entailed by the 'loss aversion bias' used by psychologists and economists to explain purchasing patterns, among other things? Put in economic terms, it means that a person would demand more to give up something that he already has than he would pay to acquire the very same thing anew. In the classic experiment, people who refused to pay $10 to acquire a mug, having been given it, refuse to sell it for $10 – which should obviously count as a good deal given their first judgement.[29] In the present context, the thought is that immigrants – who otherwise attach little, if any, value to their citizenships of origin (had they not been birth citizens already, they often would not have gone to any trouble to *acquire* those citizenships) – will typically start valuing them (or at least value them more highly) when asked to give them up. This could at least partly explain the strong reactions against the citizenship renunciation requirement, reactions much stronger than those against other naturalization requirements.

Notice that the reluctance to give up citizenship of the sending state that is induced by the loss aversion bias does not actually account to a *considered, well-defined* preference for retaining that citizenship. One is talking not of reflective preferences but of flawed judgements deriving from cognitive biases (or, at best, of adaptive preferences that are not a measure of autonomy in the end).[30] How much moral weight one should attach to such judgements remains an open question. My aim is just to raise awareness of the fact that focusing on immigrants' *preference* to continue being members of their sending states' communities does not provide such a strong argument against the citizenship renunciation requirement, as it might be first thought.

IV Default Rules and Dual Citizenship

Having discussed the requirement of citizenship renunciation, I now turn to the case where naturalization *does* result in dual citizenship – that is, when (1) the receiving state does not impose a citizenship renunciation requirement and (2) the sending state *does not* have any provisions for loss of citizenship *ex lege*. Drawing on the literature on choice architecture and nudging, I will point out that in this case dual citizenship arises

---

[29] Or take this story: 'A wine-loving economist we know purchased some nice Bordeaux wines years ago at low prices. The wines have greatly appreciated in value, so that a bottle that cost only $10 when purchased would now fetch $200 at auction. This economist now drinks some of this wine occasionally, but would neither be willing to sell the wine at the auction price nor buy an additional bottle at that price' (Kahneman, Knetsch, and Thaler 2000, p. 159).
[30] See Elster 1986.

purely from a *default* rule, and that one might therefore object to dual citizenship on the grounds that it does not express the *active choice* of the individual. I criticise this legal setup governing matters of citizenship and propose a reform that would correct the problem by introducing an element of choice alongside the default rule.

A   What Are Default Rules?

Default rules are part and parcel of our everyday existence. And, in many ways, that is a good thing. Without them people would be forced to decide much more often than they would like to, and continuously deciding could stand in the way of their everyday life activities and priorities. Default rules settle the matter on people's behalf. In some instances, the default arrangement can be subsequently altered by people if they so wished; that is, they can *opt out*. For example, when making an online purchase an online account may be automatically created for customers without their express action or choice, the customers having nonetheless the option to delete the account afterwards.

What is interesting about default rules is that they lead to outcomes that are very stable. Despite having the freedom to opt out, people stick by the default, even when they do not have any particular preference for it. To get a sense of how powerful default rules are, take one example provided by Cass Sunstein:

In 2011, I helped to organize a White House conference on information disclosure. Conference materials were sent out in advance to the three hundred registrants ... In those materials, people were told that unless they specifically requested otherwise, they would receive the healthy lunch option. The materials explained: 'Healthy options for lunch include, but are not limited to, a bean sprout and soy-cheese sandwich on gluten-free soda bread.'

Most people are not enthusiastic about the idea of bean sprout and soy-cheese sandwiches, and it is doubtful that many people actually wanted them. But eighty percent of attendees failed to opt out. On the morning of the event, the participants were not exactly thrilled to learn that most of them had 'selected' the bean sprout and soy-cheese sandwich for lunch. The good news is that people were not held to their apparent 'selections'; they ended up with pretty good sandwiches. Still, it is noteworthy that the well-educated participants ended up signing up, *by default*, for a quite unappealing meal.[31]

Default rules are inherently 'sticky'. This stickiness derives from psychological effects such as an 'endowment effect' (people value something more because they had it in the first place: the source of 'loss aversion')

---

[31] Sunstein 2013a, p. 12, emphasis added.

or a 'status quo bias' (caused by inertia or procrastination). Sticking with the default rule is also effortless compared with opting out, which may be somewhat demanding of time or money. But above all, opting out requires people's attention, and people are often oblivious to default rules.

Default rules have attracted much attention, thanks to the role they can play in policy making.[32] Human cognitive biases – such as an endowment effect or a loss aversion bias – can be cleverly exploited by policy makers to make more palatable policies that do not have public support, yet are to the people's benefit. Of course, what is to people's benefit is decided by the policy makers themselves, qua 'choice architects'. (Not surprisingly, one line of attack against 'nudging' focuses on precisely this point.) Another advantage would be that default rules do not restrict people's freedom, insofar as opting out is always available *at a low cost*.[33] Still, insofar as default rules are very sticky and opting out is rare (perhaps because it is costly, especially of people's scarce attention), one can nonetheless say that even when they are seemingly transparent (which is not always the case) default rules entrap people, playing on their psychological limitations.

Sunstein distinguishes three choice modes: *impersonal default rules*, *active choosing*, and *personalized default rules*. Different choice modes can apply to different types of choices. There are choices that do not matter much for most people, and that perhaps can be put on automatic pilot: for example, choosing one's seat at the cinema or in the plane.[34] But there are also choices that matter a lot in terms of their impact on people's life prospects. Such choices may include choosing one's university degree, choosing which career to pursue, or choosing which state one is a *citizen of*. Furthermore, because it also permits the exercise of political rights, the latter also impacts *other people*'s lives as well, through the coercive consequences that one's vote carries.

B   *Dual Citizenship by Default*

Following naturalization, dual citizenship often comes 'by default'. Take for example migrant K, who left birth state A to take permanent residence

---

[32] Glaeser 2006; Sunstein 2013a, 2001; Willis 2013. See also Sunstein 2013b and Thaler and Sunstein 2009.
[33] This is the sense in which nudging represents '*libertarian* paternalism' (Thaler and Sunstein 2009).
[34] Certainly, there are people who cannot wait to opt out and change the assigned seats. Such people may take pleasure in expressing their preferences on any occasion. If they do not already have a preference on any given matter, they *form* one. Sunstein points out that the formation of preferences entails effort. True. But we must not forget that there are people who might actually enjoy making such efforts, regarding them as opportunities to exercise their freedom of choice and agential control. See Sunstein 2013a, p. 19.

in state B. Suppose state B does not make naturalization conditional on citizenship renunciation. Also, state A allows, *ex lege*, its citizens to retain their citizenships when they naturalize elsewhere.[35] Thus K will automatically continue being a citizen of A when taking on the citizenship of state B. K will then become a dual citizen 'by default', thanks to A's default rule providing for automatic retention of citizenship. K can, of course, 'opt out', that is, give up citizenship in A. This would entail an additional effort on K's part. Whereas K's citizenship in B is the result of active choosing (naturalization), K without doing anything continues to be a citizen of A *ex lege*, by virtue of this state's citizenship law. Thus one can say that K becomes a dual citizen *by default*, since the laws are set up in such a way as to automatically allow her to retain citizenship of A, without her express request or consent.[36]

I think it reasonable to say that, from a moral point of view at least, it would be better for dual citizenship to arise instead through an *active choice*. Out of respect for people's agency, states should allow individuals to make an active choice between *being* or *not being dual citizens*. A rule that mandates *automatic preservation* of former citizenship upon naturalization elsewhere involves no such choice. To be sure, people can escape their dual citizenship status, but the fact that this presupposes an opt-out (with all the costs that opt-outs entail) may psychologically prevent them from doing so (as discussed in connection with loss aversion above). One advantage of changing the default rule giving rise to dual citizenship would be to give individuals (at least those having joined another citizenship community) the chance to *voluntarily* and *reflectively* endorse or reject their birth citizenships – and to do so for the first time, since that status had previously been imposed on them at birth, and hence cannot be said to have been voluntarily acquired.

Notice also that in such a situation – where one would choose between being a dual citizen (that is, remain *also* a citizen of one's birth state) and not being a dual citizen (that is, be a naturalised citizen of one's state of residence only) – the structure of choice would be different in one important respect from that created by naturalization conditioned on

---

[35] Typically, but not always, this is done deliberately to 'entrap' individuals in their role as citizens of their states of origin.

[36] Carens briefly debates an 'opt in' as alternative to the automatic grant of citizenship to the *children of immigrants*. He considers such an alternative undesirable and unjustifiable. His brief footnote does not address the case of children of émigrés (indeed, in many cases citizenship allocation is not automatic but dependent on submitting an application) or the case of individuals who naturalize, as I do here (see Carens's original manuscript, 2013, ch. 3, n. 3, omitted in the published edition). I thank the author for making the manuscript available to me before its publication.

renunciation of previous citizenship. In the latter situation, the stakes of the choice are high: whether one chooses to continue being citizen of one's birth state has implications for one's becoming citizen of one's state of residence as well; one cannot, in this situation, acquire the latter citizenship without renouncing the former. The choice circumvents dual citizenship, but it does so by forcing a person to trade *mono-nationality* in one state for *mono-nationality* in another. The change of default rule I propose entails the same choice between continuing being a citizen of one's birth state or not doing so, but this choice does *not* have any implications for one's status in the state of residence: the individuals making this choice are already citizens of their states of residence, and the question is simply whether they want to retain their birth citizenship as well; their choice is between *dual citizenship* status and *mono-nationality*. The difference between the two contexts of choice is important. Under my revised default rule, an individual's decision to forgo dual citizenship status would reflect her attitude toward her birth citizenship and that alone, whereas where naturalization is conditional on renouncing citizenship elsewhere, her decision would reflect how valuable the one citizenship is to her relative to the other. Also, we can assume that individuals would more gladly give up their birth citizenships if this were presented to them as a free choice that was altogether *irrelevant* to their naturalization in their states of residence.

But to what extent is the use of default rules appropriate at all in citizenship matters? Default rules work best when people do not have diverse preferences. When they do have diverse preferences, one-size-fits-all default rules are inefficient solutions, for they are no longer good proxies for people's actual preferences. When this is the case, it is best to *ask* them to express these preferences and decide on their own. Now, immigrants come 'in all shapes and sizes' (from the asylum-seeker and refugee to the prosperous businessman and cosmopolitan intellectual); each has their own personal story of immigration, and each has different reasons for leaving their home country. Insofar as they do, states can expect these people to relate differently to their states of origins and to their birth citizenships.

As I pointed out above, because of the inherent constraints on the freedom of choice arising from loss-aversion bias, conditioning naturalization on citizenship renunciation is also a bad strategy for finding out how people truly feel about their birth citizenships. True, asking them to make an active choice between being a dual citizen or not might not tackle their loss-aversion bias completely (they would, after all, still be 'losing' their birth citizenships). But at least this choice context involves fewer limitations (operating both consciously and unconsciously) on one's freedom of choice, since there are no trade-offs between one's birth citizenship and naturalization in one's residence state.

Furthermore, when it comes to regulating dual citizenship, states should not be satisfied with suboptimal solutions, especially if those solutions will have negative consequences, as Chapters 5 and 7 will show dual citizenship to have. The negative impact of multiple citizenship could be reduced *by removing legal defaults favouring dual citizenship* and replacing them with a *system of active choosing in citizenship matters*[37] – one based on international legal cooperation at the level of ministries of internal affairs, so as to minimise all burdens associated with an active choice.

C Reform

States might, for example, add an element of choice in the legislation allowing individuals to express their clear choice in favour of or against dual citizenship, alongside the opt-out options they already have available, as previously discussed. For example, after naturalization in the receiving state (or perhaps even as part of the naturalization procedure in that state[38]), migrants could be asked to explicitly communicate their preferences with regard to dual citizenship by filling a simple form. They could tick a box to continue being a citizen of their sending state or another box to discontinue being a citizen of their sending state. They could communicate their intention directly to the receiving state, which would then forward that request on their behalf to their sending state. The system would establish a new rule: the direct choice between being a dual citizen or not.[39]

Notice that my critique of the opt-out with respect to multiple citizenship should not be read as a defence of using opt-in as regards citizenship

---

[37] Ideally, such a system would afford as many options as possible. One example might be a global citizenship that is not parasitical on national citizenship (as European citizenship is on that of member states), if only we could find a way to successfully set it up.

[38] Although I think this would be less preferable for the obvious reason that it might be mistakenly *perceived* by applicants as a constraint on their freedom of choice, even if it would not actually be so.

[39] According to Rainer Bauböck, a citizenship regime with an emphasis on individual choice is the only one that could better adapt to individual circumstances. Furthermore, political communities are based on consent. Such consent should figure more prominently in citizenship laws. 'Assigning legal status to categories of persons defined by broad criteria such as residence, territory of birth and descent will inevitably create normative mismatches with the endless variety of individual circumstances. This is one reason why a defensible citizenship regime must provide for individual choice ... Just as immigrants should not be automatically naturalized against their will, so emigrants must have an option to renounce their citizenship', argues Bauböck (2009, p. 485). Cf. de Schutter and Ypi 2015.

matters indiscriminately, regardless of any social context. Indeed, the exclusive and pervasive use of opt-in rules for citizenship has been as a way of depriving individuals of their just entitlements – and hence as a way of excluding certain categories of people from equal membership. Take France, for example. Prior to 1993, second-generation immigrants born on French soil were automatically granted French citizenship. Subsequent to reforms of the nationality law in France in that year, however, sometime between the ages of sixteen and twenty-one, they had to declare their will to become French citizens in order to be granted citizenship.[40]

Of course, opt-in and opt-out policies use different defaults. The first does not grant citizenship as a matter of course (people have to opt in); the second does grant citizenship as a matter of course (people have to opt out). Yet neither of those defaults requires an active choice between the *two* options, of being or not being a citizen.[41] One can subsequently apply for citizenship (opt in) or renounce citizenship (opt out), to be sure, but only after a particular status (non-citizen or citizen) has been *imposed* on them by the default rule. I am merely advocating that the active choice *in both directions* should become the default. That is to say, one should be free to choose the status of being either a citizen or a non-citizen, a dual citizen or a mono-national, instead of having one or the other status imposed by default and then having the possibility of changing it, at a higher or lower cost.

One needs, however, also to contemplate the case of someone who, failing or refusing to fill the form I mentioned as a solution, does not express a choice between the two options. What would happen then? The sending state would still need to have a secondary default rule to rely on as back-up in such cases. It could, for example, take naturalization to imply renunciation of original citizenship unless the émigré communicated

---

[40] Bertossi and Hajjat 2013.
[41] That citizenship must be based primarily on choice and consent is also argued by Martin (2002, pp. 49–50), and Schuck and Smith (1985), who all emphasize the importance of making voluntary expatriation (i.e., renunciation to citizenship) more readily available to people, sometimes by reducing the material disadvantages that come with it (Martin 2002). These disadvantages can, of course, translate into a loss of rights. Hence, Schuck and Smith (1985, pp. 123–4) argue that those who choose to stop being citizens of a state should nonetheless be permitted to remain permanent residents of that state, with all the rights this status entails. They argue that those who wish to expatriate themselves should be 'able to exercise their right to renounce citizenship more knowledgeably, meaningfully and readily' (p. 7). They have in mind not only multiple citizens, but citizens of a single state as well: 'If the person chose permanent resident status, as our proposal would permit, and did not acquire a new nationality, he or she would be literally stateless' (p. 124). Their proposal entails thus that states should not prevent people from becoming stateless, if this is their will.

otherwise within, say, a year or two. Such reform would likely decrease the number of dual citizens. Yet it would also ensure that dual citizenship has a powerful meaning, which it now often lacks. Theorists complain about plural citizenship pointing to a weakening, lightening of citizenship, and making people's citizenships little more than 'citizenships of convenience'.[42] This reform would transform multiple citizenship from a citizenship of convenience to a citizenship (largely) of choice.

[42] Joppke 2010; Spiro 2008a.

4   Multiple Citizenship by Investment

In the previous two chapters I have shown how multiple citizenship is morally problematic on account of the ways it was acquired by birthright (Chapter 2) or naturalization (Chapter 3). In this chapter I will focus on a third, and last, mode of acquisition of multiple citizenship: investment. Even states that usually block the occurrence of dual citizenship by imposing a citizenship renunciation requirement upon naturalization, such as Austria, waive this requirement in the case of naturalization by investment, allowing investors (but not other candidates for naturalization) to become dual nationals. As with birthright and naturalization, the arguments I will rally in this chapter against investment-based citizenship have a broader application. They apply not only to the distribution of multiple citizenship on that basis but to the distribution of citizenship on that basis *tout court*. But the effect of those arguments will be to shut down yet another avenue by which multiple citizenship might be acquired.

States have always granted citizenship on the basis of exceptional individual achievements, of course. Thomas Paine, for example, was granted honorary French citizenship by the Girondists in the wake of the French Revolution, only to have it revoked when the Montagnards took power. (Of course, Paine was lucky to have lost only his French citizenship and not also his head.) According preferential treatment of this sort to some people may or may not be problematic. But a state explicitly granting citizenship on the basis of nothing but *financial* capital invested in that state makes the grant of citizenship an oblique *trade* – yea, a *sale* of citizenship. Meet investor citizenship.

The market logic has permeated nearly all domains of human life. Among the things that we can buy today are pregnancy services, friendship, sex, queuing time, kidneys, and the right to kill endangered species.[1] Selling citizenship seems innocuous by comparison. It does not compromise a person's body integrity, it does not breach taboos or clear social

---

[1] Sandel 2012.

norms, it does not deplete the commons. At first glance, nothing seems lost, alienated, or violated, as in the other cases just mentioned.

Investor citizenship also seems to be a clear win-win situation. The state thereby attracts or retains foreign investors, increasing its tax base. Investors who thereby obtain citizenship decrease their costs (in terms of paperwork, time, and money) and boost their profits (thanks to opportunities to own or engage in businesses available only to citizens). For those who can afford it, premier residence programs can be also an easy shortcut to naturalization. Yet no matter the reasons for doing it, these are ways of 'buying' one's way into the citizenry.

But *should* states put citizenship on sale? What should stop them from doing so, blind nationalist considerations apart? Investor citizenship might be economically advantageous for all concerned. Yet one might think that conferring citizenship should serve purposes very different from boosting the treasury.

Such objections are not without precedent. The *sale of civic status* has long aroused protests. My strategy in this chapter is to recall what was traditionally said against the sale of *noble titles*, and to consider how those arguments may extend, by analogy, to the sale of citizenship. The analogy is imperfect. Nonetheless, these two practices of selling civic status are surprisingly similar in a great many ways. As I will show, the practice of selling citizenship is not only *similar* to that of selling honours but is also *wrong in analogous ways*.

I   The Rise of Economic Citizenship

Naturalization procedures are complex, nowadays. Individuals have to meet a wide range of requirements when joining a new community: residence requirements, language and social knowledge requirements, moral requirements (penal clearance), and financial requirements (stable income stream). Not so investors, however. Investor citizenship makes citizenship readily available to them simply upon investment. Although the practice is increasingly common, details vary across countries. Some countries may waive *some* naturalization requirements (for example, residence, as in premier residence programs); others may waive *all* requirements. In the latter case, investor citizenship amounts to the 'outright conferral of citizenship' upon investment.[2]

The practice can also be more or less institutionalized. In some countries authorities have the absolute discretion to grant citizenship to investors on

---

[2] Dzankic 2012b, p. 1. See also Dzankic 2012a, 2015; Shachar and Hirschl 2014.

Multiple Citizenship by Investment 57

grounds of economic achievement (as a form of honorary citizenship).[3] Austria and Montenegro, for example, have loosely regulated investor citizenship programs, so the authorities' discretion often kicks in. These countries do not specify the exact amount or type of investment required. At the same time, in both, important naturalization requirements (like language, residence, and renunciation to previous citizenship) are waived when citizenship is acquired via investment.[4] This might be thought peculiar, insofar as both of those countries normally have very tough naturalization requirements.

Other countries – like the Commonwealth of Dominica and St. Kitts and Nevis – have developed detailed citizenship-by-investment policies. In both, the exact amount and type of investment are specified, as well as all other administrative fees. The rights and duties attached to the citizenship are also specified.[5] The most recent countries to put their citizenship on sale or to consider doing so are Malta and Cyprus.[6] Even when countries do not have investor citizenship programs, they often nonetheless have premier residence programs for investors (United States, United Kingdom, Australia, Singapore, Canada, Belgium, Hungary). Some countries, like Austria, have both. Upon investment, premier residence lifts one important naturalization requirement: residence.[7] Hence, as a result, investors benefit from fast-tracked, facilitated naturalization.

This practice has come under public scrutiny because of its association with corruption (influence peddling by politicians),[8] tax evasion, and extradition (where one buys a new citizenship in order to cleanse one's record or escape prosecution).[9] Nonetheless, the argument (with an economic flavour to it) mainly offered in favour of investor citizenship is the following: by naturalizing these individuals, states can decrease the

---

[3] Dzankic 2015. Of course, what counts as 'exceptional achievement in the national interest' is to be decided by state authorities alone. But to get an idea: a Saudi hotel investor and a Russian singer were thought to meet these criteria and were granted Austrian citizenship. See Mahncke and Ignatzi 2013.
[4] See Dzankic 2012b, pp. 11–15.
[5] Ibid., pp. 8–9. In St. Kitts and Nevis investors have two options: investing in real estate or in the Sugar Industry Diversification Foundation.
[6] Cyprus considered offering Cypriot citizenship as compensation to Russian investors having their deposits levied during the economic crisis. The goal, of course, was to keep Russian money in Cypriot banks. See *Der Spiegel* 2013. Malta, on the other hand, amended in 2013 its Citizenship Act to put Maltese, and by extension European, citizenship on sale for €650,000. See Balzan 2013 and Dzankic 2015 for discussion.
[7] Dzankic 2012b, pp. 3–6.
[8] One Austrian politician, for example, promised Austrian citizenship to a Russian investor in exchange for €5 million investment and a donation to the party (Dzankic 2012b, p. 12).
[9] Former Thai Prime Minister Thaksin Shinawatra, convicted for corruption, received Montenegrin citizenship and, most importantly, its passport after investing in Montenegrin tourism. The case sparked much debate (ibid., p. 13).

58 Acquisition

shared costs of membership for the other members (albeit perhaps only in the short term, as I will later point out). Investor citizenship may generally be regarded as a good thing, insofar as its benefits greatly exceed its costs.[10]

This is an important argument in favour of selling citizenship, especially for poor countries with small populations, which could not raise more revenue through taxes even if they wanted. There may be others. Hence it is important that I fully acknowledge from the outset that all the arguments I put forward against investor citizenship should be understood as *pro tanto* reasons against it, which depending on the context may be overridden by other considerations, such as the one just mentioned.

II Selling Honours: The Historical Record

The sale of *civic status* did not begin with contemporary schemes for the sale of citizenship. Long before the emergence of the modern state, and hence of citizenship as we know it, another status was put on the market: *noble* status. Purchasing honours (peerages) was a widespread phenomenon from the Renaissance forward. For the nobility, it represented the culmination of a deep crisis.[11] Both France and England saw a rapid increase in the ranks of the nobility from the sixteenth century onward. Many commoners literally started 'buying' their way into the aristocracy. The phenomenon of 'cash for honours' – or 'temporal simony',[12] as it was also called – took various forms.[13] A rich commoner could use his money to acquire noble status in any of these ways: he could buy an ennoblement letter;[14] he could buy a seigniorial estate that would entitle

---

[10] Buchanan 1965; Frey and Eichberger 1999 discussed in Dzankic 2012b, pp. 2–3.
[11] The nobility was already impoverished by the religious wars and by the administrative reforms of the Crown. See Bitton 1969.
[12] Mayes 1957, p. 35.
[13] Our more recent history is also full of 'cash for honours' episodes. David Lloyd George was involved in a scandal involving the sale of peerages, leading to the adoption of the Honours (Prevention of Abuses) Act in 1925. In 1976, another British Prime Minister, Harold Wilson, produced upon his resignation his 'resignation honours' (known as the 'lavender list'), full of dubious, to say the least, individuals proposed for peerage. Finally, in 2006, the House of Lords Appointments Commission rejected several individuals nominated for life peerages by Prime Minister Tony Blair. They had made substantial donations to the party just before their nominations. Many of the donations turned out to be loans to the party. See *Guardian* 2007 and Kennedy 2016.
[14] Merchants and farmers would buy a seigniorial estate and be recognized nobles upon payment of the *franc-fief*. See Bloch 1934, pp. 43–4. In England, too, the composition of the landed elites changed. Profits from trade and law came easily, and these profits could be used to buy seigniorial estates from an expanding land market (ancient Crown lands and former assets of the monasteries were put on sale). But the *new* landed elites demanded also social recognition of their new positions, to the exasperation of the *old*

him to ennoblement; he could use his fortune to marry into a poor but noble family;[15] he could buy an office, thereby being entitled to noble status (*noblesse de robe*).

In James I's England, the old landed aristocracy quickly denounced the trade of honours by the king and its acolytes. They not only found it downright offensive ('how could one place the *dignity*[16] of the nobility on the open market?'[17]). The practice often went hand in hand with the corruption of the court. Also, once knighthoods were put on the market, knighthood fell into contempt and knights started seeking higher titles, at which point higher titles too were put on sale.[18] The result was a spiralling inflation of honours. In both England and France, the resentment of the aristocracy toward the Crown mounted. The old birth aristocracy never came to accept those having bought their way into its ranks as equals. At the same time, even the newly anointed 'cash' nobility came to recognize the reputational costs and limits of the sale of peerages – eager to keep their competitive advantage over others,[19] they hoped to stop others from buying titles too.[20]

---

landed elites, who wanted precedence in the distribution of status. See Stone 1958, pp. 47, 50.

[15] What the French called '*mésalliance*'. Often, bankrupt old nobles had to marry their progeny to rich bourgeois. For the latter, noble status was the 'last frontier' of social advancement. The marriage was an exchange: money for noble status.

[16] Peter Berger proposed a conceptual distinction between *honour* and *dignity*. First, honour had a strong class dimension. A quintessentially aristocratic quality, it was the product of feudal hierarchies operating on the basis of institutional norms and roles (Berger 1970, p. 340). Yet, second, honour also bore a more universalistic dimension, regulating every person's relationship to his or her community, and the idealized norms of that community (ibid., p. 341). With the rise of the bourgeoisie, the concept of honour expanded, and eventually became meaningless (ibid.). In the modern consciousness, it was gradually replaced with dignity. While dignity was, in contrast, severed from institutional norms and roles, it still fulfilled the same function of regulating one's relationship between self and the community (ibid., pp. 342–3). However, as the quote in the text shows, the historical sources and studies I rely on in this chapter do not always reflect this fine distinction between honour and dignity. For that reason, when talking about the sale of peerages, I will use honour and dignity interchangeably. When discussing the contemporary sale of state membership, I will refer to honour's modern analogue, dignity.

[17] Mayes 1957, p. 21.

[18] Stone 1958, p. 52.

[19] The extension of the franchise brought about a similar situation: 'Middle-class people, once given the vote, wanted to conserve institutions that they had formerly been inclined to attack. Most of the new voters wanted, not to challenge the aristocracy, but to win recognition from it: once they had their rightful position they did not favour further adventures' (Brock 1973, p. 319). Similarly, the newly ennobled sought to win the acceptance of the old nobles by discrediting the process (sale) by which they themselves had acquired their own peerages.

[20] See Arundell 1603.

III Lessons from the Sale of Honours

To be sure, cash for honours testifies that social mobility was possible at least for rich commoners at that time. But the debate surrounding it testifies also to the perception that money was *the wrong way* of acquiring social status. Two points stand out in these debates. First, noble status should not be distributed for sordid, pecuniary reasons. Second, money does not make one worthy of ennoblement. Below I will point out some respects in which the sale of citizenship to investors is similar to the sale of noble titles to commoners and, more importantly, how it is also problematic in analogous ways.

A Merit and Reciprocity

At the core of the critique of cash for honours lay a defence of *merit*. The sale of honours precluded noble status from tracking merit exclusively. The association of birth with merit is puzzling at first: what does noble (hence inherited) status have to do with merit? But it becomes clear once one grasps the peculiar understanding the nobility had of 'merit'. It is very different from our present, common understanding of it.[21] The nobles' meaning of merit went beyond considerations of personal virtue, and was largely relational.[22]

In France, merit could arise only from a long-term personal relationship to the Crown. The recognition of merit was the unique prerogative of the king.[23] A man of merit[24] – a nobleman, that is – was worthy of his status as recompense for past services he and his ancestors had given the king. Merit was thus grounded in a *long-standing* gift relationship with the king.[25] Noble status (as inherited status) was a proof of strong bonds and entrenched obligations to the Crown created by past services and gratifications.[26] The sale of honours was bound to clash with this very

---

[21] According to the *Oxford English Dictionary*: 'the quality of being particularly good or worthy, especially so as to deserve praise or reward'.
[22] Smith 1996, p. 21.
[23] Ibid., p. 7.
[24] This conception of merit, corresponding in theological discourse to the notion of *condign* merit, entailed a reciprocity relationship, contrary to *congruous* merit, which entailed virtuous qualities. This distinction was important enough to figure in the 1694 French Academy's dictionary (Smith 1996, pp. 20–1, n. 31).
[25] At the time there was a general reverence for all things long-standing or ancient. The British constitution, for example, was respected by people for its having been in place since time immemorial (Pocock 1987).
[26] Notice also that noble title – passed from generation to generation – accounted for a single continuing being (e.g., under the name of Earl of Oxford) transcending the mortal bodies of individuals taking this title in every generation (e.g., the first, second, third, ...

particular understanding of merit. Sure, giving the king money in exchange for a noble title might be termed as 'granting him a service' or 'doing him a favour'. But this did not say anything about past commitments and services to the Crown which alone could evince merit.[27] Important was the *timing* of such exchanges. To confer merit, as the nobles understood it, such exchanges should have taken place on multiple occasions, over hundreds of years. Becoming a nobleman immediately upon the first payment of cash failed to say anything about the *past*. And most importantly – taking the long-standing past to be the only true indicator of what was to come – it failed also to say anything about the *future* of these relationships.

In England, too, noble status was a hallmark of personal merit.[28] And its sale was depriving 'the Crown of the fairest means of *rewarding deserving* servants by making nobility appear cheap'.[29] Quite bafflingly, even those making the purchase were aware of this moral pitfall. One purchaser of honours defended his new acquisition as follows: 'he observed *merit to be no medium to an honorary reward*, that he saw divers persons who he thought deserved it as little as he (either in their persons or estates) by that meanes leap over his head, and therefore seeing the market open and finding his purse not unfurnished for it he was perswaded to ware his mony as other men had done'.[30]

So money did not make one worthy of noble status. Does money make one *worthy of citizenship*? Arguably not, and for broadly the same reason. Like the old nobles, one might well take merit to arise from a long-standing relationship to a community. Such relationship would presuppose repeated interactions and exchanges spanning, if not generations, at least (for foreign-born, would-be citizens) a great many years. Under this understanding of 'merit', conferral of citizenship would recognize robust relationships (social, political, *and* economic) to a community of citizens. Just as one's long-standing commitments and services to the Crown made one worthy of nobility in olden times, so too might one's long-standing commitments and relationship to a community be what makes one worthy of acquiring an additional citizenship today.

---

*n*th Earl of Oxford). This approach to noble persona is similar to that toward the king's persona. The authority of the king lay in two personas: his mystic persona (*corpus mysticum*) and his mortal persona (*corpus naturale*) (Kantorowicz 1997).

[27] Under this understanding of merit, it was plainly impossible for commoners (even rich ones) to *ever* be worthy of noble status. Noble status was inherited status *exclusively*.
[28] Stone 1958, p. 60.
[29] Mayes 1957, p. 36, emphasis added.
[30] Ibid., emphasis added.

Indeed, an important task of naturalization tests is to prove the existence and robustness of these relationships. Residence requirements, in particular, put on emphasis on their *duration*.[31] Temporality counts. Merit is subject to a test of time, today just as in the seventeenth century. Here is a reason that should be so. Robust relationships to a community are a measure of *equal standing* in that community – and surely it is equal standing that citizenship should reflect in the end, not big purses. Status (whether noble or citizen status) should always mirror social realities. Yet if there are no 'robustness tests' in investor citizenship (beyond that of the pocket), formal status becomes a broken mirror of these realities.

Besides its link to their conception of merit, the old nobles had an additional reason for insisting on duration. Long-standing gift relationships bound one to the Crown by duties of *reciprocity*. Seen in this light, the *duration* of relationships mattered because only the passage of time permitted repeated interactions, which were the true test of reciprocity.[32] Buying status on a spot market is, of course, a one-off transaction. There was thus a worry that the 'pocket nobility' will fail to reciprocate the king for its new privileges. If privileges were bestowed in exchange for a one-off monetary payment, then there would be no room for debts of gratitude.[33]

Reciprocity was a key value in the relationship with the king. Nowadays reciprocity is a key value in the relationship with the state. A lack of reciprocity may lead to the dissolution of the state or to the breakdown of state institutions in times of hardship. One task of citizenship is to promote reciprocity among community members. But if states want citizenship to foster reciprocity, then granting citizenship on the basis of short-term investments might be a bad idea.

First, because the investors' main concern will be their profits. Sharp investors will try to further their own interest at all costs (forgoing duties

---

[31] The passage of time can determine the allocation of rights in different ways. Think first of usucaption, or acquisitive prescription (*longa enim possession ius parit possidendi*). Property titles could be acquired by prescription: continuous possession of land granted the possessor property rights. Think second of the French Civil Solidarity Pact (PACS). Personal relationships have to be enduring enough to qualify for such unions. Think third of ongoing rules-based regularization regimes. Illegal migrants can escape deportation and legalize their status if they have lived long enough in (and in peaceful communion with) a community. In all cases, relationships (to land, to a person, or to a community) have to be robust enough to endow the parties with rights (and duties). Duration is a proxy (not perfect, but nonetheless relevant) for such robustness.

[32] Axelrod and Hamilton 1981; Trivers 1971.

[33] This point did not go unnoticed. As one nobleman remarked: 'yt when he first sets up you may bring your wench to his house and do yor things there; but when he grows rich, he turns conscientious and will sell no wine upon ye Sabbath day' (quoted in Stone 1958, p. 61).

of reciprocity in the process). If citizenship comes to reward investors, then indirectly it comes to reward the pursuit of short-term self-interest. Second, a history of past interactions creates robust obligations and a sense of responsibility toward one's peers. Special relationships create special duties.[34] These are absent in the case of someone just deciding to buy citizenship one day, for business reasons (whereas such relationships are much more often present in the case of someone following the standard naturalization route). Citizens-by-investment can, and many will, retain their original residences abroad, not relocating to their new state of citizenship. The lack of interactions (past or future) with the new community will prevent the emergence of any sense of obligation or any fellow feeling toward investor citizens' new co-nationals.

But the problem may lie not with investors per se, but with *market* relationships. Markets do reward a concern, not for selfless reciprocity, but for self-interest. And the logic behind the mode of distribution of a good may also contaminate its mode of its use. Having acquired their citizenship through the market, investors could follow the same market logic in their citizen capacity. If so, in times of hardship when citizenship is no longer profitable to them, investors may just defect. They may transfer their capital elsewhere and forget all about the special duties they have *qua* citizens. In the market, dissatisfaction is expressed by exit. In democracies it is supposed to be expressed through voice.[35] Investors will prefer exit to voice insofar as they are thinking and acting as economic agents rather than as citizens.

A similar worry was expressed, in olden times, about the pocket nobility. Was the cash bond enough to ensure that the nobleman will stick by the king in case of war, sacrificing himself if necessary? It seemed not: the sale of honours allowed for all debts owed to the Crown to be monetized and thus also extinguished by the money transfer. So, if the king thought that by selling honours he was potentially increasing the ranks of his supporters, he was obviously wrong. At most it put him in a more precarious situation than before: relying on people who will have little incentive to prove themselves reliable in such situations.[36] Perhaps it is worth noticing that selling honours was self-defeating for the other party as well. Nobility was first and foremost a state of *distinction* – of being born in a noble family. Scarcity made nobility highly valued and

---

[34] For duties of citizenship, see Lazar 2010; Scheffler 1997.
[35] Hirschman 1970.
[36] Machiavelli ([1532] 1882, ch. 12) objected to mercenary armies on the same ground: these are soldiers who will easily defect to the opponent, if he bids higher. Buying more soldiers could thus do more harm than good.

desired. Now, those buying noble titles were doing it partly with the intention of distinguishing themselves from the masses. They wanted to purchase a status distinction. But their plans backfired. Commodification led to an inflation of honours, depreciating nobility to the point of it ceasing to be the state of distinction it once was.

Similarly, a community might try to get rich by selling citizenship. It might profit, at first. But that community would be selling citizenship to the wrong people: individuals whose only reason for buying it would be pure profit maximization. Investors will use their new citizenship to improve profits; these profits may be deposited into offshore accounts to escape taxation. So, although a nation might be better off economically immediately upon engaging in such an exchange, it may not be in the long term. The investor will try to cover her initial costs of buying the citizenship and make profits beyond that, perhaps in ways detrimental to the national economy. For those reasons, in the case of both pocket nobles and investor citizens, we would be dealing with *self-defeating exchanges* – exchanges that undermine their own purpose. As such, we have one good reason for blocking them.

But maybe markets are not altogether incompatible with reciprocity. They might simply promote a *different kind* of reciprocity. Returning a favour extinguishes all standing debts of gratitude that arise from gift giving, for example. No subsequent duties of reciprocity survive the return transaction. Everyone has done his duty. Yet this does not mean that there is no reciprocity in market relationships. Quite the contrary. In market exchanges, one *instantly reciprocates* for what one gets. As Marx put it, under the market reciprocity is a 'natural precondition of exchange'.[37] What is the problem then?

Markets are not primarily concerned with reciprocity. Reciprocity appears purely as a by-product of the pursuit of self-interest.[38] The problem of markets – in Marx's view and later in Cohen's too – is that they fail to promote '*communal* reciprocity'.[39] Communal reciprocity can be understood as mutuality, yielding one another services as in a gift relationship ('I care that you care for me'). Whereas market reciprocity is ensured by cash rewards, communal reciprocity is ensured uniquely by *caring for human beings*. It turns on the relationship with the other members of the community – with the other members of the jazz band,

---

[37] Marx 1973, p. 244.
[38] In Marx's (1973, p. 244) words, 'the common interest which appears as the motive of the whole is recognised as a fact by both sides; but, as such, it is not the motive, but rather it proceeds, as it were, behind the back of these self-reflected particular interests, behind the back of one's individual's interest in opposition to that of the other'.
[39] Cohen 2009; Vrousalis 2012.

in Cohen's example. In this sense, communal reciprocity is a club good – a good enjoyed by all and only members. To be sure, gift relationships are characterized by greater uncertainty: one does not know if, how, and when the other will reciprocate. Also, there are no mechanisms for enforcing reciprocation. Gift relationships are based on *trust*. Communal reciprocity thus requires mutual trust. In the market, by contrast, little trust (except in the due enforcement of the law of property and contracts) is required: one knows how and when the other will reciprocate; there are clear rules and mechanisms for enforcing reciprocity (as in contracts, for example).[40] Market reciprocity is less about mutual trust and more about mutual satisfaction of interests. But trust is hard to gain, which makes it so dear to us. And for this precise reason, communal reciprocity may be more valuable than its market counterpart.

Now, by selling citizenship a state makes it clear that it is equally content with one type of reciprocity (market) as another (communal). Yet there are good reasons for not being. First, gift relationships might surprisingly promote a better satisfaction of needs. The fact of not knowing how and when the other will reciprocate may ultimately be a good thing. The world is uncertain: one cannot know what exactly one will need, and when exactly one will need it. Gift relationships are underspecified, and this is in fact a comparative advantage they have over contracts. Go back in history again. The king was often not sure whether he would need an army or shelter, and when. Entering a gift relationship with the nobleman was thus more useful to him than entering a cash one (in which the nobleman would reciprocate instantly and in cash necessarily). Think now of investor citizenship. When selling citizenship, the list of expectations has already been drawn (and satisfied) on both sides.[41]

Second, market reciprocity (as by-product of the pursuit of self-interest) cannot prevent the dissolution of societal bonds, or indeed of the state itself, in times of hardship when individual survival is at stake. Communal reciprocity, however, might.

If *citizenship* is to further robust reciprocity, it cannot be put on sale. The investor's relationship with the community will be of a purely contractual sort. And, as such, it will fall victim to the traps discussed above. In particular, market reciprocity will be unable to prevent the citizen-investor from defecting (with all her capital) when times get tough.

---

[40] Contracts enforce reciprocity by establishing rights and duties on both sides. Yet an emphasis on rights will undermine the other pillars of reciprocity, such as trust or affection; in other words, 'standing on your rights gets in the way of sitting down at the table' (Goodin 1993, pp. 510, 511–13).

[41] Standard naturalization, on the other hand, is designed to prove that the applicant is already in a *de facto* gift relationship with the community he wants to join *de jure*.

B   Fairness

From our perspective at least, the sale of peerages can also be seen as unjust, insofar as not all commoners had equal opportunities to advance socially in that way. Only *rich* commoners were upwardly mobile through that route. By the same token, investor citizenship may likewise be unjust insofar as putting citizenship on sale discriminates against the poor. All otherwise identically situated individuals should have equal opportunities of becoming citizens, no matter their financial situation.

While it is true that the poor might not have exactly the same opportunities to acquire citizenship (that is, via investment), they nonetheless have other opportunities to do so (via standard naturalization). So, in the end, an apologist for investor citizenship might say, both rich and poor can naturalize one way or another. But outcomes are not everything. Selling citizenship is problematic in two ways. First, investor citizenship makes available to the rich and *only to the rich* an extra naturalization route, over and above the standard one that is available to the rich and poor alike. Second, the naturalization-by-investment route waives important requirements, such as residence, language, and renunciation of previous citizenship. Those requirements loom large in the standard naturalization route, which is the only one available to the poor. States are making some 'pass under the yolk', but not all. Not only do the rich have *more* naturalization routes available; they have also *smoother* routes.

Some might object to what was said above, thinking that discrimination is inherent in standard naturalization as well. Think of language or history tests. Highly educated people have the upper hand and nobody seems bothered by that fact. Quite the contrary, there are voices claiming that such tests should be made harder to pass, with the positive consequence of 'adopting' better quality citizens. If it is not problematic to discriminate on the basis of education, why should discrimination on the basis of money pose a problem? Why object to discrimination against the poor, but not to discrimination against the uneducated?

Surely, one discrimination does not excuse the other, however. States should reduce, not multiply, forms of discrimination. And in any case, these two forms of discrimination are different in relevant respects. First, discriminating on the basis of education is less degrading than discriminating on the basis of money: at least education is a deeper and more stable attribute of the person, unlike merely contingent and perhaps fleeting facts about his pocket.[42] Second, there are good reasons to

---

[42] That is so, because one's education stays with its possessor one's entire life, whereas money goes in and out of one's bank account. But some might think that it is more

discriminate on the basis of the first, which do not apply in the case of the second. How well one performs in naturalization tests is an indicator of that person's capacity to integrate in the community. Competence in such tests is the best proxy states have for such capacity. Money might guarantee that one is a successful entrepreneur.[43] But money alone is not a good indicator of an individual's capacity to fit that community more generally. Third, one does not get citizenship for education directly, as one gets citizenship for money directly in investor citizenship. Education will undoubtedly make it easier to pass the naturalization tests. But one gets citizenship exclusively for performing well in naturalization tests, not directly for the diplomas on one's wall.

Yet some will argue that money is indeed a good indicator of one's quality as citizen. There are financial requirements in the standard naturalization route too, after all. Deep pockets guarantee that one can contribute to one's and one's fellow nationals' welfare. And contributing to the common good surely makes one a good citizen. There was even a time when property and financial status qualified one for holding political rights. If money does count, why is investor citizenship a problem?

Here are just a few reasons. First, nowadays one no longer thinks that voting rights should be conditioned upon property holdings; why then provide a fast track to citizenship (and hence grant political rights) on the basis of money? Investor citizenship might have made sense in the political context of the nineteenth century but not in that of the twenty-first. Second, the aim of financial requirements is to prove economic integration in the labour market and financial independence – to guarantee, in other words, that one will be a contributor to the commonwealth and not a drain on it. In standard naturalization, the financial requirement is of a cloth with the various other requirements; like the other requirements, it is a measure that that individual will be on a broadly equal footing with the other members of the community.

---

degrading to discriminate on the basis of education than financial status, precisely because it is *enduring* over time. That reaction makes sense when we are talking about enduring attributes that an agent cannot voluntarily acquire or avoid. But that is obviously not the case with education. While I believe all discrimination is wrong, I also think that some forms of discrimination are worse than others. One is discriminating against people for features that are outside their control and hence arbitrary (such as gender, race, ethnicity, sexual orientation). Another is discriminating against people on the basis of features that largely depend on social and political structures or arise from structural, background injustice (i.e., from unequal opportunity). In light of this, we might say that *overall* (i.e., for more people and to a greater extent) education is a less arbitrary feature than financial status.

[43] Some of the skills required by citizenship (reading, writing, calculating) are also required by entrepreneurship. Yet knowledge beyond these skills is required to pass citizenship tests.

In investor citizenship, by contrast, financial requirements go way beyond what is minimally required for economic integration. Furthermore, they take precedence over (if not displacing altogether) other naturalization requirements, like language or culture tests. Yet money does not guarantee integration in those other respects, of course. Nor does it guarantee that the individual will necessarily contribute more economically. By comparison to other professionals, investors are, after all, particularly well situated to maximize individual profits by avoiding taxation.

C   Signalling

At this point one might wonder whether citizenship, or honours before it, really 'says something' about its possessor. Honours certainly purported to do so. That is why their sale created two problems by allowing wealthy commoners (merchants, traders, pirates, and such like) to join easily the ranks of the nobility.

First, noble status no longer testified to particular features that had long been associated with it. A true *gentilhomme* had to be detached from all things material – money included – and animated only by higher pursuits. The main quality of the nobility was *magnanimity* (*libéralité* in French, that is, freedom from selfishness) – the capacity to give 'when giving is called for and without self-interest'.[44] After all, if the First Estate served God and the Third Estate its own interests, the Second Estate was supposed to serve the sovereign.[45] For that, the nobleman had to be generous and capable of great sacrifices. In the case of the birth nobility, ancestry was proof of the lineage's past generosity and a promise of future generosity. But commoners lacked such ancestry and generally used their talents only for their personal advantage, in particular, for increasing revenues.[46] Conferring a noble title on someone who could not rise to the moral expectations associated with it seemed like a bad idea.

The 'moral community' constituted by the old aristocracy thus felt threatened by the sale of honours.[47] Their sale made it possible for honours to be acquired by individuals of dubious character, not just dubious origins. In England, for example, the old aristocracy objected variously: to the ennoblement of Philip Stanhope, convicted for sodomy and pardoned for murder; to that of Robert Lord Rich, a famous pirate

[44] See Smith 1996, pp. 30, 29, 31.
[45] Ibid., p. 43.
[46] Ibid., pp. 43–4.
[47] Le Roux 2011.

Multiple Citizenship by Investment 69

(in spite of the king's loathing of pirates); and to that of Sir William Grey, involved in a customs-evasion scandal.[48] The House of Commons complained that honours were abused by 'people most odious to the commonwealth by their extortion, usury, and other ungodly kind of getting'.[49]

Moreover, selling honours associated noble status with qualities that were profoundly anti-noble. Materialistic pursuits, now suddenly rewarded by grants of noble titles, had been long considered incompatible with the noble condition. In France, for example, the reaction against the cash nobility was largely anti-bourgeois in form. Anti-bourgeois satires repeatedly emphasized the stark contrast between the true noble and bourgeois qualities (such as egoism, opportunism, ambition, or entrepreneurial spirit).[50] When bourgeois commoners became noblemen, the result was hilarious and often grotesque. Wealth and its display in an effort to emulate noble life did not make one a true *gentilhomme*. Neither did it grant him equal standing among noble peers.

Fast forward a few centuries. Today it is harder to figure out how citizenship says anything about one's character in a way similar to how noble status spoke about character in the seventeenth century. The analogy between the sale of citizenship and the sale of honours may seem to fall rather flat in this respect, unless we are willing to see nations as special moral communities (as some political theorists do) or see citizenship as embodying communal values and requiring the exercise of distinct moral virtues.[51]

Talk of 'citizenship virtues' easily leads to murky waters that I shall here largely avoid. Yet note one respect in which (naturalized) citizenship might, at least on its face, be thought to speak to questions of character. That is penal clearance as part of the naturalization process. Its main aim is to ensure that citizenship is allocated to those of 'good character'.[52] Penal clearance is the only purely (and openly) moral requirement for naturalization. It expresses the view that citizenship belongs to individuals exhibiting certain moral qualities considered important by that community (which may, of course, vary from one community to another).

---

[48] Mayes 1957, pp. 24–9. The fact that Stanhope was convicted for sodomy but pardoned for a serious wrong like murder is problematic in itself, but here I shall let that pass.
[49] Mayes 1957, p. 36.
[50] See Molière's *Le Bourgeois Gentilhomme*, *La Comédienne*, and *George Dandin* and Boileau's *Fifth Satire*. For discussion, see Alter 1970.
[51] For a view of the nation as moral community, see Miller 1995; for a discussion of citizen virtues, see Pettit 1997.
[52] See, for example, Australia's naturalization requirements (www.border.gov.au/Trav/Citi/Appl/What-documents-do-you-need/good-character-and-offences).

Beyond that, naturalization procedures also aim to identify certain *competences* making one fit as citizen. Tests of language, history, and culture aim to ensure the applicant can easily integrate into that community. Citizenship may not say much about an individual's character, as honours did in the past. Yet if we look at the aforementioned naturalization requirements, we can see that citizenship acquired in that way is at least supposed to give some clues about one's competences and moral compass.[53]

Return, now, to investor citizenship and remember that standard naturalization requirements are waived when citizenship is acquired upon investment. In this latter case, citizenship can no longer convey reliable information about the character or civic competence of its beholder. At most, it may convey information about the investor's depth of pockets or entrepreneurial skills. But money alone is a poor indicator of good character or civic competence.

The second problem historically associated with selling honours is that it created confusion. That was for a simple reason. All group memberships, indeed all social labels, act as markers.[54] The main use of such markers is to facilitate social cooperation by imparting information. Often one needs to interact with people without having much information about them. Under uncertainty, labels (memberships included) reduce information-seeking costs and risks, provided their signalling is reliable, that is, they impart some *relatively reliable* information about their beholders. Yet the 'inflation' of titles made the nobility practically undistinguishable from the richer elements among the masses. One could not know, looking at the title, who is a true noble and who not.

An important guarantee of the reliability of the information conveyed by membership is the *mode of distribution* of that membership.[55] Different groups devise various tests and procedures for ascribing membership.

---

[53] Some might disagree that the requirements and tests of naturalization are the right ones for proving one's moral compass and competence, or indeed whether one's moral compass and competence should matter at all in the grant of citizenship. These are legitimate worries, but they require wholly separate analyses. For the sake of this chapter, I assume that naturalization requirements serve their purpose, at least to some extent. As I point out elsewhere (see Chapter 3), I agree that some conditions imposed on citizenship acquisition may be illegitimate. Yet, as I argue in Chapter 8, I believe that such an assessment should be more nuanced and focus on each subcategory of citizenship rights instead (e.g., political or economic rights, rights of residence, rights of free entry and exit).

[54] Bowles and Gintis 2011; Gintis, Smith, and Bowles 2001.

[55] Groups are often required to establish who is a 'true' member and who is not. Usurpers and pretenders are everywhere. A good means for identifying usurpers is finding out how they came to be members in the first place. Finding this out can be expensive in terms of time and resources, however.

Their role is to track certain *qualities* or *features* in individuals that are considered desirable and important by the group, and that are widely associated with the members of that group. Groups set up *distribution criteria* for their membership aimed at selecting only those individuals truly exhibiting the traits and qualities sought by the group. The problem arises when one membership, usually associated with some qualities and features, comes to be distributed in a new way that tracks other different qualities and features. In the case of honours, for example, their sale made it difficult for a noble title to convey reliable information about a title holder. It cast doubt on what information was to be conveyed by anyone's title, for no one could be sure anymore whether any given nobleman's title testified to noble qualities and a long-standing relationship with the king, or merely to deep pockets.[56] That explains why distinctions between old and new nobility were staunchly kept, if only at the symbolic level (in dressing codes, seating rules, and so on).[57]

Citizenship is one marker among many. It, too, says something about the individual bearing it, albeit in fewer circumstances than honours did, and perhaps less obviously and less successfully so. But some might nonetheless be suspicious of the analogy between noble title and citizenship for another simple reason. As an egalitarian status, citizenship is simply *not* supposed to distinguish its possessor from the rest of people, like noble title did. However, this critique has its own fault: it overlooks the fact that while 'internally inclusive' (and egalitarian), citizenship is also 'externally exclusive' (and inegalitarian).[58] I already mentioned how citizenship acts as a marker of character or competence, at least in standard naturalization, a process that is meant both to welcome newcomers into the group (that is, to include) and to make clear where the boundaries of the group lie (that is, to exclude those who do not exhibit character and competence). Travelling is another instance in which one's citizenship acts like a marker. All travellers are stopped at the borders by people with guns and asked for their passports. Those citizens of the state pass easily; but non-citizens, not so. Why? Because in the state's mind, citizenship says something about its possessor, leading border authorities to let some in or demand additional guarantees or information (visas or other special provisions) from others.

---

[56] Which led Louis XIV order a verification of all noble titles (*recherche sur la noblesse*) at a certain point.
[57] New nobles were standing at council meetings, while the 'true' nobles were seated. The former's wives often had to wear distinctive hats (Bitton 1969, pp. 100–1).
[58] Brubaker 1992, p. 21.

States take citizenship and the information it conveys seriously. The problem when allowing different modes of distribution of citizenship, each tracking different qualities and features in an individual, is that thereby citizenship ceases to be a reliable marker. If the distribution mode of citizenship changes, and a category of 'investor citizen' is introduced, then citizenship can fail to convey the same reliable information it used to convey about its beholder. Investor citizenship might be a reliable marker of wealth. But, as I have said, one can doubt it is also a reliable marker of good character or civic competence more generally. Therefore, citizenship as such can easily convey *false information* about its beholder. In everyday interactions, simply knowing that one is a fellow citizen will not tell us whether one is of good character or competent or just plain filthy rich.

D   Social Values and Meanings

Putting honours on the market also inherently downgraded noble status. When subjected to 'undignified haggling', honours seemed 'cheap'.[59] Commodification dislodged particular values and meanings nobility used to have. It could no longer be valued as a status of distinction, be associated with spiritual virtues, or indicate the existence of a meaningful relationship with the Crown, for example. Why this happened is simple. Different types of transfer (gift, exchange, cash transaction) attach different values and meanings to the same good. 'Given freely', a good may convey one meaning; 'given for money', it may convey another. By affirming one particular value and meaning for a good, commodification can undermine other values and meanings that that good would have had when distributed otherwise. Take a classic example. Some object to prostitution for implicitly devaluing the desired good ('bought sex is not the same').[60] Freely given sex is more valuable (and perhaps more enjoyable) precisely because of the 'freely' part. And not only because it makes a difference to the pocket. Freely offered sex has a different meaning from sold sex, one that is *particularly* valued in our societies. Similarly, putting on sale citizenship may change the value and meaning citizenship typically has.

A particular value and meaning that would be undermined by commodification is that of citizenship as human right. Citizenship is first and foremost *the right* to have rights. All people are *entitled* to citizenship (at least one citizenship) as equal human beings. Citizenship is thus a human

[59] Mayes 1957, p. 35.
[60] Hirsch 1977, p. 87.

right.[61] The right to have rights is not only inalienable (one cannot sell or renounce it), it is also universal (everyone has it). This means, of course, that one need not buy this right. There is no point acquiring a right to something if one already has that right beforehand. Buying citizenship implicitly presupposes that, prior to the transaction, one has no claims to it.[62] In the case of the investor, this will most certainly be true. Were investors prevented from buying citizenship, their human right to citizenship would not be violated. It would not, because their birth citizenship was granted to them in virtue of this human right; and as I have argued in Chapter 2, that human right applies to only *one* citizenship (usually the birth one). But the fact remains that in the transaction, the purchased citizenship does not have this value of human right.[63] Transacted citizenship cannot fulfil the value of a human right; citizenship, as a good secured in a transaction, cannot achieve its full potential.

This might not seem problematic insofar as citizenship can still fulfil this important value when granted to stateless refugees or to birth citizens. If so, then the purely economic valuation of citizenship imposed by investor citizenship may nonetheless *coexist* with other different values and meanings citizenship may have (its human right value included) in other instances. Take food. It may be valued as a means of subsistence, but also as a means of pleasure, say. The value of food for a Swiss eating caviar is certainly different from the value of food for a Biafran eating rice. One might say that in the case of the Swiss, food fulfils its value not as means of subsistence, but as means of pleasure. And one might think that the former meaning – of food as supporting life – is more important than the latter. Yet both meanings coexist peacefully. What is the problem then?

First, states may want all members of the community to share a *common meaning and value* of citizenship – it is something that unites all members, after all. The meaning of citizenship would then have to be the same in all instances. This could be a good idea insofar as allowing different values and meanings of the same good might create confusion, as pointed out earlier. Take the sexual analogy. One can have sex with

---

[61] Arendt 2004; United Nations 1948; *Perez v. Brownell*, 356 U.S. 44 (1958), at p. 356: 'Citizenship *is* man's basic right, for it is nothing less than the right to have rights.'

[62] Similarly, Okun (1975) makes the distinction between the spheres of dollars and of rights. Rights are precisely proofs against sale and purchase.

[63] If the investor would be stateless, the situation would be very different, however. Citizenship would have in this case the potential to be valued as a human right. But then states should grant the investor citizenship precisely as a matter of right – that is, for free rather than conditioned on investment – if citizenship is indeed to fulfil its role of human right in this case.

74   Acquisition

both one's spouse and a prostitute, and sex would have a different meaning with each. Bought sex is different from freely given sex. Maybe one can keep these meanings separate. But if one's spouse finds out about the prostitute, they will wonder what is the *real* meaning of sex for their spouse, after all. They will wonder whether sex with them is valued differently by their spouse from sex with the prostitute, or not.[64] And if one is not a schizophrenic, can he hold unto both meanings of sex at the same time without confusing them?

This leads us to the second point: one meaning of the good may slowly contaminate the others.[65] Take the example of food I gave earlier. The danger of thinking primarily of it as satisfying the gluttony of the rich would be to forget that it is also needed for the survival of the poor. The more glamorous meaning may come to drive the less glamorous one. And the conflation of meanings can easily have unwanted practical consequences. In the case of citizenship, thinking of it as satisfying the desire for profits may lead us to forget that it is first and foremost a human right – that is, it should satisfy the basic needs of people, not desires for profits. States might become reluctant to grant citizenship to stateless refugees, and more inclined to grant it to rich investors. Insofar as each state can grant a limited number of citizenships and faces a decision as to whom to distribute them, such value shifts[66] may have serious negative effects on the respect of human rights. The above should not come as a surprise. Markets are blind to our reasons (and whether those are based on need or desire) for seeking to acquire a good, and that is true whether that good is food or citizenship.[67] Desires may take precedence over needs, if backed by bigger purses. Yet the primary purpose and value of some goods (like food or citizenship) may come from serving needs.[68] When this is the case, it may well be a good idea to keep them off the market.

---

[64] This might create a coordination problem between the spouses in the end; they would no longer know what to expect from each other. Here is where a common shared meaning comes in handy: by creating concordant mutual expectations, *conventions* prevent coordination problems. See Lewis 1969, pp. 24–51.

[65] Or have a domino effect, in Margaret Jane Radin's (1996) words.

[66] The value shift in commodification is perhaps best explained by Walzer (1983, p. 97): '[O]ften money fails to represent value; the translations are made, but as with good poetry, something is lost in the process. Hence we can buy and sell universally only if we disregard real values; while if we attend to values, there are things that cannot be bought and sold. Particular things: the abstract universality of money is undercut and circumscribed by the creation of values that can't easily be priced or that we don't want priced.' See also Sandel 2012.

[67] Several features characterize market interactions: want-regarding character, impersonality, unrestrained pursuit of self-interest, and prevalence of exit over voice (Anderson 1990).

[68] That citizenship first and foremost responds to needs can be seen in its automatic allocation to individuals upon birth. Newborns do not *want* it; they *need* it. So too

But selling citizenship might be downgrading in other ways too. What can one say about a group deciding to treat its membership as merchandise? Is the group downgrading itself in any way? The nobility saw the sale of noble titles as a blow to its honour as a group. It was in the end just undermining everybody's self-esteem, old and new nobles alike. Today's citizens might be attached and proud of their citizenships just like nobles were attached and proud of their noble titles. If so, selling citizenship may be damaging the self-esteem of the citizen community. The sale implicitly equates group membership to a pile of money. The problem is not that citizenship is sold too cheaply. The issue is not the price, low or high, but rather selling it at all. Some things are above cash. And on those things (the self-esteem and dignity of a group) one just cannot put a price tag.[69] A state putting citizenship on sale risks undermining its citizens' respect in the state and in themselves as members of it, just as monarchs undermined the nobility's respect in the nobility and in themselves as members of it when trading honours.

E Political Consequences

Last but not least, selling honours raised two additional problems: it involved corruption and it implied the dangerous trade of political power.

Take first corruption. Profits often went into private hands. Offensive as the sale of peerages was to the old aristocracy under any condition, it was all the more so when the fees went to courtiers instead of the exchequer.[70] Likewise today, one might not have a problem with selling citizenship per se, yet one might have a problem with where the money from the sale goes. Commodification (of noble or citizen status) might be all right for the good purposes: boosting the king's treasury or boosting national budgets. But it is not for lining private pockets.

In the sale of honours the moral problem was twofold. First, the nobility may have had a problem with honours being sold by intermediates (favourites) and not by the king himself. In this sense, the problem

---

stateless persons. See also my discussion of the allocation of citizenship upon birthright in Chapter 2.

[69] In Kant's (2012, 4: 434–5) words: 'What has a price can be replaced by something else as its equivalent; what on the other hand is above all price and therefore admits of no equivalent has a dignity. What is related to general human inclinations and needs has a market price ... but that which constitutes the condition under which alone something can be an end in itself has not merely a relative worth, that is, a price, but an inner worth, that is, a dignity.'

[70] 'Much speech of new barons to be made for monie, which were the lesse to be misliked yf yt came to the Kings cofers', wrote John Chamberlain to Dudley Carleton, in 1615 discussing Sir Dormer's acquisition of a barony for £10,000. The money it seems went to Lord Sheffield, not to the exchequer. Mayes 1957, p. 22.

76   Acquisition

was not that noble title was 'prostituted' (sold), but that it was 'pimped' (its sale was intermediated). Second, the nobility may have had a problem not with 'pimping' honours per se, but with something different: *abuse of power or corruption*. Take the sexual analogy here:

(a) A pimp might have an agreement with a prostitute to trade her sexual services. He can agree with her on a price and negotiate on her behalf with prospective clients. One might or might not think this (pimping) wrong.
(b) The pimp negotiates with a client on a price above that previously agreed with the prostitute, and without her knowledge or consent pockets the extra money. The pimp abuses thus his power (given by the prostitute) to negotiate and trade her sexual services in order to draw unentitled benefits. One might think (b) wrong irrespective of whether one thinks (a) wrong.

In a similar way, the sale of honours was historically intermediated by the king's favourites. But these favourites may have had the king's permission to negotiate and sell honours on his behalf; if so, they were acting as his pimps. That in and of itself may have been a problem. But over and above that was the further problem that they would often cash in the fees themselves: they were *abusing* their power (even where that power was royally granted) to traffic in honours.

Commodification will be accompanied by corruption especially when no clear rules are set. The sale of peerages was not a formally institutionalized practice. It was a disorganized trade often contaminated by favouritism. Many times, it went on behind the king's back. The bulk of the sale of peerages was intermediated by the royal camarilla, who – in the absence of clear rules or supervisory agencies – would also pocket the money for themselves.[71]

Now consider the sale of citizenship. First, just like the king's favourites, state officials and bureaucrats may be acting as 'pimps' when selling citizenship to investors. This might be a problem in itself. Yet some states fail to have clear and precise rules when selling citizenship. Sometimes literally everything is left to the discretion of the authorities. Other times there are rules, but they are fuzzy. All this, in turn, favours abuse of power and corruption.[72] In the absence of clear rules surrounding investor citizenship, state officials and bureaucrats could easily abuse

---

[71] Mayes 1957, pp. 26–9. One of the kings' acolytes (Buckingham) was impeached on the charge that he forced a man to purchase baronial dignity.
[72] See the notes from Section I for corruption scandals involving the sale of citizenship.

Multiple Citizenship by Investment   77

their power to 'pimp' citizenship in order to draw unentitled profits personally or to promote their own narrow political agendas.

Take next the *trade of political power*. Ennoblement did more than just grant symbolic status. It granted political power: the right to sit in the British House of Lords or in the French Estates. Noblemen also sat in the king's law courts and at council meetings. They were in a position to dispense justice and to block the king's edicts. For these reasons, in England, the nobility feared that its new 'additions' would deprive it of the respect and support in disputes with the Crown.[73] Indeed, it did not take long for the Commons to complain that honours were abused through their 'mercenary acquisition'.[74] The sale of peerages was dangerous for putting 'mercenaries' in positions of political power and of administering justice.

Similarly, today, selling citizenship entails more than selling mere formal status. It amounts to the *actual* sale of *rights and duties* attached to this status. Some of the rights and duties citizens have are generally thought to be inalienable. Consider these examples: military duties, juror duties, and voting rights.[75] Nowadays (if not always before)[76] those are thought of as rights and duties that cannot (or should not) be put on the auction block. But if one thinks that such rights and duties entailed by one's citizenship cannot be bought and sold, then by extension one should also think that citizenship itself cannot be bought and sold. This would obviously be the simplest and cleanest way to object to investor citizenship. The sale of citizenship would implicitly put on the auction block rights and duties that individually are unsellable in the first place. If states do not sell such rights and duties separately, then surely states should not be selling them in 'packages' under the label of 'citizenship'.

The longer route would be to point out the ways in which selling political rights violates democratic equality and is utterly inefficient. Scarce commodities – life, health, and citizenship included – 'should be distributed less unequally than the ability to pay for them'.[77] So too,

---

[73] Mayes 1957, p. 35. At the same time, however, the Crown used the sale of peerages to strengthen the court party in the House of Lords (Mayes 1957, p. 33). Besides money, and political domination, another goal of the 'inflation of peerages' was to undermine the pride the old nobles got from their titles (Mayes 1957, p. 36).
[74] Letter to the House of Commons, cited in Mayes 1957, p. 36.
[75] See Radin 1987; Rose-Ackerman 1985; Walzer 1983.
[76] For reasons of space, I address only *political* rights and duties. A discussion of military duties would be obsolete: the professionalization of armies renders these duties superfluous today. There was a time, however, when such duties were 'dead' serious. Selling exemptions from military duties then (e.g., during the American Civil War) allowed money to make the difference between life and death.
[77] Tobin 1970, p. 264.

implicitly, the political rights and duties attached to citizenship. Economic inequalities are ubiquitous, to be sure; yet ubiquitous as they are, they should not be allowed to spill over into political inequalities as well. A market in political rights (just like a market in votes) would, on one hand, concentrate power in the rich.[78] A market in political duties would, on the other, concentrate burdens in the poor. The distribution of resources would dictate the distribution of political power. Public matters would thus become private business.[79]

Selling political rights and duties would be also politically inefficient. Blocked exchanges serve the important function of controlling the externalities that exchanges can produce.[80] Take the tragedy of the commons dilemma: everyone has a right to the commons, yet everyone making use of this right will simply destroy the commons altogether.[81] The logic of the market (exalting the pursuit of self-interest) will most likely endanger the 'we' approach to the commons. Putting political rights on the market would similarly empower corrupt politicians in pursuit of self-interest rather than the common good. Those having 'bought' their political power will use it to recover their initial costs and well beyond, to compensate them for the *entrepreneurial risk* they took. Although citizens, investors who simply bought their citizenship will relate to their newly acquired political power in a purely entrepreneurial way. And this self-interested and economistic use of political power could have negative externalities for the other citizens.[82] Political power gives us *power over the commons*. A purely economic approach to political power – as the one promoted by the sale of citizenship – is problematic for encouraging the depletion of the common pool of resources.

But selling citizenship would be also another way of 'selling out the nation'. Political rights and duties are relational: they are rights and duties *to someone*, not something.[83] When voting or when holding political office, citizens are exercising political power over their national peers.

---

[78] Ibid., p. 269.
[79] Walzer 1983, p. 99.
[80] Epstein 1985. One reason for blocking the sale of certain goods would be that selling them might be self-defeating. By transacting a good, we might be losing the preconditions for enjoying the benefits of the transaction thereafter. For example, if one sells oneself into slavery, one will not be able to make use of the received cash, for by becoming a slave one would implicitly lose property rights over oneself and one's belongings.
[81] Hardin 1968.
[82] Investors might use their voting rights as to restrict the other citizens' access to social benefits, for example.
[83] Tribe (1985, p. 333, emphasis added) argues that 'rights that are *relational* and *systemic* are necessarily inalienable: individuals cannot waive them because individuals are *not their sole focus* '.

Political and civil duties (to vote, to serve as a juror) are also duties citizens have toward fellow group members. Such relational rights and duties cannot be bought and sold, precisely because in being relational they pertain to (special) relationships between *particular* individuals. Therefore, they cannot be transferred to someone else, by cash transfer or otherwise.[84]

IV   A Clarification

I have examined the sale of honours to show *mutatis mutandis* that investor citizenship is problematic. The analogy might to some seem ill-suited. How can an elitist, privileged, and exclusivist status *par excellence* be compared with modern citizenship – an inclusive, democratic status that was supposed to break the class barriers instated by feudalism? To them, all of the similarities that I have pointed out will seem incidental or utterly exaggerated.

Others might take the analogy for more than it is. Am I implying by this comparison that today's democratic citizenship system is as perverse as the honours system? From a global perspective, does not citizenship maintain the birth privileges of a group in a way similar to honours? The privilege is still there, only the subject of this privilege has changed; the boundaries of the privileged group have only expanded from a class (the aristocracy) to a mass (the so-called nation). In this sense, citizenship is more similar to feudal membership than one might think.[85] The citizenship system based on *jus sanguinis* leads to entrenched inequalities, if not within nations, then across them. Even worse, some might take the analogy to be a disguised defence of birth or class privileges. Why refer to values that are dear to us today when discussing a profoundly corrupt system, if not somehow obliquely to defend it?

For all such interlocutors, a clarification is in order. The chapter does not aim to defend or glorify in any way the honours system or to demonize or idealize our present citizenship system. My recourse to the historical case of selling honours is purely instrumental. By appealing to this analogy, this chapter aims to show that the market logic undermines values that are (or are thought to be) common to both systems – values like merit, reciprocity, or political efficiency. As corrupt as it was, the

---

[84] Notice that hiring a nanny does not amount to *transferring* altogether parental duties. We are instead merely paying someone else to *discharge* the duty that still belongs to us.

[85] According to Joseph H. Carens (1987, p. 252), citizenship is 'the modern equivalent of feudal privilege – an inherited status that greatly enhances one's life chances. Like feudal birthright privileges, restrictive citizenship is hard to justify when one thinks about it closely'.

honours system was paradoxically founded on values akin to those that ground our political systems nowadays. Democratic and national revolutions have just extended the relationships to which these values apply from relationships between members of the same social group to relationships between diverse social groups composing the nation.

Our *ideal* of democratic citizenship is diametrically opposed to the feudal honours system. When discussing the pitfalls of investor citizenship, I have looked upon particular values and principles typically associated with this ideal, like reciprocity and equality. Yet our *practice* of democratic citizenship today is far from this ideal in many ways. Its reliance on birth circumstance is one of them.[86] Yet just because our practice of citizenship has colossally failed to match the ideal does not mean that states must move entirely to the opposite direction. Investor citizenship is definitely a step back from our ideal of democratic citizenship, seriously prejudicing values such as fairness and equality. It is not the first such step and probably not the last either. But this does not mean that we should not be morally concerned about it. We should be concerned about this step, just as we should be about all other steps back from the democratic citizenship ideal.

It should also be emphasized that the comparisons between investor citizenship and ordinary naturalization requirements are not in any way prescriptive. By that comparison, I do not imply that naturalization requirements today are in line with our ideal of democratic citizenship. Far from it. Yet if ordinary naturalization requirements derail (to a greater or lesser extent[87]) our citizenship ideal, investor citizenship rips up the tracks *entirely*, as I have argued. Even if things are bad as they are, why make them worse?

V   Conclusion

As has been shown, there are plenty of arguments against the practice of investor citizenship. Allocating citizenship on the basis of financial power is likely to subject the very idea of citizenship to derision, just as putting a price on honours did in the case of noble status.

Yet perhaps we should not object (or maybe just not *so* strongly) to the idea of allocating certain *economic* rights that are the privilege of citizenship conditionally on investment. Good investors could, through their investments, do a lot of good for a country that needs those resources, at least in the short term. The size of their pockets might be a good indicator

---

[86] For a critique of the emphasis on birth circumstances, see Shachar 2009.
[87] Just how much is beyond the scope of this chapter, but see Chapter 3.

of how good investors they are, and thus of how much use they could make of those citizenship-conditioned economic rights to benefit both themselves and their new fellow citizens.

Buying economic rights outright – that is, using money to buy the power to make more money – would be a more candid type of transaction. Buying citizenship *tout court* for the sake of benefiting from the economic rights associated with this citizenship has, as I have pointed out, additional problematic aspects: for example, it also entails buying political rights, thus political power, together with the economic rights associated with citizenship. These problems would be averted if states were to *unbundle* the component rights of citizenship and distribute them separately. It would then be less objectionable to allocate economic (but not political) rights on the basis of capital. I discuss this proposal at length in Chapter 8.

Investor citizenship almost invariably leads to multiple citizenship, a fact of signal importance in the context of this book. Investors are already citizens of one state, and they are buying an *additional* citizenship for their own financial purposes. Distributing economic rights and those alone on the basis of investment would allow these people to acquire extended economic rights in various countries *without* becoming also citizens of these countries as well, that is, without becoming multiple citizens. That would at least reduce the unfair advantages that come from buying citizenship and thereby from becoming a multiple national as well (see my discussion in Chapter 7).

Part II

Consequences

Having explored the various grounds for acquisition of multiple citizenship, we will now turn to its consequences, at both the national (Chapters 5 and 6) and global levels (Chapter 7).

Chapters 5 and 6 examine the domestic consequences of multiple citizenship for democratic decision making. They focus, respectively, on two mechanisms legitimizing collective decisions: *deliberation* and *voting*. What distinguishes multiple citizens from other categories of migrants is the fact that they enjoy political rights simultaneously in two or more political communities. It is thus important to explore whether this double exercise of political rights, peculiar to multiple citizens, affects collective decision making in either of those modes and, if so, how. While Chapter 5 will discuss the ways by which multiple citizenship can undermine the consistency of collective decisions, Chapter 6 will examine whether multiple citizenship brings the boundaries of the demos closer to or further from those ideally prescribed by varying principles for constituting the demos (the affected interests principle, the legally subjected principle, and the unaffected interests principle).

The final chapter of this part of the book, Chapter 7, will examine the global consequences of multiple citizenship. It will assess how well multiple citizenship answers to global justice concerns and examine its consequences for global equality. It will argue that the grounds for allocating multiple citizenship are morally objectionable from a global egalitarian perspective, and will also point out how multiple citizenship is problematic in both non-ideal[1] and ideal settings.[2] The chapter will mainly focus on the interaction between the norms regulating the distribution of multiple citizenship and the international norms regulating double taxation. It will argue that this interaction risks increasing global inequalities and will propose a solution, reforming the OECD Model Tax Convention according to prioritarian considerations.

---

[1] I.e., when there are noticeable differences among states, in terms of wealth, resources, and other factors determining people's life opportunities and choices.

[2] I.e., when there is complete equality among countries with respect to wealth, resources, and other factors determining people's life opportunities and choices.

5 Multiple Citizenship and Collective Decision Making

Collective decisions may draw their legitimacy from two sources: the procedures by which they were made and their quality. With respect to the latter, a decision may be deemed 'good' if it promotes the welfare of the decision makers. But it may also be deemed 'good' for exhibiting certain epistemic qualities, for example, tracking the truth or being grounded in coherent collective judgements.

Individual judgements can be coherent with respect to different frames of reference that emerge during public deliberation and guide decision making. But in order for those individual judgements to add up to a coherent collective decision (via majority rule), they must be guided by a *common* frame of reference.

This is not an entirely new point. John Stuart Mill, for example, pointed out how difficult it is to unite members of different nationalities under the same free government. Diagnosing the reason for that, Mill said that a 'still more vital consideration' than their lacking 'fellow-feeling' and 'the sentiment of nationality' is the fact that

> *especially* if they read and speak different languages, the *united public opinion*, necessary to the working of representative government, cannot exist. The *influences which form opinions and decide political acts are different* in the different sections of the country ... The *same* books, newspapers, pamphlets, speeches, do not reach them. One section does not know what opinions, or what instigations, are circulating in another.[1]

Put in more abstract terms, the problem Mill points to – that of a collective of people who must decide together but whose ways of thinking about the decision are systematically different – is familiar to social choice and political theorists, who stress the importance of common frames of reference in guiding collective decision making. Drawing on their insights, I will in this chapter point out how multiple citizenship may undermine collective rationality by exposing people to multiple, and

---

[1] Mill [1861] 1975, pp. 381–2, emphasis added.

potentially conflicting, frames of reference when exercising their political agency through voting or deliberating in multiple states at the same time.

If people vote having in mind different conceptions of what they are voting for, then the outcomes yielded by majority rule will be meaningless. If people vote having in mind different understandings of what they are voting for,[2] then aggregating their votes to make sense of their collective will is nonsensical. Majority rule is a meaningful decision-making procedure only under bounded disagreement. And that is what multiple citizens' participation in political processes in two very different places at once threatens to undermine.

I Multiple Citizens as Political Agents

The *rights* of immigrants in the receiving states have been in the academic spotlight for quite a while now.[3] Immigrants' *duties* toward their receiving communities have been considerably less so.[4] So, too, have the rights these immigrants still hold in and duties they owe to their *sending* states. In the scarce literature devoted to them, these rights and duties are labelled 'external citizenship'.[5] Among these rights and duties, the exercise of political rights – external voting – has received most attention.[6]

The academic views on external voting are mixed. Some say that external voters are innocuous.[7] Others that external voting is deficient democratically.[8] Still others say that it gives rise to negative externalities affecting the communities of the sending states. That may be because external voters are more prone to vote irresponsibly or to support nationalist parties. And where external voters constitute external kin minorities, they may well serve as a fifth column of their kin state.[9] Of course, diasporas can do harm in other ways too – through *direct support* of nationalistic and paramilitary groups, for example.[10] But there are reasons to think that they

---

[2] For example, when the same party sends mixed signals and electoral messages about its intentions, as with 'dog whistle' politics (Goodin and Saward 2005).
[3] Bauböck 1994; Carens 2008.
[4] For an exception, see de Schutter and Ypi (2015), arguing that citizenship is a burden that must be shared by immigrants with their receiving communities.
[5] Bauböck 2005, 2009.
[6] Bauböck 2007b; European Commission for Democracy through Law 2011; Grace 2004; International Institute for Democracy and Electoral Assistance 2007; Østergaard-Nielsen 2008.
[7] Guarnizo et. al. 2003.
[8] López-Guerra 2005. I discuss external voting extensively in Chapter 6.
[9] Bauböck 2010.
[10] According to the World Bank, 'the strongest effect of war on the risk of subsequent war works through diasporas. After five years of postconflict peace, the risk of renewed conflict is around six times higher in the societies with the largest diasporas in America

might do harm even just through participating politically in the state from which they came.

There are other reasons, however, for supposing that external voting might prove beneficial to the sending states.[11] After all, people usually migrate to places that are not only more prosperous than their homelands but also more democratic. Exposure to a more democratic political culture and to political institutions placing greater emphasis on citizen rights and political accountability could, in principle, turn émigrés into important agents of change vis-à-vis their origin countries. Émigrés would be better at screening out incompetent or corrupt politicians, while also setting higher standards for them. Bottom line: external voters could constitute a political avant-garde, enlightened by liberal democratic political principles and values and able to improve the prospects of their countries through their votes.[12] At least some evidence, however, points in the opposite direction: instead of supporting the expansion of liberal values at home, diasporas support undemocratic political forces, such as extreme right-wing parties.[13]

Now, while not all external voters also have citizenship in their present place of residence, dual citizens nonetheless make up a significant proportion of these external voters. They hold political rights in *both* sending *and* receiving states. Does this make a difference for their political participation and for their impact on the quality of collective decision making? If so, how? Is their political participation in the sending state any different because of their being *citizens* of the receiving states as well (instead of merely residing there as temporary or long-term migrants)? Conversely, does the exercise of political rights in the sending state interact in any important way with their political participation in the receiving state?

My argument about how dual citizens' political agency might undermine collective decision making assumes that dual citizens do indeed participate politically in both of their states, through voting and/or public deliberation. Whether this is indeed the case, empirically, remains an open question.[14] As other commentators have remarked, concerns about

---

than in those without American diasporas. Presumably this effect works through the financial contributions of diasporas to rebel organizations' (Collier and Hoeffler 2000). Paul Collier further argues in *Exodus* (Collier 2013) that migration has deleterious effects on both sending and receiving states. Such claims are contested, however, by other economists.

[11] Brand 2013.
[12] Shain 1999.
[13] Koinova 2009.
[14] Existing debates among citizenship scholars and normative theorists commonly emphasize the benefits *naturalization* brings for the integration and political participation of immigrants in their receiving state (e.g., Blatter 2013; de Schutter and Ypi 2015;

the political nature of dual citizenship are 'the most speculative and the least quantifiable'.[15] Some claim that dual citizenship facilitates integration and political participation.[16] Others claim the exact opposite.[17]

The few studies so far reported have produced mixed results. One study, for example, shows that among Latino immigrants in the United States, first-generation dual citizens are less politically connected than their counterparts who are citizens of the United States alone.[18] The political disconnectedness of dual citizens does not hold, however, beyond the first generation.[19] Another study concluded that dual citizenship does not have significant influence on the likelihood of voting among Latinos and blacks, but it increases that likelihood among whites and Asians.[20] Such studies exploring how dual citizenship affects political participation in the *receiving* states are thus inconclusive. Furthermore, none of those studies addresses how dual citizenship affects the same individuals' political participation in their *sending* states.

Such studies also focus mainly on the individuals' likelihood to vote, disregarding other forms of political participation. We do not know just how much a second citizenship affects political socialization in general, and public deliberation and preference-formation specifically, in both sending and receiving states. The closest we have is a study using European Social Survey data to explore non-electoral modes of political participation in the receiving state, and the role citizenship plays in such political engagement. While the study does not draw a distinction between dual and single citizens, it concludes that foreign-born citizens of the receiving state (many of whom will be dual citizens in the sending state) are more politically active than foreign-born residents (most of whom will be mono-nationals who are citizens of the sending state alone).[21]

Thus, although the evidence is mixed and far from conclusive, there are at least some indications that multiple citizens do indeed participate politically in both of their states, both electorally and otherwise. If so, what might we expect the effects to be?

Prokic et al. 2013). Fewer studies, however, focus on how a second citizenship affects political participation. For exceptions, see Escobar 2004; Rumbaut 1994; Staton, Jackson, and Canache 2007b.

[15] Schuck 1998, p. 234.
[16] Escobar 2004; Guarnizo, Portes, and Haller 2003; Jones-Correa 2001; Schuck 1998; Spiro 1997; Spiro and Schuck 1998; Yang 1994.
[17] See Geyer 1996; Huntington 2004; Renshon 2001.
[18] Staton, Jackson, and Canache 2007b; on the first point, see also Cain and Doherty 2006.
[19] Staton, Jackson, and Canache 2007a.
[20] Ramakrishnan 2005.
[21] Just and Anderson 2011.

II Voting, Deliberation, and Collective Rationality

Collective decisions made by majority voting or public deliberation are legitimate in part by virtue of the inputs that go into these processes – the citizens' preferences and views. They are also legitimate in part because of how these citizens' preferences and views are treated in the process of decision making: they are given equal weight and equal consideration. Last but not least, collective decisions made by majority voting and public deliberation are legitimate because they are supposedly 'better' decisions than those that would have been reached in other ways[22] (such as flipping a coin, drawing a lot, or putting the decision in the hands of one or a limited number of individuals).[23]

Of course, collective decisions can be deemed 'good' or 'better' than other decisions in various ways. In this chapter I focus on one quality that makes collective decisions 'good': their embodying *logically coherent collective judgements*. To be sure, we would like collective decisions to be epistemically good in other ways as well. For example, we would like collective decisions to track the truth (to be 'correct'). Fortunately, when it comes to voting by majority rule, there is a good chance that that will be the case. As the Marquis de Condorcet proved in 1785, a majority vote among a group of independent voters, each one of them more likely to be right than wrong, will be even more likely than any of those individuals alone to reach the correct decision. Even better, this likelihood increases quickly with the number of such voters.[24]

But while majority rule may be good at capturing the truth in its results, it is less so at yielding logically consistent collective decisions. At the same time as discovering the biggest strength of majority rule, Condorcet also discovered one of its biggest weaknesses: the so-called Condorcet paradox.

A *The Condorcet Paradox: How Majority Rule Can Yield Inconsistent Collective Decisions*

The paradox consists in the following: if one takes a set of perfectly *rational* or *consistent* (that is, *transitive*) *individual* preferences over the full

---

[22] See Estlund 2009.
[23] The distinctions I am drawing correspond roughly to the concepts of 'input', 'throughput', and 'output' legitimacy. See Scharpf 1999 and Schmidt 2013.
[24] Political scientists have expanded Condorcet's jury theorem beyond its traditional assumptions. See, e.g., Grofman and Feld 1988; List and Goodin 2001. For an extensive study of Condorcet's jury theorem, see Goodin and Spiekermann 2018.

range of relevant options, and aggregates them using pairwise majority voting, one can end up with *irrational* or *inconsistent* (that is, *intransitive*) *collective* preferences.

For example, given a set of options (a, b, c), suppose that John prefers (a) to (b) to (c), Mary prefers (b) to (c) to (a), and David (c) to (a) to (b). Majority voting over pairs of options will not, in this case, give rise to a consistent collective preference ordering: (a) will be preferred to (b) by two votes (John's and David's) to one (Mary's); (b) will be preferred to (c) by two votes (John's and Mary's) to one (David's); yet (c) will be preferred to (a) by two votes (Mary's and David's) to one (John's). Majority rule is thus unable to guarantee full rationality in collective decision making insofar as consistent *individual* choices can coexist with inconsistent *collective* choices.[25] The paradox delivers thus a serious blow to democracy – as social theorists (like Black and Riker) pointed out – casting doubt on the meaningfulness of decisions made by majority rule.[26]

B   *From Aggregating Preferences to Aggregating Judgements*

The Condorcet paradox applies to preference orderings and does not look behind them. However, in most decision contexts complex judgements and reasoning underlie people's votes. There too, an analogous problem can arise with majority rule: it might aggregate perfectly coherent sets of individual judgements or reasons into incoherent collective judgements and reasons.

To see how, notice that individual preferences, just like other attitudinal states, are propositional; that is, they can take the form of propositions (for example, 'A is preferred to B', 'B is preferred to C', and 'A is preferred to C'). And just like preferences, propositions expressing preferences or propositions expressing a wider range of attitudinal states – like judgements and beliefs – can be aggregated as well. Unsurprisingly, when using majority rule to aggregate judgements on logically interconnected propositions, the same problem arises: logically consistent *individual* judgements can give rise to logically *in*consistent *collective* ones. In the case of propositions, the decision problem is known as the *discursive dilemma*.[27]

---

[25] Riker 1982, p. 1.
[26] Black 1948, 1998; Riker 1982.
[27] On judgement aggregation theory and the discursive dilemma, see Kornhauser and Sager 1993, 2004; List 2012, 2011a, 2011b; List and Pettit 2004; Pettit 2001.

Multiple Citizenship and Collective Decision Making 91

Table 5.1 *Aggregating judgements*

	p	$p \to q$	q
Citizen A	True	True	True
Citizen B	True	False	False
Citizen C	False	True	False
Majority	True	True	False

To get a better sense of the discursive dilemma, take the following example.[28]

Imagine we have a set of logically interconnected propositions:

p: The state's revenues are relatively stable.

$p \to q$: If the state's revenues are relatively stable, then the state should continue investing in big infrastructure projects.

q: The state should continue investing in big infrastructure projects.

Now take the set of judgements in Table 5.1, on the propositions above. While all the individual judgements are logically coherent, notice that the majority's collective judgement (in the bottom row) is that (1) the state's revenues *are* indeed relatively stable; (2) in that case, the state *should* continue investing in big infrastructure projects; *and yet* (3) the state should *not* continue investing in big infrastructure projects!

If we had a set of propositions (p, q, r), where p and q played the role of premises or inference rules for a conclusion (r), majority rule could deem in a collective judgement the conclusion r false, while at the same time deem the premises and inference rules as true. This shows again the limits of majority rule: the collective judgement reached by majority rule would not reflect the logical entailment between premises and conclusion that would be present in the majority of individuals' judgements.

We could think of p and q as reasons for a decision r. Seen in that light, the discursive dilemma shows that majority rule might sever the connection between *collective reasons* and *collective decisions*. Political theorists in the Rawlsian tradition have long emphasized that in order to be legitimate, collective decisions must be publicly justified. The problem posed by majority rule is thus relevant for public justification, and has implications for the concept of *public reason*.[29] If our collective decisions do not

---

[28] This example is inspired by List 2012, p. 182.
[29] On the theory of public reason and public justification, see Rawls 1993, 1997 and Quong 2011, 2013a, 2013b.

answer to a set of collective reasons, then our decisions not only lack justification, but may even be nonsensical or meaningless.

C   *Why Consistency Matters*

It is worth explaining at this point the multiple grounds on which – from a democratic perspective – inconsistent collective decisions are problematic. This is for three reasons.

First, if collective decisions are cut loose from the collective reasons underlying them, then the basis for democratic contestation is undercut.[30] Citizens must have 'access to the reasons supporting those decisions' in order to 'be able to contest the soundness of those decisions or the degree of support they offer to the decisions made'.[31] Yet, as pointed out when discussing judgement aggregation, following majority rule the acceptance of a conclusion does not go hand in hand with the acceptance of its premises (reasons); quite the contrary, it might coexist with their rejection. Consistent collective outcomes and reasoning, in contrast, serve an important democratic function, favouring opposition and contestation.

Second, inconsistent collective decisions are problematic because they make it hard to distinguish any 'collective intention' behind collective outcomes. Structurally, the problem of inconsistent collective judgements is very similar to that of 'dog whistle' politics. If a party promises different things to different people, and wins the election on the basis of mixed messages, then its victory does not add up to much in substantive policy terms.[32] Inconsistent collective judgements reached by majority rule suffer from the same lack of substance.

Third, inconsistent collective decisions are problematic also insofar as individuals expect collective decisions to be action guiding. Collective decisions giving incoherent or conflicting guidance cannot do that.[33] Moreover, incoherent decisions will be hard to justify, especially when imposing serious costs (coercion being one of them) on individuals.

D   *Avoiding Inconsistency: Single-Peaked Preferences, Unidimensionally Aligned Judgements*

An important advantage of decision making by majority rule is, of course, that it allows for a *plurality* of diverse inputs (be they preferences or

[30] See Pettit 2001, pp. 281–4.
[31] Ibid., p. 281.
[32] Goodin and Saward 2005, p. 473.
[33] List 2012, p. 197.

judgements) to be taken into account. The drawback, however, is that this diversity of opinion can undermine collective rationality. Satisfying all three requirements of democracy – pluralism, majoritarianism, and collective rationality – at the same time can be a challenge.[34] Yet it is possible, at a small cost for pluralism: if pluralism and diversity of opinion stay *within bounds*, then deciding by majority rule does not pose any problems for collective rationality. As it will become clear below, a community can easily rein in pluralism by letting *common* frames of reference guide its decisions. This is, of course, simply Mill's point quoted at the beginning of the chapter.

Now, the problem of incoherent collective decisions does not arise, of course, where there is unanimity and people all have exactly the same preferences or the same judgements. Moreover, inconsistent collective outcomes are more likely to occur in more heterogeneous groups – when there is high disagreement among decision makers.[35] So the question is: How can a community make rational collective decisions in the absence of any *substantive* agreement on what the members' preferences, judgements, or reasons for a decision should be? The trick is to contain (or bound) pluralism and diversity of opinion without eliminating it altogether.[36]

In the case of *preferences*, for example, this amounts to ensuring that disagreement among voters remains 'well structured'.[37] Even if voters have diverse preference orderings – that is, even if they substantively disagree about what option(s) they should prefer – their preference profiles can nonetheless all display the same underlying structure. One structure that was shown to ensure consistency in decision making is *single-peakedness*. When individual preferences are single-peaked, the collective preferences emerging by majority rule are guaranteed to be consistent.[38] Preferences are said to be single-peaked if there is a way of ordering all the available options on a left-right axis, such that each individual's preferences arranged on this axis have the following profile: there is a single peak (individuals' most preferred options) with their less preferred options ranking lower the more distant they are from their most preferred options.

Similarly, in the case of judgements, if judgement profiles are *unidimensionally aligned*, then aggregating these individual judgements gives rise to consistent collective judgements. Judgement profiles are unidimensionally

---

[34] This constitutes the 'democratic trilemma' in List's (2011b, p. 275) terms.
[35] List 2012, p. 195.
[36] In List's (2011b, p. 282) words, 'democracy cannot get off ground unless pluralism in the relevant group or society is sufficiently limited'.
[37] Black 1948.
[38] Ibid. Arguably, it is enough for 75 per cent or less of individual preference profiles to be single-peaked for the probability of a Condorcet cycle to approach zero (Niemi 1969).

94 Consequences

aligned if individuals accepting one proposition are either all to the left or all to the right of those rejecting it.[39] This should be the case for all propositions on which individuals pass judgements.[40] Such an alignment suggests, according to his proponent,[41] that there is some common underlying cognitive or ideological dimension structuring these individuals' judgements. The more homogenous and cohesive a group is, the more likely its judgements are to satisfy this condition, and the more likely it therefore is to reach consistent collective judgements by majority rule. And if groups are not cohesive in this respect, they can enhance their cohesiveness and thus the consistency of their collective judgements by deliberating, as I will point out below.[42]

E *The Need for Structured Disagreement or Meta-Agreement*

The two structural conditions mentioned – single-peakedness and unidimensional alignment – represent forms of *minimal agreement* that frame collective decisions. In the absence of substantive agreement among individuals, these weaker forms of agreement can ensure that collective decision making by majority rule would be immune from the incoherencies that would render it meaningless. In other words, in order for people's substantive disagreement to make any sense, they must first agree on what this disagreement is all about.[43]

According to List, both single-peakedness and unidimensional alignment can arise out of some *deep-level consensus* among voters – what he calls 'meta-agreement' or 'agreement at the meta-level'. Both indicate some background cohesion of substantively different individual preferences and judgements.[44] While disagreeing on what the first best, second best, or *n*th best option is, individuals can nonetheless agree on what structures these options – that is, on what is at stake in the choice they make and on how all these options are arrayed in relation to that choice.

When people agree on the frame structuring their options, they agree at the meta-level, although they may well still have different preferences with respect to those options. Individual option rankings may be different,

---

[39] In a unidimensional setting, and *mutatis mutandis* in a multidimensional setting.
[40] List 2012, p. 195.
[41] Ibid.
[42] Ibid., pp. 195–7.
[43] This is exactly what Riker (1982, p. 128) has in mind when saying that '[i]f by reason of discussion, debate, civic education and political socialization, voters have a common view of the political dimension (as evidenced by single-peakedness), then a transitive outcome is guaranteed ... This fact will not prevent civil war, but it will at least ensure that the civil war makes sense.'
[44] List 2002.

while the reference points underlying these rankings are the same. Similarly, as regards judgements: while people may hold different judgements, there may exist a common underlying dimension structuring those judgements. If the set of propositions under evaluation is framed by a common issue dimension, then for every proposition in this set all people rejecting it will be either to the left or to the right of those endorsing it.[45]

Although it hasn't been directly discussed in the public justification literature,[46] we could well imagine how a meta-agreement would look in the space of reasons. Imagine that, from a set of available reasons for a decision X, different people would endorse different reasons, yet they would all agree on how the reasons in that set hang together – for example, that endorsing reason (a) means rejecting reason (b) while at the same time also endorsing reason (c). They agree thus on how reasons hang together or cluster in the justificatory reason space of decision. Suppose that different individuals would agree on what sort of reasons are relevant for a decision (religious, political, scientific, and so on) while subscribing to very opposite views along the same spectrum of reasons. For example, an anti-religious party and a Christian-democratic party can endorse different reasons for action, yet their reasons can share the same doctrinal space. In other words, they see the relevant reasons in play as clustering together in the same way; their perceptions of the reason space are framed and structured along a common dimension (the existence/non-existence of some divine higher order, in our example).

What common frame of reference should structure our preferences or judgements can, of course, be a morally charged question. Nevertheless, meta-agreement – agreement on the frame of reference guiding a decision – is significantly less demanding[47] than its counterpart, substantive agreement, which has been the focus of political philosophers like Rawls,[48] legal scholars like Sunstein,[49] and public reason

---

[45] And *mutatis mutandis* for a well-aligned set of issue dimensions.
[46] See note 50. The most public justification theorists do is discuss two models of public reason: a *consensus* model according to which they endorse the same reason A underlying decision X, and the *convergence* model whereby individuals each endorse different reasons (A, B, C, etc.) underlying decision X. (See, e.g., Vallier 2011.) Yet there is no mention of how different reasons may hang together at a meta-level of justification.
[47] List 2002, p. 73.
[48] In Rawls's (1993, pp. 133–72) overlapping consensus, citizens agree on conclusions without necessarily agreeing on the premises supporting these conclusions. They share thus *some* judgements, but not *all* judgements. It is clear, however, that although *incomplete*, the overlapping consensus represents a *substantive* agreement, not a meta-agreement. For a discussion of the overlapping consensus, see List 2002, pp. 76–7.
[49] Sunstein 1995. He talks of 'incompletely theorized' or 'incompletely specified' agreements over a course of action (or conclusion) combined with persistent disagreement over the reasons for that action (or premises). Structurally reminiscent of

theorists,[50] as well as deliberative democrats.[51] How to achieve it is the focus of the next section.

F   Structuring Disagreement through Deliberation

The existence of common frames of reference among individuals is a good way of ensuring that the collective decisions reached by majority voting among them will be logically coherent. But how do these common frames structuring disagreement emerge? A series of studies have shown that deliberation can play precisely this function: empirical findings from Deliberative Polling show that deliberation can induce single-peakedness among preferences by increasing meta-agreement.

Drawing on data from two Deliberative Polls, List, McLean, Fishkin, and Luskin showed that levels of single-peakedness are higher post-deliberation than pre-deliberation.[52] This effect was greater the more individuals had deliberated and the lower the salience of the topic. The authors' explanation was as follows. Group deliberation generates a common dimension or conception of the issue involved in the collective decision, which frames and structures all available options. (For example, an issue might be framed in ideological terms, as expressing a confrontation between liberalism and conservatism, or as entailing trade-offs between economic growth and environmental conservation.) Group members then identify their preferred options within this common frame.

---

the Rawlsian overlapping consensus, Sunstein's agreements are also substantive, albeit limited in their scope.

[50] Public justification and public reason theories revolve around substantive agreement at the level of *reasons* underlying political decisions. In order to be legitimate, collective decisions must be justified by appeal to reasons all citizens can share; that is, individuals must agree on both conclusions and premises supporting these conclusions. See Quong 2011, 2013a, 2013b; Rawls 1997; Vallier 2011; Vallier and D'Agostino 2013; Wall 2010. Although very demanding, such justificatory substantive agreement has its strengths: not only does it facilitate collective rationality by ensuring consistent collective judgements, but it also ensures that a minimal political morality (based on the Golden Rule) among citizens is respected (see Goodin 1992).

[51] Substantive agreement is ideally sought by deliberative theorists as well. When arguing that deliberation should 'transform' or 'launder' individual preferences, so as to facilitate consensus, deliberative democrats have substantive agreement in mind. According to Elster (1986, p. 112, emphasis added), e.g., 'The core of the theory [of deliberative democracy] ... is that rather than aggregating or filtering preferences, the political system should be set up with a view to *changing* them by public debate and confrontation. The input to the social choice mechanism would then not be the raw, quite possibly selfish or irrational preferences ... but informed and other-regarding preferences. Or rather, there would not be any need for an aggregation mechanism, since a rational discussion would tend to produce *unanimous preferences* ... Not optimal compromise, but *unanimous agreement* is the goal of politics on this view.' See also Goodin 1986; Gutmann and Thompson 1996; Habermas 1995, 1996..

[52] List, Luskin, Fishkin, and McLean 2013. See also Farrar et al. 2010.

Several frames of interpretation may be available for the same decision (for example, that at stake in the decision is not economic growth versus environmental sustainability but rural development versus urban expansion), so it is important for group members to *agree on what the relevant frame for their decision problem is supposed be.*

The results are not surprising. It was already known, for example, that deliberation increases cooperation by framing individual choice in a particular way.[53] By putting forward 'we-frames', constructing collective interests and public reasons, or inducing a sense of collective agency, deliberation nudges individuals to be more cooperative than they would otherwise be.[54]

G   *Recap and the Role of Citizenship*

The discussion above invokes some relatively technical notions. Thus it is perhaps worth summarizing, in simpler terms, the important points from the sections above. What matters is the following. Citizens must first agree on what they are disagreeing about in order to make rational collective decisions. In other words, there must be a minimal level of consensus or cohesion around a common frame of reference guiding their collective decisions. In colloquial terms, they should 'see the big picture' or, better yet, 'see the *same* big picture'. Only then will citizens be able to make coherent, meaningful collective decisions.

Luckily, securing this big picture agreement comes more easily than securing a substantive one. I explained above how deliberation can structure disagreement, leading deliberators to internalize common frames of mind. The members of deliberative groups will conceptualize alternatives similarly, even though their rankings of these alternatives will vary. Such agreement will be the result of some combination of information sharing, learning, and various pressures of group dynamics.[55]

It is not inappropriate to think of political communities as being akin to deliberative groups. Being an official member of the national community – that is, being a citizen – increases one's opportunities (and indeed one's civic duty) to engage in public deliberation with other members. One's access to channels and fora of deliberation is often a function of one's social capital, particularly one's networks. In virtue of being deeply socially embedded, citizens can engage more easily and more deeply in deliberation than non-members. Being deeply socially embedded also

---

[53] Dawes, McTavish, and Shaklee 1977; Orbell, van de Kragt, and Dawes 1988.
[54] Dryzek and List 2003, pp. 12–16.
[55] List, Luskin, Fishkin, and McLean 2013; Luskin and Fishkin 2002.

gives them more incentives for doing so.[56] Engaging in deliberation with fellow nationals, citizens' preferences and choices are likely to be affected by the same structuring influences on opinion – by the same newspapers, discourses, pamphlets, and so on, as Mill points out.

On the one hand, citizens' preferences and judgements are likely to be structured by the common frames of interpretation emerging from public deliberation to which they, as citizens, are party. Those who are members of the same political community are likely to see the big picture broadly in the same way, even when disagreeing substantively on the details. Accordingly, their preferences, although different, are likely to be single-peaked along the same frame of reference. This is all to the good. By fostering deliberation, citizenship will tend to promote meta-agreement among fellow citizens, and thus also promote logically coherent collective decisions.

On the other hand, however, it is likely that different political communities will end up having different frames of reference for their collective decisions. That is in part because the political institutional settings and political culture (party system, ideological cleavages, electoral system, and so on) in which collective decisions are made differ for each community, and so do the interests of each community. But frames of reference for collective decisions also differ from one political community to another in part because the boundaries of political communities are fairly closed and their compositions are fairly stable, making the distinctions between political communities relatively enduring.

---

[56] Although migrants may have a stronger reason to engage in deliberation than citizens, because they have more to gain by doing so. It may be the only way they have of exercising political influence where they live, unlike citizens who also have a vote there. Furthermore, for migrants, engaging in deliberation could be a way of gaining social and political recognition, recognition that has already been granted to citizens. So migrants would *need* deliberation more than citizens do. The fact remains, however, that at the community level citizens have more opportunities for deliberation (there are fewer legal, cultural, and social barriers to participation in deliberation; for example, only citizens can be part of a jury, assist the debates of the parliament in some countries, be a party member, etc.). Who *is* taking part in deliberation is one thing, who *should* take part in public deliberation is another; I bracket such issues here. It is enough to say that citizens should first and foremost (but maybe not uniquely) deliberate with one another. The fact remains that cooperation (and deliberation, as an instance of cooperation) is generally driven by reciprocity. If most cooperation is driven by the fear of counter-retaliation (see Goodin 1992), then citizens have a reason to deliberate with other citizens, who by their votes have the power to coerce, but not with migrants who lack this power. The right to exercise political power, belonging uniquely to citizens, will put those people in a situation to reciprocate and thus to cooperate. Yet, because migrants have few, if any, political rights, there are fewer incentives for citizens to engage in an exchange with them.

Moreover, it is fairly plausible that, as a result of closed deliberation inside each political community, the differences between these communities and their frames of references would increase rather than decrease. Suppose we have two political communities with two *different* frames of reference, x and y. Say that for each community, its dominant frame of reference guiding decisions is endorsed by 55 per cent of its members, with the rest of the members from each community supporting another frame of reference (z) that is common across the two political communities. Over time – due to pressures of conformism, informational and reputational cascades, and herd behaviour[57] – closed deliberation among fellow citizens inside each community may increase the support enjoyed by the dominant, but very different, frames of reference (x and y),[58] from 55 per cent to more for each dominant frame inside each community, to the disadvantage of the alternative frame (z) that is common across them. In virtue of this, we could say that over time, the two political communities would become more dissimilar.

III How Multiple Citizenship Could Undermine Collective Rationality

What happens when the boundaries between the deliberative groups constituted by political communities get blurred? What happens if some individuals are members of two deliberative groups at the same time? With the above distinctions and connections in mind, I will now return to discuss how *multiple citizenship* can undermine collective decision making by disrupting meta-agreement – that is, the common frames of reference that must guide decision making in a community. I will focus on meta-agreement at the level of *preferences*, but what I will say applies *mutatis mutandis* to judgements or reasons as well.

A   Deciding in Two Countries

How and why is multiple citizenship a problem for meta-agreement? The type of challenge presented by multiple citizenship is, in general terms, a

---

[57] See Ash [1955] 2011; Banerjee 1992; Bikchandani et al. 1998; Kuran and Sunstein 1999.
[58] My discussion here focuses on the endorsement of a common frame of reference (i.e., of meta-agreement) rather than the endorsement of any particular substantive view. However, I do rely on studies (see Sunstein 2000, p. 178; 2002, p. 92) showing that in the presence of common identity, solidarity, and affected ties among group members, closed deliberation inside that group will enforce the support for the substantive view that is already most widely supported inside that group. I see no reason why the same effect would not be present at the meta-level of decision making as well.

common one. We engage on an everyday basis in deliberation inside various different groups of which we are members. We have different conversations with different people. The pressure toward agreement within such groups is ubiquitous. And sometimes our chance of agreeing with some people is undermined by our commitment to doing the same with others.

Deliberative Polling showed that deliberation could promote meta-agreement at group level, thereby structuring disagreement and ensuring that the group will reach coherent collective decisions. Yet those Deliberative Polls targeted *closed* deliberative groups. They did not explore potential problematic *inter*-group dynamics, like those caused by membership in multiple groups. Thus we do not know what happens if some individuals are members of more than one deliberating group, that is, if they are involved in deliberation inside different groups with different opinion structures. We simply do not know whether meta-agreement inside one deliberative group could be undermined when some group members are exposed to countervailing deliberative pressures and alternative frames of reference within another deliberative group. But it might be undermined.

Is meta-agreement contingent upon *bounded* deliberation? Arguably, that might well be the case, as I point out below. First, however, let us see how that might relate to dual citizens.

Different political communities may well, when deliberating, posit different frames of reference for the decisions they confront. In technical terms, the preferences of members may be single-peaked within each community, according to the structuring dimension that community agrees upon when deliberating. But that structuring dimension might be different in different communities. Dual citizens, in virtue of their dual membership, are likely to be engaged in deliberation within two different political communities. They will have to reach a meta-agreement with their fellow nationals from two different communities, perhaps a different one in each community.

The problem is that meta-agreement within one group may be undermined if some of its members (dual citizens) are exposed to counter-deliberation in another group. A dual citizen's choices and preferences may be consistent with the frame of reference of one community, but inconsistent with the frame of reference of the dual citizen's other community. If political communities posit different structuring dimensions of their options (which is entirely possible, even likely), then perfectly single-peaked preferences according to one community's structuring dimension will become non-single-peaked when shifted to

Multiple Citizenship and Collective Decision Making 101

the other community's structuring dimension. Meta-agreement in one community will thus be endangered by some members' preferences being shaped by the meta-agreement of another community.

Take the following example:

Dual citizen K is member of two deliberative groups: the political community of state A and political community of state B. Far away, in state C, following civil unrest this state's dictator decides to wipe out a large portion of the population to keep the reins of power. The members of the political communities of states A and B are asked to choose between several options on how to handle the situation. The options are:

(a) do nothing
(b) joint military intervention in state C, only under UN mandate
(c) military intervention by state A in state C
(d) joint economic sanctions (embargo) imposed on state C
(e) joint diplomatic sanctions (exclusion from IOs) imposed on state C
(f) placement of military arsenal of state C under international control.

Upon deliberating on these options, the political communities of states A and B come up with different ways of looking at the set of options that they have. The political community of state A, suppose, frames these options in terms of their impact on the civilian population, while the political community of state B frames them in terms of their potential efficiency in undermining the dictator.

Suppose that according to A's community, the options above would be ordered from worst to best according to their impact on civilians as follows: c<b<a<d<e<f. Military intervention will most infuriate the dictator, who will retaliate on the civilians in a desperate attempt to preserve power – so the number of victims will be the highest under this option. On the contrary, option (f) would entail bargaining with the dictator, who, let us presume for the sake of argument, will stop the civilian killings but retain power.

According to the frame used to conceptualize the choices among state B's community, in contrast, the correct ordering of the options would be: a<e<f< d<c<b. Doing nothing will further empower the dictator, while military intervention under UN mandate would be the option most likely to terminate his stay in power. (The other options would loosen his hold on power to greater or lesser extents.)

Dual citizen K, upon deliberating with fellow nationals within state A – the state K resides in – formulates the following rank of preferences: c<b<a<f<e<d, meaning that her most preferred option is (d), while the least preferred is (c). K's preference profile would be single-peaked with respect to the meta-agreement within state A, as shown in Figure 5.1.

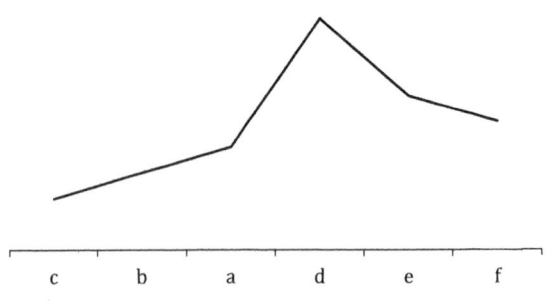

Figure 5.1 *K*'s single-peaked preference profile in *A*.

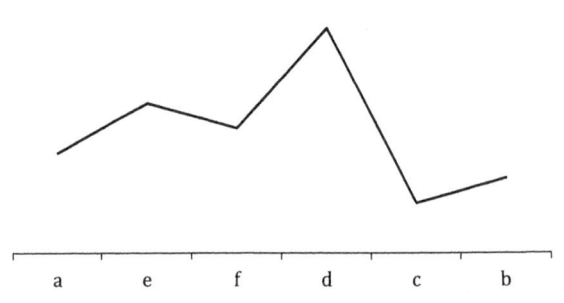

Figure 5.2 *K*'s non-single-peaked preference profile in *B*.

While *K*'s preference ordering (c<b<a<f<e<d) is perfectly consistent with (a single-peaked ranking within) state *A* community's way of conceptualizing the options, it would not be consistent with (not single-peaked ranking according to) state *B* community's way of conceptualizing the options. *K*'s preference profile in *B* would look like Figure 5.2. Meta-agreement within state *B* would be disrupted by the inclusion of *K*'s preferences, which are not single-peaked with respect to the ordering of that community. And the reason they are not is that *K*'s preferences have already been structured according to the meta-agreement from state *A*.

To be sure, in the example above the two communities make collective decisions on policy choices directly. However, some might rightly point out that it rarely happens for political communities to take a vote on each policy decision they face. Most national elections are ones in which the political community entrusts one party (or a coalition of parties) to make such policy decisions for a certain period of time, without further consultation of voters in between times.

Yet national elections constitute collective decisions, too. As such, they are vulnerable to the same problem above. Instead of choosing among a set of policy options, the political community chooses among a set of political parties. Just as the policy space (that is, the set of policy options) is structured along a common frame of reference in a community, its partisan political space (that is, the set of parties running for election) is likewise structured. And while different political communities may have nominally the same type of parties (for example, liberal, nationalist, communist, socialist), they may structure their political spaces differently. That is, their citizens may choose among these political parties with different frames of reference in mind.

For example, in one community (A) the national election may be framed as a choice between liberalism and populism. There, then, the party options would be structured alongside a liberal–populist dimension. For the sake of the example, let us assume that for community A the partisan space would be structured as follows (from left to right, the left being the most 'liberal' and the right the most 'populist'[59]): the liberals, the nationalists, the socialists, and finally, the communists. Now say community B has the same political parties, but because it has a history of authoritarian rule, it frames the choice of its national election as one between authoritarianism and democracy. For B's political community, then, the party ordering would be (from left to right, the left having the party that is most strongly associated with authoritarianism, and the right the party that is perceived as most strongly 'democratic'): the nationalists, the communists, the liberals, the socialists.

To be sure, mine is only a hypothetical example. But I believe there may be many real-world examples of political communities framing their political choices differently. Considering that party cleavages are the result of the complex history and socio-economical idiosyncrasies of each state,[60] there may well be cases where the political spaces of two political communities are structured differently, although they contain nominally the same type of parties. Voting for the socialists in an Eastern European state (where that socialist party is the successor of the communist party that had a monopoly on state power) and voting for the socialists in France (where socialism traces its roots back to the French Revolution) are political choices bearing a very different meaning in each

---

[59] I am referring, of course, to how these parties are perceived or interpreted by the public.
[60] See, for example, Lipset and Rokkan 1967; Rokkan 1999.

political community. This also means that, in order for the results of the national elections to represent coherent collective judgements, persons voting in both states must keep in mind these different frames of reference each community has, and cast their vote in accordance to each (that is, according to the meta-agreement within each community).

There are at least two possible objections to what was argued above. One would be that different political communities, as deliberative groups, are actually likely to conceptualize their choices in the same way when faced with the same or similar set of options. If so, when deliberating, political communities would reach the same meta-agreement (conceptualize their options the same way), and the preferences of dual citizens would be single-peaked with respect to both communities' orderings.

But what reasons do we have for believing that the same frames of reference will emerge in deliberation in different communities? Maybe one reason would be that all political communities exhibit a great degree of ideational heterogeneity to begin with. And in any case, their boundaries (ethnic, ideological, and otherwise) are increasingly blurred in a globalizing world. The differences between communities are fading away. Information and migration flows tend to standardize not only lifestyles but also ways of seeing the world across communities.[61] This may seem to be a powerful objection to my argument, but it should be taken with a pinch of salt. What matters is whether these changes are indeed powerful enough to influence the frames of reference guiding the national elections of different political communities, which are largely the product of institutional and structural factors – such as the state's political system, political culture, and history, as well as its locally dominant political discourses. These factors are mostly fixed and unlikely to change except very gradually. At least for the moment, I think that the ongoing process of convergence between political communities powered by globalization and open borders is unlikely to override the institutional and structural factors that obstruct the emergence of common frames of references among communities.

Presently, deliberative political communities are more different than similar to one another. This is unlikely to change in the near future. Indeed, as the Brexit referendum, Trump's election in the United States, the 2016 Austrian presidential elections,[62] and the 2017 German

---

[61] Taking into account that political communities will be exposed to the same information – to the same pool of arguments and empirical data – we might expect political communities to conceptualize choices and preferences the same way.

[62] The 2016 Austrian election pitted a pro-European independent candidate against a far-right candidate. While the pro-European candidate eventually won, he did so only after the elections were held a second time. The initial elections gave him only a marginal

parliamentary elections show,[63] the political forces (over)emphasizing these differences and advocating policies meant to enforce them are becoming stronger every day. Completely open borders are to most, if not all, governments a nightmarish dystopia. A whole range of policies and institutions – from education to internal affairs – are set to work to preserve and promote the particularities (cultural, political, and so on) thought to define the community.[64] That is exacerbated by various other factors, ranging from socialization to in-group conformism and group polarization as a result of closed deliberations. Hence, despite globalization and its various cultural and ideological spillovers, it is very likely for different political communities to frame their collective decisions differently.

The second, and more important, objection to the scenario I offered above is the following. If citizenship indeed fosters deliberation, then dual citizens will engage in deliberation in *each* of their political communities. This means that dual citizens will structure or *re*structure, as needed, their preferences according to the common frame of reference endorsed by each community in deliberation. That is, a dual citizen will 'reshuffle' preferences and reconstitute judgements according to the prevailing conceptualizing dimension of each community.[65] Through *re*formulation of preferences according to the common frame of reference underlying the decisions of the second community, the preferences that dual citizens express in their second community will end up fitting perfectly with the frame of reference underlying the choices of their

---

advantage over his opponent, and following irregularities affecting a number of votes large enough to have potentially reversed the outcome, the Constitutional Court decided it best to void the election results and organize another election. See Oltermann 2016.

[63] The results of the elections saw the first far-right party (AfD) to enter Bundestag in over six decades.

[64] E.g., the defence of French republican values was a common argument in the burqa debate, and so was Danish secularism and freedom of expression in the Danish cartoon debate.

[65] It was pointed out that individuals *can* adapt their *behaviour* to different sets of social norms. They can behave at home according to the social norms and values of one community, and at work, for example, according to the social norms and values of another. (See Morton 2014.) This might dissuade some from accepting that dual citizens will have trouble *reasoning* consistently with two different collective frames of mind simultaneously. The issue at stake here, however, is different in relevant respects from the one where individuals have to *behave* according to different social codes. What is at stake here is not behaviour but rather psychological adaptation and flexibility. As Morton notices, code switching might put people under psychological stress. Cognitive dissonance will more likely occur when people have to behave according to norms and values they do not internalize. Even so, they can – indeed, will – under social and legal pressure behave as if they had internalized them. Internalizing conflicting values and norms and acting consistently according to them is difficult, if not impossible. For dual citizens, reasoning and acting – and exercising political power – according to different frames of mind will be difficult, if not impossible.

106 Consequences

fellow citizens there, even if that differs from their first community's frame of reference. Dual citizens' preferences will thus have a single-peaked profile in both political communities, ensuring thereby that both communities reach coherent collective decisions through majority rule.

But is deliberation within one community powerful enough to reorient a person's preferences in line with that community's frame, if that person's preferences are at the same time 'pulled' in a different direction by counter-deliberation promoting an alternative frame in another community? What are the real chances for dual citizens to reformulate their preferences and judgements in line with the different (even conflicting) frames of reference posited by their two political communities? We do not know. All we have is evidence that deliberation in a *closed* group induces more nearly single-peaked preferences within that group, by making group members aware of the common frame of reference that should guide their individual decisions. We do not know what happens when individuals are at the same time exposed to counter-deliberation in a second group adopting a different frame of reference.[66]

B   *A Perceptual Analogy*

In the absence of any direct empirical evidence on that matter, I shall now mount an argument by analogy. It will draw on the psychology of perception to suggest that the prospects are slim for dual citizens to be able to easily or reliably reformulate their preferences and judgements in line with the different, even conflicting, decision frames their political communities might have.

The analogy that I propose is that between optical illusions and decision frames of reference. Some optical illusions involve people being unable to perceive the multiple representations of the same image. Similarly, when deciding on political choices, dual citizens may have trouble keeping in mind two different frames of reference and reliably reconstituting their choices consistently with each. Just as it is not possible to see both the duck and rabbit at the same time in Jastrow's illusion[67] (see

---

[66] We can presume, of course, that if we have two deliberating groups, A and B, and a large proportion of individuals within each group are members of the other group as well, forming a dominant opinion cluster inside each group, the two deliberating groups would adopt the same common frame of reference. We can doubt, however, that this is the case when it comes to political communities and their citizens; we can doubt they 'share' a large enough proportion of citizens (who are multiple citizens) such that their influence on public deliberation in each community would be strong enough to homogenize these communities' frames of reference.

[67] Hill 1915; Jastrow 1899; Kihlstrom 2006.

Welche Thiere gleichen einander am meisten?

Kaninchen und Ente.

Figure 5.3 'Kaninchen und Ente' ('Rabbit and Duck'), the earliest known version of the duck–rabbit illusion, from the October 23, 1892, issue of *Fliegende Blätter*. (Available at http://diglit.ub.uni-heidelberg.de/diglit/fb97/0147?sid=8af6d821538a1926abf44c9a95c40951&zoomlevel=2, courtesy of Universitätsbibliothek Heidelberg.)

Figure 5.3), it may not be possible for dual citizens to make decisions consistent with two conflicting frames of reference.

From what we know, this extrapolation is not implausible. Let me first begin with the problem posed by optical illusions before explaining how this extends to decision making.

Some optical illusions involve ambiguous images with different representational content. That is to say that a figure can, at the same time, represent different things, and looking at that figure, people will see different things. In some of the most famous examples, some will see a duck while others will see a rabbit; some will see a young woman, others an old woman; some will see a whale, others a kangaroo. People will usually perceive only one representation of the figure. But even when they might be able to perceive both representations of the same image, they will not see both representations *at the same time*.[68] Moreover, flipping from one representation to another requires mental control.[69] What is important

---

[68] Jastrow 1899.
[69] Long and Toppino 2003; Mitroff, Sobel, and Gopnik 2006; Toppino 2003; Toppino and Long 2005. Alternatively, it can be the result of neural fatigue – but that is hardly a

for our analogy below is that, when seeing an optical illusion, people can see only *one* of its representations at a time, and switching between the representations is cognitively burdensome.

In similar fashion, the same decision can be framed differently. Different political communities, in adopting a different frame of reference guiding their decisions, will interpret the options and their stakes differently. This in turn will affect their citizens' choices. That frames of decision matter in this way is not new. Experiments in both psychology and economics have long shown that people's preferences are often influenced by how their choices are conceptualized and interpreted. These influences have been termed 'framing effects'.[70] For example, people are more likely to buy condoms advertised as effective in 'fully 95%' of the cases than when they are advertised as failing in 'only 5%' of the cases.[71] However, just as it is impossible for people to see two different representations of the same image at the same time, it may be impossible for dual citizens to bear in mind two different frames for interpreting their options. Cognitively, they may not be able to keep both frames in mind simultaneously, or switch between them reliably, in the way that is required in order for them to make a choice that will be consistent with the differing frames of reference appropriate to each of the political communities in which they vote and deliberate.

In the case of optical illusions, people are sometime able to flip between representations of the same image. Might not dual citizens similarly alternate in their mind between the decision frames of two communities, reformulating their preferences in line with each community's frame of reference when politically engaging with that community? Dual citizens have no need to relate to both decision frames at the same time, after all: they are not voting *literally* at one and the same time in both states' elections. So, what stops them from making one political choice according to one frame, and subsequently a second one according to another frame?

There are some reasons to doubt at least some dual citizens' capacity to reformulate their preferences and judgements consistently with different communities' frames, and to do so reliably depending on which community they are in at the time. Simply seeing an alternative frame requires some mental effort and control, and switching between frames

---

promising model for dual citizens who are supposed to be flipping from one frame to another in a disciplined way that tracks faithfully which national community they are voting in at the moment.
[70] Tversky and Kahneman 1981.
[71] The example is taken from Revlin 2012, p. 364.

every time one engages with a different political community requires even more. Some dual citizens might simply not make the effort. And it seems almost inevitable that even those who are trying their best will occasionally err.

Furthermore, having already internalized one decision frame – for example, one structuring of the political arena – dual citizens might psychologically resist internalizing an alternative one. It is not that they are *unaware* of the alternative frame at work in their second community, which is unlikely given that they are *ex hypothesi* exercising their political and deliberative agency in both. While aware of the second community's alternative frame, a dual citizen might still have trouble reformulating his preferences coherently within this frame, not because he is unwillingly to do so, but rather because of psychological limits in doing so. For a dual citizen who has already successfully internalized one frame of reference, reformulating his preferences according to another frame may cause him *cognitive dissonance*.

In addition, it is reasonable to suppose that a political community's common frame of reference for collective decision making will have prescriptive force, in the same way social norms do. Or, perhaps more precisely, it is likely to be supported by social norms regulating what it means to be a good citizen of that community. If so, a dual citizen might have trouble internalizing and therefore switching between different mental frames. The saying 'when in Rome, do as the Romans do' might suggest otherwise. But studies of the power of early childhood socialization indicate that the norms internalised during that stage of life are very 'sticky'.[72] When coming across norms very different from the ones they grew up with, people may therefore have trouble internalizing and reliably complying with them. Thus a dual citizen may not be able to reliably reformulate his preferences in line with a different, second, common frame of reference, so that his preferences remain single-peaked with respect to it. If he cannot, his political participation in the second community on those terms may undermine collective rationality in that community by standing in the way of its reaching logically coherent collective decisions.

To come back to an example I have used earlier, imagine a dual citizen who was born and raised in a state that is a former communist dictatorship, but who has relocated and naturalized in an old democratic state. Such a person may have trouble reformulating his political preferences when voting or engaging in public deliberation in his state of residence,

---

[72] See Sears and Levy 2003.

where the left has no history of authoritarian rule. He may nonetheless feel a certain psychological pressure, or he may even (because of his early childhood socialization in the former communist dictatorship) feel obligated to never endorse in any way a leftist party. Perhaps he might feel this as a duty owed to his birth state or to his fellow citizens there. Or perhaps he may conceive it expressively, as a way of communicating that he condemns his birth state's political past or maybe as a signal that he hasn't forgotten it. Or he may fear that, to his fellow citizens from his birth state, he will come across as a hypocrite if he shifts his preferences in one state in line with another state's frame of reference. For any of these many reasons, the dual citizen may fail to internalize the alternative frame structuring the political space of his democratic state of residence.

Finally, to what extent is the analogy I draw between people's responses to optical illusions and people's responses to different decision frames persuasive? That is up for each reader of this chapter to decide. Still, I think it is not an implausible extrapolation from what we do know. As Kahneman and Tversky remarked in their landmark paper introducing the notion of decision frames, '[i]n their stubborn appeal, *framing effects resemble perceptual illusions* more than computational errors'.[73]

IV Conclusion

To sum up, collective decisions reached by majority voting risk being meaningless unless disagreement inside a political community remains within certain bounds. The emergence of common frames of reference in public deliberation, structuring substantively different preferences or judgements, serves that function. We know that deliberation promotes collective rationality in this way, yet from the studies we have we can only be confident that it does so within closed groups. Collective rationality inside one deliberating group could arguably be undermined if some of its members belong at the same time to another deliberating group as well.

By exposing individuals to public deliberation in different political communities, and thereby to multiple frames of reference guiding collective decisions, multiple citizenship may well undermine the logical coherence of the collective decisions made inside some (or all) of a multiple citizen's communities. Drawing on insights from social choice theory, democratic theories of deliberation and public reason, and experimental psychology, my aim in this chapter has been to identify

[73] Kahneman and Tversky 1984, p. 343.

ways in which multiple citizenship *could* affect the quality of collective decisions. I argued that insofar as different political communities adopt different common frames of reference for guiding their decision making – frames that are necessary for them to reach logically coherent collective judgements – multiple citizens who are members of multiple such communities would have to reformulate their preferences and judgements according to the frame of each community. Building on an analogy between people's responses to optical illusions and people's responses to alternative decision frames, I offered reasons for doubting that at least some multiple citizens will be able to do so. They certainly seem unlikely to be able to do so effortlessly or reliably.

6 Multiple Citizenship and the Boundary Problem

The previous chapter has examined the implications of multiple citizenship for the *quality* of collective decisions. Focusing on two mechanisms of decision making – voting and deliberation – I there showed how multiple citizenship could undermine collective rationality. Despite the nefarious consequences that might thus arise from multiple citizens exercising political rights (in voting) and agency (in deliberation), one might nonetheless think there are other good moral arguments in favour of it. One might think that, as a matter of principle, the exercise of political rights[1] by multiple citizens is justified, after all.

In this chapter I will attack the latter claim by considering multiple citizenship through the lens of the *boundary problem,* or the problem of constituting the demos. After all, multiple citizens are able to exercise political rights in different states only in virtue of a choice made by those states as to how to draw the boundaries of the demos, that is, how to set up their entitlements to political rights. Had states chosen other options – which I will discuss below – the problems mentioned in Chapter 5 would never have arisen to begin with.

The boundary problem is a thorny issue for democratic theory. It is likewise for democratic practice as well, as I will show in this chapter. The boundary problem presents itself as a classical 'chicken or egg' dilemma. The question of how to configure the demos cannot be settled in a democratic way – by letting the people decide – because an election presupposes an electorate, and that is precisely what the election is supposed to decide. Since elections will not solve the problem, various freestanding principles are required instead.

One may well wonder to what extent our membership regimes are attuned to the various boundary-drawing principles democratic theorists have advanced. Do those principles inform in any way our *actual practices* of defining our communities? Or are they post hoc rationales offered to

---

[1] When talking about 'political rights' I have in mind primarily the right to vote.

justify boundaries drawn for different reasons? Or are those principles perhaps *ideals* that can never be implemented by the citizenship regimes relying, as current ones invariably do, on *jus soli* or *jus sanguinis*?

Here, however, I will focus on one particular problem that arises in applying those principles to the real world. Those principles all are designed to implement a classic, Westphalian partition of the world into mutually exclusive and jointly exhaustive units. And all of those principles operate on the (typically unspoken) assumption that every individual is going to be included in *one demos only*.

Yet, in a globalized world where people enjoy increased mobility, the boundaries of different demoi have become increasingly blurred, and communities have become '*internally less inclusive* and *externally less exclusive*'.[2] Increasingly, people live where they do not belong, and belong where they do not live, from the perspective of each of the standard principles for constituting the demos.[3] As it was recently pointed out, in the context of continuous migration, states nowadays have to square fluctuating inclusion claims with stable self-government.[4] The relevant question today is: How can democracies cope with boundary instability and mismatches between their territorial jurisdictions, citizenries, and demoi?[5]

Might the solution be to allow *multiple citizenship*, the inclusion of the same individual in two or more demoi? Can multiple citizenship be a better way of defining the demos than 'one individual, one citizenship' (mono-nationality)? In theory, multiple citizenship may be compatible with any of the expansions of citizenship that would be required by each of the various proffered principles for constituting the demos.[6] As currently practiced, however, it is not fully compatible with any of them.

I start by examining those various boundary principles – the affected interests, the legally subjected, and the unaffected interests principles – and point out how all could, *in principle*, be supportive of multiple citizenship (Section I). I next explore how multiple citizenship fares with respect to each principle, *in practice*. I argue that, contrary to expectations, multiple citizenship as presently practiced[7] is not perfectly

---

[2] Goodin 1996, p. 363, emphasis in original.
[3] Frazer 2014; Goodin 2007; López-Guerra 2005.
[4] Bauböck 2015.
[5] Ibid., p. 826.
[6] Goodin (2007) advances multiple citizenship in support of the affected interests principle, Abizadeh (2012) advances it in support of the legally subjected principle.
[7] As I argue below, it is logically possible for multiple citizenship to be coextensive with pretty much any of them. Here, however, I am interested not in the logical possibility so much as whether it is realized *in practice*, i.e., whether multiple citizenship as presently practiced can answer the demands of the theory.

congruent with any of the examined principles (Section II). My next step is to inquire into the reasons for this repeated failure. I point out that one salient cause of this failure is the Gordian knot between state membership and the exercise of political rights. Severing this knot would better serve whichever principle states favour for how to constitute the demos (Section III).

I Three Boundary-Drawing Principles: Affectedness, Subjection to Law, and Unaffectedness

Who should be included in the demos and why? I will examine three principles, as ideal types, and point out how all justify an expansion of the demoi, which could in principle be accomplished with the help of multiple citizenship. (Which one of the aforementioned principles we should prefer, all things considered, for the distribution of political rights requires a separate discussion and is not the central focus of this chapter.)

A The Affected Interests Principle

Take, first, the affected interests principle. In its pure form, *all and only those affected* by a political decision should have a say in that decision. By 'those affected' theorists generally mean those having interests at stake[8] in a decision.[9] The principle, very seductive in theory, is very demanding in practice, however. First, its application would seem to require a reconfiguration of the demos with every single policy choice.[10] Citizenship, in contrast, is a relatively permanent status, too rigid to admit of such constant reconfiguration. Second, one cannot know prior to making

---

[8] Rainer Bauböck offers his 'stakeholder' principle as an alternative to the affected interests principle, but in truth it is merely a variant on it. As Bauböck (2007b, p. 2422) describes it, the stakeholder principle 'expresses first the idea that citizens have not merely fundamental interests in the outcomes of the political process, but a claim to be represented as participants to that process'. As such, the stakeholder principle seems tautological in claiming that those who have political rights (citizens) should have political rights. Second, he argues that '[i]ndividuals *whose circumstances of life* [objectively: Bauböck 2009] *link* their future well-being to the flourishing of a particular community should be recognized as stakeholders in that polity with a claim to participate in collective decision-making processes that shape the shared future of this political community.' But how are we to decide whether one's *well-being is linked to the flourishing of a community* if not by establishing whether their interests are affected by what happens to that community? 'Stakes' and 'interests' are, of course, definitionally intertwined: according to the *Oxford English Dictionary* a 'stake' just is 'a share or interest in a business, situation, or system'.

[9] Arrhenius 2005, p. 20.

[10] Whelan 1983, pp. 18–19.

Multiple Citizenship and the Boundary Problem   115

a decision who will be affected by that decision. At the same time, which decision is taken depends on who takes the decision in the first place. This circularity would seem to make the principle procedurally impossible.[11] These problems are not without solutions. Yet the solutions depart from the pure version of the principle.[12] These departures, in turn, seem very accommodating of an expansion of citizenship or of a dissolution of membership boundaries altogether.

As regards the procedural impossibility noticed by Whelan, it is easily solved by making boundaries superfluous, for example, by including everyone in the demos.[13] Indeed, a refined version of the principle could entail enfranchising 'all probably affected interests by any possible decision arising out of any possible agenda'.[14] That would ultimately justify giving 'virtually everyone a vote on virtually everything virtually everywhere in the world' – perhaps by making *every individual a citizen* of every existing state[15] or, alternatively, by making all people citizens of a single, global state.

The former is just a prescription for *multiple citizenship*. Its advantage would be to tackle externalities and extra-territorialities that are ubiquitous nowadays. The foundations of today's demos – territoriality, history, and nationality – already presuppose a web of interrelated and interdependent interests.[16] So does citizenship, providing a political and legal framework for the collective pursuit of these interests. Yet some affected interests inevitably always fall outside territorial, ethnic, or citizenship

---

[11] That is, who is affected by a law or policy depends on which law and policy is enacted; but at the same time which policy and law is enacted depends on who will make this decision (Whelan 1983, p. 19).

[12] One important departure is the inclusion of the unaffected alongside the affected. If we cannot include *all the affected* without including also some unaffected along the way, then it is better to include *all but not only* the affected than *only but not all* of the affected (Goodin 2007, pp. 56–9).

[13] 'Virtually (maybe literally) everyone in the world – and indeed everyone in all possible future worlds – should be entitled to vote on any proposal or any proposal for proposals. A maximally extensive franchise, virtually (perhaps literally) ignoring boundaries both of space and of time, would be the only legitimate way of constituting the demos to this more defensible version of the "all possibly affected interests" principle' (Goodin 2007, p. 55). See also Arrhenius 2005, p. 22.

[14] Goodin 2007, pp. 61–2.

[15] Ibid., p. 64.

[16] 'Geographically, people who live in close proximity to one another are typically (if not invariably) affected by the behavior of those around them. People bound by shared histories or nationalities typically (if not invariably) care about and conceive their interests as being affected by what one another does. The reason we think that territorial or historical or national groups ought make decisions together is that, typically if not invariably, the interests of individuals within those groups are affected by the actions and choices of others in that group' (ibid., p. 48).

boundaries.[17] Redefining territorial boundaries would be very difficult. Still, the expansion of citizenship remains, in *principle*, the most obvious solution for the inclusion of those affected.

B The Legally Subjected Principle

Among political theorists, the main competitor of the affected interests principle is the *all and only subjected* principle.[18] According to it, only those subjected to the laws of a state should be part of its demos. The principle is a requirement of democracy in the end: if democracy is about giving the law to ourselves, then law takers and law makers should be one and the same. If individuals are – as democratic theorists argue – entitled to political rights in order to be self-governing, then one is not entitled to them if one is not governed by the enactments made through the exercise of those rights.[19]

Now, with some exceptions, the reach of laws is territorially bounded. The effective power of laws of one state stops where the borders of another state begin. Each state has its own territorial jurisdiction, and all those living in its jurisdiction are bound by its laws and those alone. States may sometimes claim their laws to apply to their citizens wherever these may be, or even to non-citizens not on their territory. Yet a state's capacity to *enforce* such laws, extra-territorial in application, on another state's territory is nonetheless limited and dependent on the will of the latter.[20] Thus the laws of a state are generally coercively applied to and govern *only those* within its territorial borders.

---

[17] By 'citizenship' I am referring of course to the classic citizenship paradigm – that of 'one individual, one state, one citizenship'. Multiple citizenship was forbidden for a long time through international treaties and in national citizenship laws.

[18] Some might rightly object that this is an artificial divide: being 'subjected' is just a subtype of being 'affected' in the end. But if coercion requires special justification, then we have good reasons to think of the legally subjected principle in *sui generis* terms. On the legally subjected principle, see Abizadeh 2012; Beckman 2014; Blake 2013; Goodin 2016; López-Guerra 2005; Miller 2009, 2010; Owen 2010, 2011.

[19] See López-Guerra 2005.

[20] This is not to say that they can *never* be enforced. Laws, whether having extra-territorial application or not, may be enforced extra-territorially through various mechanisms of state cooperation. Think of the Interpol's Red Notice, which basically functions as an international arrest warrant, or of the European Arrest Warrant. They are all proof that (at least some) laws will be enforced extra-territorially. Even so individuals can be said to be *subjected* primarily to the laws of the state they reside in insofar as (1) one is expected to obey the laws of the state on the territory of which one is physically present and not *other* states' laws and (2) physical presence on a state's territory creates the primary potential for one to violate *that* state's laws (territorial jurisdiction-wise) and not other states' laws, placing the individual thus under the threat of the use of force from that state only.

As we speak, states deviate from the principle in two ways. First, *non-resident citizens* hold political rights without being subjected to the laws of their state. Second, *non-citizen residents* do not hold those rights while being subjected to state laws. States obstinately consider citizenship a legitimate ground of *inclusion* in the demos: citizens will almost always never cease holding political rights.[21] This gives rise to situations of external voting.[22] While the opinion of non-resident citizens should perhaps be taken into account, it does not follow that this should be done by enfranchising them.[23]

The strict application of the all subjected principle would entail thus both an *extension* and a *contraction* of the citizenry. On one side, the principle supports a contraction of the citizenry, insofar as non-resident citizens should be disenfranchised. One way of doing that would be to denaturalize them altogether; I will discuss other less radical ways in the next section. On the other side, the principle prescribes expanding citizenship to include long-term residing migrants who are pervasively subjected to the state's laws. This expansion is in principle compatible with multiple citizenship, at least insofar as the person is resident in or otherwise pervasively coercively subjected to the laws of both states.

C   The Unaffected Interests Principle

Finally, take the *unaffected interests* principle. According to this lesser-known principle, there is something to be gained from deliberately giving a vote to those who are unaffected – those having no personal stakes or prior opinions on a political decision.[24] The unaffected are capable of manifesting 'natural impartiality' as decision makers, a high-quality type of impartiality that is not available to those affected by the same decision.[25] The unaffected individuals can fulfil the role of 'impartial spectators'. They are more able to track justice in their judgements insofar as there is nothing for them in the decision they are about to make. The decision-making abilities of the unaffected are valued in the

---

[21] López-Guerra 2005, p. 226. See also Lafleur (2015) on the increasing acceptance of external voting. Yet there are a few exceptions to this rule; e.g., states like the United Kingdom or Canada disenfranchise their emigrants after living abroad for more than fifteen and five years, respectively.
[22] Bauböck 2007b; Brand 2013.
[23] López-Guerra 2005, p. 223.
[24] Frazer 2014, p. 380.
[25] Ibid., pp. 380–3.

judiciary and in arbitration courts.[26] Why restrict their decision power to those spheres only?[27]

Of course, some unaffected people are already inevitably included in the demos that decides on any given issue, due to the fixity of citizenship and variability of interests. Non-drivers have a say on driving legislation, non-parents on parental rights and duties, and non-taxpayers on the rates at which others will be taxed. The unaffected interests principle, however, aims at the *systematic* and *intentional* inclusion of people who will not be affected, precisely because they will not be affected. How many need be included? Not necessarily 'all and only'. *Some* can be enough to secure impartial decision making.[28] If *only* those unaffected are making the decision, it would be superfluous to include *all* of them as well: any number would do insofar as under a veil of ignorance individuals are interchangeable; a decision made by one unaffected is as impartial as a decision made by a million unaffected.[29] If we relax the 'only' requirement, however, we need to specify how many unaffected should be included in the demos alongside those affected to preserve impartiality. In principle, we could aim for the inclusion of *just enough* unaffected so as to ensure that collective decisions are *overall* impartial – for example, include $n+1$ unaffected in the demos, where n is the number of affected decision makers.[30]

How could the inclusion of the unaffected be implemented? One proposal would be that of reciprocal agreements between states. They would function in the following way. If the citizens of state A are affected by a political decision X but those of state B are not, then the citizens of state B would be empowered to make that decision. State A's citizens would do the same for state B's citizens: they would decide on issue Y, which affects the citizens of state B but not themselves. This amounts to a

---

[26] Judges, for example, have to recuse themselves in case of conflict of interest. Conflict of interest is also a problem for politicians (accumulation of mandates is banned for this very reason). It is also common to try to disqualify witnesses in front of the jury by showing they may be biased, and bias is neutralized by requiring 'hostile' witnesses to answer only by 'yes' or 'no'.

[27] Frazer 2014, pp. 390–1.

[28] As Frazer (2014, p. 394) seems to imply, without mentioning a number or proportion, or even enunciating a principle for determining one: 'Impartial spectators may not only be participants in political discourse, but may also participate alongside the affected parties in decision-making procedures such as elections.'

[29] Its *correctness*, however, is a function of the number of decision makers (see Goodin and Spiekermann 2018.)

[30] Tanasoca n.d. In principle, states could vary the number of unaffected for each political decision (perhaps depending on its importance, as well as the number of affected voters), although I have already commented on the difficulties of reconfiguring the demos with every political decision.

swap of electorates.[31] But the two states could also swap representatives instead, as proposed by Philippe Schmitter and Jeremy Bentham before him.[32]

As for the voters' swap, notice that it is already happening. Some French citizens vote in American elections, just like Hungarians vote in Italian elections, and Argentineans in Australian elections.[33] I am referring here, of course, to *dual* citizens. *Multiple citizenship* could thus in principle promote the inclusion of the unaffected.

II Multiple Citizenship and Boundaries: An Assessment

At least *in theory*, then, multiple citizenship can be easily squared with all three principles for constituting the demos. But how well does it fare with respect to each *in practice*? Is multiple citizenship coextensive with all, some, or none of these boundary principles?

A *The Affected Interests Principle*

As previously discussed, the affected interests principle might justify enfranchising everyone, everywhere.[34] That would simply entail making everyone a *multiple citizen*. In theory, then, multiple citizenship seems perfectly suited to implement this particular demos principle. But what chances does it actually have of doing so in practice?

According to the spirit of this principle, what kind of affected interests should be enfranchised? In answering this question, it is perhaps easier to think of what kind should *not* be enfranchised. And it turns out that precisely these interests get enfranchised through multiple citizenship, as I argue below.

States should *not* on these grounds enfranchise people with *no affected interests*. This comes as obvious. The problem, however, is that some of

---

[31] This is Frazer's (2014, pp. 394–5) proposal.
[32] Schmitter 1997, pp. 303–6. Bentham (2002, sec. II, art. 10, pp. 231, 250, emphasis added) made a similar proposal in his *Project of a Constitutional Code for France*: 'From the capacity of being elected no human creature whatsoever shall be excluded.' He further explains in his *Observations*: 'In France it seems to be no uncommon opinion that M. Necker, a Citizen of Geneva, is not of all men the least deserving of the confidence of French men ... Were the French and English legislature *to interchange a few Members*, there could not be a more powerful means of wearing away those national antipathies and jealousies which as far as they prevail are so disgraceful and so detrimental to both countries.'
[33] Of course, what combinations are possible depends on what countries permit the accumulation of citizenships, as well as external voting (the exercise of political rights by non-resident citizens).
[34] Goodin 2007, p. 64.

the objective circumstances on which we might rely as proxies for affected interests are not actually reliable in tracking the existence of such interests. Consider, for example, the case of *birthright* multiple citizens. They have inherited multiple different citizenships from their parents or grandparents.[35] In virtue of birth circumstances alone (as opposed to preexisting affected interests) such people are included in the demoi of multiple states.[36] But multiple citizens usually grow up and reside in one of their states of citizenship, developing certain interests there. Their welfare and everyday life will, most likely, be largely dependent on the decisions of one state's government (considering also their everyday subjection to the laws of this state), as well as being unavoidably intertwined with the welfare and everyday lives of their co-nationals there. At the same time, by holding the citizenship of another state or states, they get to be included in another demos or demoi as well, without necessarily so much having stakes there. Think of third- or fourth-generation migrants. They can be citizens of a state they do not reside in, hardly speak the language of, and have never even visited. They may know very little (almost nothing) about this state's history and culture or about its current state of affairs, its economic and political situation, and so on.[37] In other words, they could *have nothing to do* with this state, except being citizen of it.

This should not be too surprising. It is, after all, bound to happen if individuals inherit citizenship just like they inherit family furniture.[38] They do not need it, they do not use it, yet they keep it. In this case, however, their citizenship – demoted to the status of old furniture or perhaps promoted to the status of family heritage – does not answer to affected interests. Merely holding the passport of a state does not

---

[35] Indeed, in some cases, one can apply for citizenship by descent and thereby be granted citizenship on the basis of distant family ties (e.g., by establishing their grandparents' citizenship). At the time of writing, states like Ireland, Italy, Israel, Poland, Spain, and Hungary had such provisions, whereas other states (e.g., the United Kingdom and Canada) limited citizenship by descent to one generation only.

[36] True, newborns do not get to exercise their political rights the very moment they become citizens (i.e., at birth). Yet their citizenship guarantees that they will do so, no matter what, when the time comes. Put it otherwise, their political rights are dormant until reaching voting age. But upon reaching this age, there is no further conditionality on their exercise. Plus, the source of these rights is the person's birth citizenship uniquely. Inasmuch it makes sense to say that political rights were granted upon birth. The problem is, of course, that thereby people get included in the demos, interests or *no* interests at stake. Certainly, disenfranchisement is possible but only in special circumstances, for example, when required by a court in cases of felony, bankruptcy, or corruption, or on the reason of mental illness (Blais, Massicotte, and Yoshinaka 2001, pp. 44–50).

[37] True, so too may other citizens born, raised, and residing there.

[38] See also my critique of birthright citizenship in Chapter 2.

necessarily entail having an interest at stake in political decisions made there. At most, it points to a *potential* interest. Now, enfranchising *possibly affected* interests (that is, actually existing interests that *could be affected* by any given decision) is a sound proposal. But enfranchising possibly affected *potential* interests (that is, interests that *could exist* but do not) is harder to square with the affected interests principle. And that is precisely what multiple citizenship at least sometimes does, in no small part because of the grounds used in its allocation (see Chapter 2 for a general discussion).

Enfranchising affected interests that are *dead* or *dying* could also be a problem. This is the second sort of interests that mistakenly get enfranchised by multiple citizenship. Unsurprisingly, people's interests change over time. Over the course of a lifetime some interests die out, others are kindled. As a permanent status, however, citizenship cannot be conferred and then withdrawn in response to this volatility.[39] One becomes part of the demos once and for all, even when one's interests there may be dead or dying.[40] In the case of *naturalized* dual citizens,[41] for example, citizenship in the state of origin may well be a reminder of past – 'dead' – interests. A migrant may well have had interests in her state of origin, before deciding to build a life elsewhere and shortly after resettling. It is unlikely, however, for all of her interests to have survived her move, resettling, and naturalization in another state. It is unlikely for her wellbeing to still be substantially and unavoidably dependent on the decisions of her state of origin, after she has spent many years elsewhere.[42] Also, after many years spent elsewhere, still being citizen of her origin state may be all that is keeping 'alive' what would otherwise have

---

[39] The state's prerogative to withdraw citizenship is generally seen as illegitimate (for discussion, see Gibney 2013b and Lenard 2018). Yet on the present analysis, what has traditionally been considered as a great virtue of citizenship – its permanence – also constitutes one of its major drawbacks.

[40] Of course, one may in principle renounce one's birth citizenship after naturalizing in another state, in order to comply with the affected interests principle. However, not all states accept citizenship renunciation. Also, it may be unreasonably difficult for someone – either psychologically (see my discussion of loss aversion in Chapter 3) or materially (because of high exit charges imposed by the state one is leaving) – actually to do so. Finally, the affected interests principle is supposed to guide the actions of states in deciding whom to enfranchise; it is therefore arguably a 'category mistake' to say that an individual should internalize a principle that is not addressed to her to begin with and renounce her birth citizenship to comply with it.

[41] I.e., birth citizens of one state having acquiring a second citizenship through naturalization in another state.

[42] Notice that when talking of dual citizens, it is harder to argue that their well-being depends on the well-being of their relatives from their birth state. Simply because in many cases, these individuals would have already taken advantage of family reunification policies to bring their families with them after naturalizing elsewhere.

normally been extinguished interests. The problem here is that citizenship is too damn stubborn to cut the life supply of these dying interests the migrant – now dual citizen – may have in her state of origin. In this way, citizenship can make people 'prisoners' of these largely former interests.[43] Surely, the interests of many third- and fourth-generation migrants – now dual citizens – in the states of origin of their ancestors are, at most, *fading* interests. Such fading ties should be given purely symbolic recognition perhaps. But they have at best a very weak claim to being enfranchised under the affected interests principle.

Finally, enfranchising *strategically cultivated* affected interests could be problematic as well. When implementing the affected interested principle, we should be wary of such interests that may *deceptively* call for enfranchisement. The worry is that people might *strategically cultivate* interests so as to gain more votes and have more political power. Such strategically cultivated affected interests would present much the same moral problem as expensive tastes. Moral theorists generally think people should not get more resources just to satisfy their expensive tastes.[44] That would be particularly the case if such tastes were *deliberately* cultivated purely in order to extract more resources.[45] Similarly, one could think people should not get more votes just because they have deliberately cultivated affected interests simply in order to get those extra votes. Strategically cultivated (affected) interests would have a *world-to-mind* direction of fit, whereas the affected interests we would presumably[46] want to enfranchise by upholding this principle would have a *mind-to-world* direction of fit. While the former affected interests would be a *faciendum* (something 'to be brought about', 'to be made true'), the latter sort of affected interests would be a *factum* (a fact, something that is antecedently true

---

[43] In this sense, multiple citizenship pays tribute to the doctrine of perpetual allegiance according to which being citizen of a state was a lifetime affair.
[44] Dworkin 1981.
[45] Arneson 1989.
[46] I say 'presumably' because others might interpret the spirit of this principle differently. My view is that, insofar as we take the aim of this principle to be the *fair* distribution of political power, we would object to any attempts, on the part of individuals, to take unfair advantage of this principle – such as strategically developing interests merely as a way of gaining more political power. Also, another danger would be for the principle to mirror and amplify in its application existing inequalities in other dimensions. For example, those having fewer opportunities in life (e.g., economically deprived individuals, those having fewer chances to explore the world, travel, invest, migrate, or resettle) might naturally end up having fewer affected interests at stake in decisions around the globe. If so, they would also end up having significantly less political power than other individuals, if the principle were to be applied. It would be possible then for social and economic inequalities to spill into political inequalities as well, through the operation of the affected interests principle.

of the world).[47] This more general distinction helps us better distinguish between those interests that are worthy of enfranchisement and those that are not.

Suppose we were to cancel existing voting rights and reallocate them all anew strictly in accordance with the affected interests principle. But suppose we left the allocation of all other rights of citizenship exactly as they currently are. In this (admittedly fanciful) scenario, who would be in a position to strategically cultivate affected interests in any particular place? I believe that would be those who have all the other rights of citizenship in that place. After all, all those other rights of citizenship make it easier for one to develop and pursue interests in a state; it first provides people with *opportunities* to have interests at stake in that state, which, if pursued, would lead to fully fledged interests. Furthermore, the mere fact of being citizen of a state incentivizes one to cultivate and pursue certain interests there. As holders of several citizenships, multiple citizens have more opportunities and incentives to strategically cultivate affected interests in this way.[48] For example, a multiple citizen may choose to use the citizenship right she has to buy land and become a farmer in several states, a case in which she will end up having an (affected) interest in all of those states.[49] It is likely this interest would not have emerged had the individual *not chosen* to make use of her citizenship rights this way.

Such use of citizenship rights represents a problem for both the affected interests principle and multiple citizenship. First, some people – multiple citizens – have more opportunities than others to develop affected interests, which may be unfair in the end were we to implement the principle. Second, if the principle were to be followed to the letter

---

[47] See Velleman 1992, p. 8.
[48] In some countries, for example, only citizens are allowed to own certain sorts of property, such as farmland. Restrictions on foreign land ownership were imposed, at the time of writing, by the Czech Republic, Hungary, Latvia, Estonia, Lithuania, Slovakia, and Poland. See European Commission 2008; Swinnen and Vranken 2008. In other countries, only citizens are allowed to own shares in national companies.
[49] Some authors like Bauböck pointed out that the enfranchisement of *instrumental* interests is problematic and cannot ground a moral claim to citizenship (Bauböck 2009). Enfranchising purely *material* instrumental interests would also undermine democratic values. My objection, however, is not against the interests' instrumentality. (Indeed, most of our interests are instrumental). Rather, I object to deliberately developing interests by using one's citizenship opportunities. Such interests *do not precede* but are rather *consequential* to membership, whereas the affected interests principle would require the opposite (that one becomes a member in virtue of one's interests, rather than one having interests in virtue of being a member). To talk of citizenship as enfranchising affected interests would be thus to talk of a self-fulfilling prophecy, insofar as citizens will have interests precisely in virtue of their being citizens.

(that is, in my fanciful scenario, if votes are redistributed solely on the basis of affected interests), multiple citizens would, by deliberately exploiting their citizenship opportunities, come to be included in the demoi of multiple states – and they would do so on the basis of what could be counted as 'cheating' from the point of view of the principle. In other words, by strategically cultivating interests in multiple states with the help of their multiple citizenships there, they would be able to 'cash in' more votes around the world in virtue of the all affected principle than other people.[50]

B   *The Legally Subjected Principle*

As shown above, the legally subjected principle prescribes both a contraction and an expansion of the current citizenry. In theory, multiple citizenship is consistent with the principle. Naturalizing non-citizen residents in their state of residence would make them citizens there, as well as being citizens of their state of origin if they were allowed to retain their original citizenship there at the same time.[51] In practice, however, things are more complicated than that. That is not only because (as some might be quick to point out) at any given point in time, one can be physically present in only one place, and hence one can be said to only be systematically and pervasively subjected to the law (in an *omnibus* way) and government of only one state. It is rather because historically, not logically, multiple citizenship proved to be *incompatible* with the principle of enfranchising all and only those who are subject to the laws of the state. But let us take it one step at a time.

Dual citizens make up one important category, among others, of non-residing citizens. They normally make their permanent residence in only one of the states of which they are citizens. Not residing in the other state, they are *not* systematically and pervasively subjected to that state's laws.[52] Yet by holding political rights there, they are nonetheless part of that state's demos. Such *inclusion of those non-subjected* is

---

[50] Of course, the subsequent political inequalities may be problematic irrespective of the 'cheating', that is, irrespective of how they emerged. For a discussion, see Goodin and Tanasoca 2014.

[51] I.e., insofar as the laws of *both* the state of origin and the state of residence permit dual citizenship.

[52] In other words, they are 'permanent emigrants' of this state. López-Guerra (2005, p. 216, emphasis added) starts his exposé with precisely this point: 'No doubt citizens who are *only temporarily* abroad – tourists, students, transient workers, government officials, military personnel and so on – should retain the right to vote in their home country. But should an emigrant who has lived for, say, twenty years in a foreign country, with no intention of returning to her country of origin, also retain that right?'

obviously one deviation from the principle that says to enfranchise all and only those subjected to the state's laws. The second deviation is the *exclusion of those subjected* from the demos. The former is the case of long-term or permanent *immigrants*, who are subject to the law of a state without having a say in this law. While theirs is a case of political *under-inclusion* according to the legally subjected principle, the case of non-residing citizens being included in the demos is a case of political *over-inclusion* with respect to the same principle.[53] From the perspective of the legally subjected principle, both cases are democratically problematic.

Now, to be sure, dual citizenship was successful in tackling under-inclusion. The problem, however, is that it solved the underinclusion precisely by creating further overinclusion, thereby backfiring from the point of view of the legally subjected principle. By doing that dual citizenship acted as a double-edged sword and imposed constraints on the perfect application of the principle. How is that?

Immigrants who are long-term residents in a state of which they are not citizens constitute double trouble for the legally subjected principle. In order to have a say in laws to which they are subjected, they need to become citizens there. Otherwise, while being subjected, they would be excluded from the demos of their state of residence (the state of immigration). And if they retain citizenship in their state of origin, they would be included in the demos of the state from which they emigrated without being subjected to the laws there.

One obstacle to immigrant inclusion has long been the citizenship policy of the receiving states. Some immigrants were wary of naturalizing insofar as in order to do so they were required to renounce the citizenship of their state of origin. Hence, to promote immigrant inclusion, immigration states lifted the ban on dual citizenship. Even if dual citizenship could not ensure that immigrants were systematically and pervasively subject to the laws of their sending states (nothing could, except relocating there), it could ensure – in line with the principle – that they be included in the demoi of the receiving states.

Yet dual citizenship also compromised the *perfect application* of the legally subjected principle, which could be achieved only if individuals were included in the demos of their receiving state *as well as* excluded from that of their sending one – that is, only if dual citizenship status

---

[53] Of these, some might be illegal migrants. Obviously, in their case, the primary obstacle for political inclusion is their illegal status, and only after that the lack of formal inclusion (citizenship). Depending on the residence state's regularization policy, such migrants may at one point have the opportunity to legalize their status.

would have been precluded.[54] That could be achieved only if the receiving states granted naturalization on condition of citizenship renunciation *or* if the sending states insisted on their émigrés losing their birth citizenship upon naturalizing elsewhere.

But what tended to happen was for the sending states to also adjust their citizenship laws as to allow their non-residing citizens to keep their citizen status upon acquiring another citizenship elsewhere, that is, to allow them to become dual citizens. The sending states preferred bearing what would be considered a democratic deficit according to the legally subjected principle, in hopes of cashing in more dollars from remittances.[55]

So, in the end, and much like other second-bests, multiple citizenship prevented the worst-case scenario (that individuals be enfranchised in their sending state and disenfranchised in their receiving state), but failed to ensure the best case one (that they be disenfranchised in their sending state and enfranchised in the receiving one). If so, it seems then that multiple citizenship may not be fit for redesigning demos boundaries according to the legally subjected principle either.

C   *The Unaffected Interests Principle*

Is multiple citizenship better cut out for implementing the unaffected interests principle? I previously hinted that, reminiscent somehow of an electoral swap of voters between states, it might be. Dual citizens can indeed vote, as members of one state, in another state's elections. But what is also important is that they do so in virtue of being citizens of that latter state as well. This is not *automatically* a problem for their unaffectedness, and hence their impartiality. Take Jeremy Bentham, Joseph Priestley, and Thomas Paine's French citizenships. (They were all made honorary citizens of France, by the National Assembly, on 26 August 1792.) Although a French citizen, Bentham urged the French National Convention to free its colonies.[56] In spite of his newly acquired citizenship – and perhaps in no small part thanks to his philosophical skills – he was still able to speak his mind as an impartial thinker.[57] In Schofield's

---

[54] The other possibility would have been to simply disenfranchise them in their sending states; that is, to ensure that their citizenship in the sending state is politically meaningless (López-Guerra 2005, p. 228).

[55] These states took for granted that citizenship would indeed make a difference for the remittances flow, which may, of course, not be true, as I point out in Chapter 7.

[56] Bentham 2002, pp. 289–316.

[57] Quite interestingly, Bentham (2002, p. 291) starts his discourse by reminding the French that he is one of them ('Your predecessors made me a French citizen: hear me speak like one') only to continue by revealing the driving force behind his reasoning: 'I begin with justice: it stands foremost in your thoughts.' To be sure, invoking his French citizenship

words, his writings, at that time, were those of a 'highly intelligent commentator who was relatively uncommitted in terms of the party politics of the day'.[58] So was Thomas Paine when voting in the French Convention as an MP – and that almost cost him his head.[59] Their citizenships did not therefore undermine their impartiality – they could still defend values that were, at the time, considered anti-French, or that conflicted with the most salient political forces of the moment and their interests. But in their case that was possible precisely because they did not have any vital interests at stake in French affairs, as most French citizens at that time usually did. For them citizenship was nothing more than a symbolic status. But this is not always the case with citizenship.

Indeed, most people do not become dual citizens through *honorary* citizenship. At the same time, honorary citizenship today is not what it used to be: pure symbolic recognition of extraordinary personal achievements. Some states, like Austria, use it as a cover-up for another category of citizenship: investor citizenship. That might not be such an 'honourable' practice to begin with (as I have argued in Chapter 4). But more importantly, it shows how even honorary citizenship has become inextricably tied to various material interests. While, as I have argued in the discussion of the affected interests principle, many dual citizens (honorary or not) will no longer have interests at stake in their birth states, or may have fading interests there, *not all of them* will be altogether *un*affected by the political decisions of those states. Hence while dual citizenship makes it practically possible for the citizens of one state to vote in the elections of another state, it creates the possibility that they might *not* do so in all impartiality. Remember in that connection my analysis above of how citizenship may sustain fading interests or may incentivize people to develop interests in a state.

Thus, there will also be some cases where dual citizens will be doubly partial, rather than being impartial with respect to one of their state's political decisions. If K, a dual citizen of states A and B, has an A-specific agenda when voting in A and a B-specific agenda when voting in B, voting according to his state-specific interests in each of the states would make him just *doubly partial*.[60] Things would be very different, however,

---

is rhetorically a good way of making the Convention endorse an *impartial* viewpoint that could have been easily dismissed as repugnant for clashing with French interests, as recognized by Bentham himself: 'What is least pleasant among them [reasons], may pay you best for hearing it. Were it ever so unpleasant, better hear it while it is yet time, than when it is too late, and from one friend, than from a host of enemies.'

[58] Schofield 2004, p. 384.
[59] Which is ironic, considering he was a fierce opponent of the death penalty.
[60] Remember that natural impartiality can be espoused only by a person having *no* interests at stake in a decision: 'Without any interests or pre-existing preferences, one simply has no reason to favour one of the affected parties over any other' (Frazer 2014, p. 392).

if K, citizen of A, were able to vote in B's elections *without being citizen* of B, or if K, citizen of B, were able to vote in A's elections *without being citizen* of A – that is, if we could therefore prevent dual citizenship, without precluding dual voting. Being able to vote in both A and B, while being a citizen of only one state (A), would mean that K can vote as an affected party in state A, while also being 'naturally' impartial when voting in state B where he is not a citizen. But obviously in this case K would simply not be a dual citizen at all. To be sure, enfranchising otherwise unaffected foreigners could be a way of including the unaffected in our demos. But notice that *naturalizing* them in the course of enfranchising them risks blowing away whatever natural impartiality they may have had at first.

In today's interconnected, integrated world, there might be yet other ways by which dual citizens would be incapable of remaining impartial. In the above example, spillovers between states A and B could undermine K's impartiality. If there are political spillovers between A and B, such that what happens to state B will affect state A as well, then when K will vote in B's elections, she will do so as an *affected* party – not in virtue of her B-specific state interests (for K may have none), but instead in virtue of her interests in state A that will be affected by what happens in state B. Spillovers may be reciprocal (where A's decisions impact B *and* B's decisions impact A), or they may be one-sided (where A's decisions impact B, *without* B's decisions impacting A or the other way around, of course).

Spillovers of people – dual citizenship – are symptomatic of spillovers of other sorts (for example, political or economic). Spillovers will be more common between neighbouring countries, countries with complex common histories, or countries engaged in multi-level institutionalized cooperation. And, not coincidentally, these are precisely the countries that favour dual citizenship policies. First, dual citizenship often targets external kin minorities, groups of people belonging ethnically to one state and territorially to another; often enough these two states are *neighbouring* states.[61] Second, the countries with a rich common history will be tempted to use dual citizenship as an instrument of reparative justice or of marking their historical, and in some cases cultural, bonds. Third, political and economic interdependence puts pressure on even the more reluctant states to relax their citizenship policies with respect to dual citizenship. Germany, for example, while generally averse to dual citizenship, allows citizens of other EU states to keep their previous citizenships upon naturalization.

[61] Bauböck 2010.

Even with respect to the unaffected interests principle, therefore, it seems that multiple citizenship cannot guarantee a perfect implementation.

III Untying the Gordian Knot: Citizenship-*sine*-Political Rights, Political Rights-*sine*-Citizenship

I explained previously why multiple citizenship does not much help to bring demos boundaries into close conformity with those ideally prescribed by each of the aforementioned principles. Multiple citizenship risks enfranchising also non-existing, dying, or strategically cultivated affected interests – affected interests whose enfranchisement would not bring any real gain in terms of democratic legitimacy. It fares poorly with respect to the legally subjected principle as well, insofar as multiple citizens are included in the demos of at least one of their states of citizenship while inevitably being non-subjected with respect to this state's laws. Finally, multiple citizenship is not effective for the inclusion of the unaffected: those members of one state voting in the elections of another do so in virtue of citizenship there, at least some being thus likely to be affected and to vote partially as well. But *why* exactly is multiple citizenship not of any help in implementing these principles when initially at least it seemed like a good idea?

Notice that its failure is in each case due to the *rigidity* of citizenship as such, as it is currently conceived. Multiplying citizenship will not change its substance. Citizenship is a *permanent* status,[62] and it *unavoidably enfranchises its beholders*. In consequence, people having no affected interests, or who previously *had* affected interests but no longer do, may be included in the demos nonetheless. The problem is thus that one becomes a citizen *once and for all*, irrespective of other considerations. But, of course, in itself that would not be such a big deal if citizenship did not also enfranchise *by default*. For if citizens did not automatically hold political rights, then multiple citizenship would not risk enfranchising non-existent, dying, or strategically cultivated affected interests. The same goes for the legally subjected principle. If dual citizens would not standardly hold political rights in both of their states, then overinclusion would not necessarily be an issue for one of their states where they do not reside. And finally, in our example above pertaining to the unaffected interests principle, what compromises K's impartiality is that, in addition to holding political rights in both states, she also holds all other benefits attached to her state memberships. Had K not been a citizen –

---

[62] See Chapter 2 for my proposal of citizenship renewal.

had *K* been prevented from being affected by and benefitting from the consequences of her political choices – *K* would have a good chance of being an impartial decision maker.

One obvious solution would be thus to *unbundle* the rights and duties involved in citizenship, and to detach political rights from the bundle. Then *citizenship-sine-political rights* and *political rights-sine-citizenship* could be distributed *separately*. There is nothing all that shockingly original about the proposal. Take property rights. This rights category is made up of several distinctive rights, which are often distributed separately to different people according to different mechanisms and criteria.[63] The right of exclusive use can, for example, belong to a person – the tenant – without that person also having the right of transfer (this right belongs to the landlord uniquely). In the same way the rights (and duties) that constitute the category of citizenship rights (and duties) could be distributed separately to different people. This would leave open the possibility for one to vote without being citizen of a state and to be citizen of a state without being able to vote there. So far, however, political rights have been essentially inseparable from citizenship[64] – indeed, they have been one of its main incidents.

This leads us to the second issue: Is it better to draw the boundaries of the demos by distributing citizenship as it is presently construed, or by distributing political rights separately (political rights-*sine*-citizenship)? As I argued in my discussion of multiple citizenship in relation to the three main principles for enfranchisement, the first option is not as promising as it might first appear.

Yet the question of this choice has not received much attention from those having reflected on the matter so far. Whelan refers to both when discussing the boundary dilemma, acknowledging the distinction in passing without much reflection on it.[65] Similarly, Goodin reiterates the distinction without further probing.[66] But, as previously argued, this

---

[63] These property rights are distinctive not only in practice, but also logically. See Goodin 1990; Honoré 1961; Waldron 1985.

[64] To be sure, it is not all that uncommon for resident foreigners to vote in local elections, but these rights do not extend to national elections as well, nor do they represent the norm across the world.

[65] He asks, 'who may participate? Or, how do we determine membership in the group whose members are entitled to participate? ... [H]ow do we delimit the group within which, for purposes of making a particular decision, votes are to be counted and a majority preference identified? Or, to note a distinction passed over above, how are *citizens*, those with the right to be counted, distinguished from other persons?' (Whelan 1983, p. 14, emphasis added).

[66] 'Ordinarily, the "all affected interests" principle is taken to be a standard for defining the *scope of membership* in the demos. Alternatively, or additionally, it might be used to delimit the *scope of the "decisional power"* of the demos' (Goodin 2007, p. 62, emphasis added).

is one little detail that really matters. States not only have a choice between different boundary-drawing principles (the affected interests, the legally subjected, or the unaffected interests principle); they have also a choice between what is being distributed in order to implement these principles. Most important, however, their *choice of what to distribute* has consequences for their *choice of the principle* according to which they wish to define demos boundaries. For example, if states opt for the unaffected interests principle, distributing citizenship as we know it may be to some extent self-defeating, whereas distributing political rights-*sine*-citizenship would not be.

States and policy makers thus have a choice between instruments to demarcate demos boundaries. They may distribute citizenship as presently cast, bundling together voting and all other citizenship rights, or alternatively they can unbundle them and distribute political rights-*sine*-citizenship separately.[67] Enfranchising individuals *without* granting them all the benefits of citizenship as presently construed *is* an option, and so is granting people all the benefits of citizenship, *minus* the exercise of political rights.[68]

Table 6.1 shows, very roughly, how full citizenship, citizenship-*sine*-political rights, and political rights-*sine*-citizenship might be distributed to different categories of people as to satisfy one principle or another. I say 'very roughly' because here I took (1) *residence* and *citizenship* to be the main determinants of one's *affectedness* by a state, (2) *residence* to be the main determinant of one's *subjection* to a state's laws, and (3) *non-residence* and *non-citizenship* to be the main determinants of one's *unaffectedness* by a state. These are all proxies and thus may not perfectly reflect the situation on the ground. Indeed, residence and citizenship might not be the best proxies for affectedness or subjection as pointed out above, or non-residence and non-citizen status the best ones for unaffectedness. As we saw in Section II.A, citizenship does not always guarantee that someone will have affected interests in a state, or may indicate a type of affectedness that is not worth enfranchising. At the same time, as pointed out above, some may contest the fact that residence uniquely determines one's subjection to a state's laws.

Thus one could easily contest the proxies I use in the table, and argue that other indicators of affected interests, unaffectedness, or subjection to

---

[67] Of course, redrawing territorial borders it another option. See Whelan 1983, p. 39.
[68] Similarly, Bauböck (2009, p. 485) argues that the rights entailed by citizenship should be differentiated between first- and second-generation émigrés. Sarah Song (2016) also proposes disaggregating citizenship rights and duties insofar as group-differentiated rights and duties are justifiable. She distinguishes between different groups of people (sojourners, residents, and members) and different grounds for allocation (coercion, affiliation, and fair play).

Table 6.1 *What gets distributed to whom in the unbundling*

Citizenship and residence status	Affected interests	Subjection to laws	Unaffected interests
Non-resident citizens	Full citizenship	Citizenship-*sine*-political rights	Citizenship-*sine*-political rights
Resident citizens	Full citizenship	Full citizenship	Citizenship-*sine*-political rights
Resident non-citizens	Political rights-*sine*-citizenship	Political rights-*sine*-citizenship	Citizenship-*sine*-political rights
Non-resident non-citizens	–	–	Political rights-*sine*-citizenship

a state's laws might be more appropriate. A more in-depth analysis could leave us with a more fine-grained categorization of individuals than the one I use in the first column of the table. However, it would not affect the main point I am trying to make: that unbundling citizenship rights would be a better solution to the challenge that migration poses to each principle, in that it would allow a more accurate implementation of whichever demos principle we decided to choose. Unbundled rights and duties would permit a more accurate demarcation of the demos.

But what consequences would such decoupling have for multiple citizenship? Allowing people to hold several citizenships with all their other benefits, minus the exercise of political rights, would render multiple citizenship politically innocuous, to be sure.[69] Allowing people to vote in several states without also being citizen of all these states would open up the possibility of giving individuals a choice between being citizen of several states without having a say in all these states, and having a say in several states without also being a citizen of all these states. To be sure, the first option would entail a certain measure of disenfranchisement (in that individuals may lose the political rights they hold in one or more states, while still remaining citizens of those states),[70] whereas the second would entail a certain measure of denaturalization (in that individuals may lose their citizenship(s) in some state(s) but still hold

---

[69] 'Politically meaningless' according to López-Guerra (2005, p. 228).
[70] To get a better grasp of the first option, think of academics affiliated to several departments. Typically, only their substantive appointment grants them a vote, whereas the courtesy appointments do not. Similarly, despite being *formal* members of two states, dual citizens would be allowed to vote in only one of them, say, where they take permanent residence and where they make most use of public goods.

political rights there).[71] Both sound bad. Yet these options would ensure that, in a world that values freedom of movement, the boundaries of our political communities stay true to our ideal principles – whatever principle one embraces as ideal for resolving the boundary problem.

The unbundling of citizenship rights and duties I proposed in this chapter is limited. Only political rights would be distributed separately; all other rights and duties presently associated with citizenship would be kept together and distributed together. We should envisage, however, also the advantages of a more radical approach: the unbundling of all those other rights and duties of citizenship as well, and distributing each *separately* on the basis of criteria specific to it alone. Indeed, we could keep the exercise of political rights as the *only* exclusive right associated with citizenship status (*citizenship qua political rights*). I discuss these more radical unbundling proposals in Chapter 8.

---

[71] I am not talking of *standard* denaturalization, however, insofar as, although stripped of their citizenship, people would still be allowed to vote.

7 Taxing Multiple Citizens and Global Inequality

Different reforms of global taxation, from the Tobin tax to Pogge's global resources dividend and Shachar's birthright levy, have been proposed to alleviate global inequality.[1] Some aim to address specific causes of global disparities: an unequal distribution of resources or an arbitrary distribution of state membership. In this chapter I focus on a particular pattern of distribution of state membership – multiple citizenship – and its consequences for global equality.

I here explore one mechanism – double taxation agreements – by which multiple citizenship impacts global equality. To be sure, multiple citizens are not the only taxpayers to benefit from these agreements. They advantage, in precisely the ways I here find problematic, any (non-naturalized) migrants who have material and business interests in her state of origin and who draw an economic benefit from both states. Still, being a multiple citizen undeniably makes it easier to benefit from such agreements to the fullest and over the long run, and hence provides one with an additional incentive to do so, by cultivating and preserving material interests in the sending state.[2] Thus I argue in this chapter that the present distribution of multiple citizenship, coupled with the current international regime governing double taxation, increases global inequality. Having established that, I then propose two potential remedies to this problem: a multiple citizenship levy and a reform of double taxation agreements.

To reiterate: I am not claiming that multiple citizenship is the *only* source of global inequality, or even a particularly *large* contributor to it. Neither am I claiming that the advantages enjoyed by multiple citizens under the double tax agreements I shall be discussing are a *major* source of global inequality, all things considered. Surely, in order to effect any great reduction in global inequality, much more needs to be done than to reform multiple citizenship and double taxation policies. Still, even if

---

[1] Pogge 2001; Shachar 2009; Tobin 1974.
[2] See also my discussion of strategically cultivated affected interests in Chapter 6.

multiple citizenship and double tax agreements do not necessarily figure very highly on the reform agenda of the global egalitarian, considerations of global inequality and the contribution of double tax agreements to that should figure prominently on the agenda of any reformer of multiple citizenship. And the latter is, of course, the central concern of this book.

I   Citizenship and Global Inequality

Objections to global inequalities come from two directions. The first is luck egalitarian. Call it the 'moral arbitrariness of birth' argument. According to this first objection, inequalities resulting from birth circumstances should be redressed because of how they came about.[3] All inequalities resulting from luck are morally objectionable and undeserved, since they are not the result of autonomous agency. A second objection, call it 'left egalitarian', draws on the intrinsic wrongness of inequality. Global inequality per se is morally objectionable, on this second account, whatever its origin.[4] Hence, it is a matter of justice to neutralize this inequality as such.[5] Whichever is our reason for neutralizing inequalities, redistributive global taxation of some sort or another is generally seen as a solution.

Ayelet Shachar makes a luck egalitarian objection to national citizenship being distributed through what she calls the 'birthright lottery'. As discussed in Chapter 2, citizenship is distributed on the basis of birth circumstances, and thus on the basis of luck – of being born on a certain territory (*jus soli*) or of being born in a certain family (*jus sanguinis*).[6] Insofar as global inequalities arise from or are maintained by citizenship, and citizenship results from unchosen circumstances like birth, those inequalities are considered by luck egalitarians as *unfair* inequalities that should be mitigated. Shachar draws an analogy in her book between citizenship and property.[7] States tax inheritances because it is unfair for some to be advantaged by circumstances that are well beyond their control. Why should they not do the same for citizenship?[8]

---

[3] See Caney 2001, 2006; Dworkin 2003; Sangiovanni 2011; Tan 2011.
[4] This corresponds to Derek Parfit's distinction between teleological and deontic egalitarians (Parfit 1997).
[5] Whatever one's preferred metric of equality.
[6] Shachar 2009, pp. 7–18.
[7] Ibid., ch. 1.
[8] See Heath 2005. As Joseph Heath rightfully argues, the advantage of being born in Japan comes not from one's access to natural resources but from the fact that 'previous generations of Japanese citizens have saved upwards of 25 per cent of their income. But why should one person, who happens to have ancestors who saved a lot, be richer than another, whose ancestors saved nothing? Thus the egalitarian case against national

For left egalitarians, however, what matters is that citizenship affords different life chances – and that is true regardless of how citizenship is acquired, whether through the luck of birth or deliberate naturalization. Citizenship is by its nature 'internally inclusive', while 'externally exclusive', as theorists of national communities rightly remark.[9] Membership works as a 'social closure'[10] and as a 'gate keeper'[11] of life prospects. Egalitarian social justice schemes implemented inside each welfare state target only those in that state; redistribution is governed by the logic of citizenship, and of states. That citizenship has the effect of producing inequality across the globe is therefore unavoidable. From a left-egalitarian standpoint, that is a good reason to neutralize the effects of national citizenship *tout court*.

II Multiple Citizenship, Inequality, and the Birthright Levy

Against this background, what can one make of *multiple* citizenship? As discussed in Chapter 1, multiple citizenship was conceptualized as an avant-garde type of membership, postnational and global in kind.[12] As such, it was supposed to bring about greater global equality as well. I will argue, however, that one has reason to fear multiple citizenship's potentially bad influence on global equality.

Consider first the global luck egalitarian argument. Shachar's proposal is to redress global inequalities by the imposition of a birthright privilege levy on the political membership of wealthy nations.[13] But if one does that, then by the same logic ought one not also impose an additional *tax on multiple citizenship* if people derive extra benefits from that?[14]

If the arbitrary distribution of citizenship affording different life chances must be neutralized, then on the same grounds one could impose a tax on multiple citizenship, when this beneficial status arises solely from luck as in

---

savings is identical to the egalitarian case against individual inheritance.' Heath makes the same point here as Shachar: we tax individuals for their inheritance, but citizenship grants access to various resources and goods that are 'inherited' from previous generations. We tax family savings; why not tax community savings at the international level?

[9] Brubaker 1992, p. 21.
[10] Ibid.
[11] While 'gatekeeping' has exclusive effects, citizenship also has 'opportunity-enhancing' effects for those included (Shachar 2009, p. 33).
[12] See Castles and Davidson 2000, p. 24; Jacobson 1998–9, p. 444; Soysal 1994, 2004, p. 335.
[13] Shachar 2009, pp. 96–108.
[14] By Shachar's logic, we ought presumably to impose a birthright levy on dual citizens twice, in respect of each citizenship. But should we not also impose a 'multiple citizenship levy' on them insofar as those multiple citizenships interact in such a way as to confer yet further advantages on them globally?

the case of birthright multiple citizenship. Individuals born into multinational families, who enjoy particular benefits from accumulated citizenships solely because of their nationally diverse blood ties, would pay a tax to those less privileged. The justification for this tax would be that, in comparison to mono-nationals, dual citizens are advantaged: however much or little one citizenship brings them, the other brings them (a lot or a little) more. A second citizenship might compensate the shortfalls of the first citizenship, acting as a safety net. Or it might magnify existing opportunities. Or it might just provide 'option value' in cases of uncertainty, where one does not know which option will eventually prove most valuable.[15] Whichever way, a second or third citizenship can certainly give its owner advantages over mono-nationals.

It is not that clear, at least from the perspective of global luck egalitarianism, whether the same should be done when multiple citizenship arises from naturalization. After all, naturalization comes as consequence of an individual choice and effort. But elements of luck, as well as choice, intervene in the naturalization process.[16] It is, for example, often a matter of luck whether a person's chosen profession is one that appears on the 'priority' list for fast-tracking immigration to (leading to naturalization in) the country in which that person wants to acquire a second citizenship. So, too, it is a matter of luck whether a person is the descendant of former citizens deprived of their membership in unfortunate historical circumstances, which can lead that state to fast-track her (re)naturalization.

Furthermore, even if we are willing to accept that the citizenship acquired through naturalization is, at least to some extent, the result of the individual's choice and effort, the fact that an individual would thereby become a dual citizen is often largely a matter of luck. First, it is certainly not the case that all states allow their citizens who are naturalized elsewhere to retain their birthright citizenships; if one's does, that is just a lucky break. Second, it is also the case, as I have argued elsewhere (in Chapters 2 and 3), that one's birth citizenship is the result of an accident of birth and thus not the result of any individual active choice. Third, when a country allows its citizens to retain their birth citizenships upon naturalization elsewhere (and thus become dual citizens), this almost invariably happens through the workings of a legal

---

[15] Arrow and Fisher 1974.
[16] Consider the case of investor citizenship or citizenship-by-investment (see Dzankic 2012a). Birth citizens of advantaged nations (those who are already pretty well off, globally) will be better able to 'buy' a second citizenship, with the resources brought by their birthright citizenship. Thus the global rich will have a greater propensity of becoming multiple citizens (and of maximizing their advantages subsequently). See Chapter 4 for a discussion.

default rule – according to which one automatically continues being a citizen of one's birth state – rather than as the result of an active choice to do so and thereby become a dual citizen (see Chapter 3 for discussion). Hence, at no point in time has a naturalized individual ever actively consented to being granted the citizenship of his birth state or to continue being a citizen of his birth state, as he has in the case of his citizenship of naturalization. Thus, one's becoming a dual citizen is always the result of luck not only because luck elements intervene in the acquisition of a new citizenship in the naturalization process, but also because it is largely a matter of luck and purely contingent whether one continues being a citizen of one's birth state and hence becomes a dual citizen.

Multiple citizenship is objectionable also from a global left-egalitarian perspective. Dividing the world into separate states and allocating *one* citizenship accordingly creates and sustains global inequalities. Permitting people to hold two or more citizenships might just widen these inequalities.[17] First, multiple citizenship can entail an aggregation of the benefits attached to each separate citizenship, giving the multiple citizen more benefits than a mono-national has. Second, as I shall go on to show, citizenship and international taxation regimes interact in unfortunate ways for global inequality. As I point out below, dual citizens can further extend the benefits brought by their citizenships via double taxation agreements, which in turn might affect their already worse-off fellow nationals.

III Interactive Effects, Extra-Benefits, and Double Taxation Agreements

Double taxation agreements are bilateral treaties between two states, aimed at avoiding the imposition of the same tax on the same individual twice.

A state's jurisdictional claim to tax income rests on two different grounds. One is the state's relationship to the taxpayer, established by residence or citizenship. The other is the state's relationship to income

---

[17] In a world in which all national citizenships promoted identical life conditions, citizenship itself would not give rise to global inequalities, but multiple citizenship still would. If national citizenships give access to equal resources, welfare, opportunities, and capabilities, then dual citizenship allows some to double their otherwise equal share. Imagine, for example, that each state would pay the exact same pension (this could apply to other citizenship benefits as well) to all its citizens over sixty-five. A dual citizen would, in principle, be able to collect two pensions, whereas a mono-citizen could collect only one. It depends on how each country sets up the rules for the distribution of its benefits, of course – but the mere possibility is evidence that multiple citizenship can remain problematic even under ideal conditions of perfect global equality.

generated on its territory. Most states both tax income at source (arising within their jurisdiction) and tax residing individuals (living within their jurisdiction). In general, people derive their only income from the state in which they reside, so there is no potential for double taxation to arise. But when this is not true, the same income might potentially be taxed twice. One state could tax it at source, on the ground that the income is generated on its territory, while a second state could tax it by virtue of the taxpayer's residence on its territory.[18]

Double taxation entails additional burdens for individuals and is generally thought to impede economic activity. While states have long opposed all interference in or limitation of their right to tax in general,[19] they have typically concluded double taxation agreements that have precisely the effect of limiting their exclusive taxing rights. Under double taxation agreements, the contracting states agree on what each state is or is not entitled to tax, and on what relief measures to provide to taxpayers when double taxation cannot be avoided.

With the mushrooming of bilateral double taxation treaties[20] came calls for a unitary legal framework that could be used as a reference point in international negotiations. Nowadays most double taxation agreements follow the OECD Model Tax Convention on Income and Capital. In settling the competing claims of states of residence and states of source, the OECD Convention confers (as a general rule, with various exceptions noted below) the exclusive right to tax to the state of residence. Insofar as that rule is followed, taxation by the state of source is precluded, thus preventing double taxation.[21]

---

[18] A few states also tax on grounds of citizenship alone, irrespective of a person's residence or source of income (e.g., the United States, Eritrea). In those cases, income could be taxed thrice: by the third state in virtue of the citizenship of the taxpayer generating that income. This might be justified by appeal to the ancient doctrine of 'perpetual allegiance'. In Blackstone's ([1753] 1893, bk. 1, ch. X, p. 370) words, birth citizenship creates 'a debt of gratitude which cannot be forfeited, cancelled, or altered, by any change if time, place and circumstance'.

[19] According to Lord Mansfield 'one nation does not take notice of the revenue laws of another'. The 'notice' doctrine was iterated in two eighteenth-century cases: *Holman v. Johnson* and *Planche v. Fletcher* (Kovatch 2000).

[20] There are also multilateral double taxation treaties like the 1996 *Convention between Nordic Countries for the Avoidance of Double Taxation with Respect to Taxes on Income and Capital* or the 1971 *Andean Pact*.

[21] OECD 2010, I-5. In cases of exceptions to that rule, double taxation can occur, and two 'methods of relief' are available: exemption and credit (ibid., I-8). Under the exemption method (preferred by European states), income taxed in the state of source shall be exempted from taxation in the state of residence, but the state of residence may take this income into account when calculating the rate at which the taxpayer's remaining income will be taxed in that state. The credit method (preferred by the United States) provides

A few types of income can be taxed by both states. Examples of that are dividends and interest, which can be taxed by both states (articles 10 and 11). But there is a limit on the tax imposed by the state of source of up to 5 per cent of the gross amount of the dividends and 10 per cent of the gross amount of the interest.

Several types of income can be taxed by the state on source alone. These include income from immovable property situated in that state and from the sale of such property (articles 6, 13, and 22 of the OECD Model Tax Convention); income from artistic or sport activity in that state (article 17); profits from firms with permanent establishment in that state and from sale of the capital forming business property of the establishment; income from employment in the private sector, if the employee was present on state territory for more than 183 days of the fiscal year (article 15); and remuneration from government service (article 19).[22] Again, insofar as taxation of these income streams is the exclusive prerogative of the state of source, further issues of double taxation on them do not arise.

Other types of income cannot be taxed by the state of source. These are royalties (article 12), private sector pensions (article 18) and gains from sale of shares (article 13), capital represented by shares and securities (article 22), and business profits that are not attributable to a permanent establishment in the state of source (article 7).[23]

As a rule, permanent establishment and physical presence in the state of source for more than 183 days of the fiscal year can give that state the upper hand in taxation, despite the general priority enjoyed by the state of residence in raising taxes.

A   What Do Double Taxation Agreements Entail for Dual Citizens?

Let us assume person K, a citizen of both states A and B, earns income in state B from private services she provides there. Suppose, however, K resides in state A (and is present in state B for less than the period of 183 days required for K to count as resident there under double taxation agreements). Then it is state A that gets to tax this income. State B loses dual citizen K as a taxpayer, despite the fact that dual citizen K still enjoys a range of public goods that state B makes available to its citizens.

---

that the tax levied by the state of source shall be credited against the tax levied by the state of residence on that income.

[22] OECD 2010, I-6-I-7.
[23] Ibid., I-7.

K takes advantage of these public goods when she pursues employment there. The judicial system protects K's labour rights and enforces other state regulations supporting her activities. K also enjoys other public goods, without which her employment would be impeded: monetary stability, political stability ensuring a predictable legal framework, labour market regulation, and so on.

The public goods K enjoys, however, go beyond ones such as just mentioned, which are strictly connected to her economic interests. As a citizen of state B, K enjoys the consular services and the diplomatic protection offered by state B. Her citizenship may also be a token of her affective ties to state B, thus providing K some sort of psychological comfort. The same comfort may come from the fact that as a citizen of state B, having thus a vote in B and a say in B's businesses, K has some means of protecting the family left behind in B, or friends there, or, who knows, maybe just the fellow citizens she still cares about (if supposing she has some romantic nationalist feelings for them).

The problem is that K does not pay for the benefits gained as a citizen of state B, be they of a material or psychological nature. Thanks to the double taxation agreements, the income K earns in B is taxed only in residence state A. Hence K does not cover her share of the costs of providing the public goods she uses in B.[24] Even if K's use of the public good does not in any way increase the cost of providing it, the dual citizen is not paying what her society in B has determined is her fair contribution to the costs of providing it, by virtue of her residence in state A, which is facilitated by her being a citizen of state A as well as B. K is *totally* free riding. When the dual citizen does not have to pay anything, fellow citizens have to cover her share of the costs for the provision of public goods.

The same remains largely true even where the double taxation treaty allows both states to claim some tax. Take the case of dividends. Dividends can be taxed by both state of source and state of residence. However, the taxing power of the state of source is limited: the tax it imposes on this revenue cannot exceed 5 per cent. Assuming that this state would have imposed a tax far greater than 5 per cent on the dividends, had it not been for the double taxation agreement, the state of source obviously incurs a financial loss as a result of this limitation. The loss seems particularly unfair when the dividends come from shareholding in a national company (the national airline, say), shareholding in

---

[24] One's contribution to the public welfare is not reduced to taxation. However, I am referring to public goods provided through public expenditures and thus dependent on fiscal contributions.

which is permitted only to citizens. The shareholding, and thus all income derived it, is made possible precisely by K's citizenship in state B; yet state B cannot fully tax the dividends. Suppose that for the dividends K has in B, this state would normally (absent the double taxation agreement) have levied a 15 per cent tax. By virtue of double taxation agreements, state B can tax only 5 per cent – thus losing 10 per cent of the income tax, which will have to be made up by the community of citizens of B. K is then at least *partially* free riding. Her fellow citizens from B will have to cover for the remaining part of the tax that this state cannot impose on K's income, and which would normally have been owed to this state.

This means that K's fellow nationals will either have to contribute more (to sustain the same level of provision of the public good) or else enjoy a lesser provision of the public good. Either way, the tax treatment accorded to dual citizen K under double taxation agreements serves to impose costs on her co-nationals in B.

Such situations created by double taxation agreements are somewhat akin to the 'tragedy of the commons'.[25] The dual citizen can enjoy the full benefits while paying only part of the costs, insofar as he contributes less than his fair share (or nothing at all) to the provision of public goods. Hence he has an incentive to support higher benefit levels (big government and strong welfarism) when voting. This vote in effect gives rise to externalities for his co-nationals. There are various things that might be logically possible for a state to do in order to control these externalities, but realistically it is highly unlikely they will be done.[26]

IV Impact on Global Inequality

I previously pointed out how double taxation agreements make dual citizens better off (enjoying the same public goods but paying less for them) at the expense of their fellow nationals from the country in which they are not resident. But what are the consequences of multiple citizenship for global equality more generally? To answer that one needs to

---

[25] Hardin 1968. I say 'somewhat akin' because in the classic, full-blown tragedy of the commons, everybody is in the same position to benefit from the commons, whereas in this case only a proportion of people (those who are immigrants and dual citizens) are.

[26] The state might consider either making the dual citizen pay in full his taxes to the state, but that would involve tearing up the double taxation agreement. Alternatively, it might consider decreasing the value of his vote proportionally to the reduction in his taxes through double taxation agreements. If he pays only a third as much in taxes as he would were it not for the double taxation agreement, his vote should perhaps count for a third of what it would normally be worth according to the principle of 'one person, one vote, one value'. If he does not pay anything at all, then, perhaps, his vote should not be counted (or should be weighted 0 under weighted voting).

know two facts: first, who has access to dual citizenship, and second, who loses from double taxation agreements. Only then it can be established who is benefitting and who is bearing the costs arising from dual citizenship. My point here will be that dual citizenship works against global equality, in each of those respects. First, those who are globally worse off are less likely to become dual citizens. Second, double taxation agreements, in their present form, disadvantage the global poor.

A   *The Poor Do Not Move*

The global poor generally do not become dual citizens. The rich do, and in so doing they expand their resources – thus potentially increasing global inequality. Start with the case of dual citizenship via naturalization. Casual empiricism is more than sufficient to reveal that those who naturalize and become dual citizens are not the most deprived individuals worldwide. The reason is obvious: residence is a requirement for acquiring citizenship through naturalization, and residence in a foreign place will not be an easy option for the poor. The travel and resettling that make residence possible (payment for flights, visas,[27] and other related expenditures) require a certain financial autonomy that poor people simply do not have. And this is true even in the case of illegal immigration (people smugglers do not offer their services for free). In the case of naturalization via citizenship-by-investment, things are particularly clear: that is an option only for the seriously rich.[28] But even as concerns *jus sanguinis* (that is, inherited) dual citizenship, for one to be born in a mixed family previous immigration of the parents is required; and because poor people can less afford to migrate, they will be less likely to confer on their children the benefits of dual citizenship.

Another reason predominantly the better off hold dual citizenship concerns the citizenship laws of different countries. For someone to become a dual citizen, his birth state must allow its citizens to retain birth citizenship upon acquiring citizenship elsewhere, while his host state must not insist on renunciation of previous citizenship upon naturalization. States that are better integrated in the world economy (states whose citizens both invest elsewhere and benefit from foreign investment) are more prone to accept dual citizenship. They simply have

---

[27] Visa regimes usually favour skilled workers (e.g., medical professionals) to cope with shortfalls of the labour force. Those are not the poorest individuals in the community. Fewer visas are granted to unskilled workers, although these people are the most vulnerable. Giving the poorest also fewer opportunities to migrate diminishes the probability for them to become dual nationals.
[28] See Chapter 4.

more incentives to do so. States that are better economically integrated globally are also richer states. Thus, citizens of rich and developing countries will have increased access to dual citizenship. This reasoning seems borne out looking at the citizenship laws of many African states. Many of the poorest states, whose citizens might benefit the most from dual citizenship, ban this practice.[29]

Theorists already observed this trend: the richest world citizens are the first to endorse a cosmopolitan ethic and enjoy the benefits of globalization, plural membership included. Richard Falk, for example, bemoans the global financial elite that is made up of global citizens who support cosmopolitan reformist schemes, but lack a global civic sense of responsibility.[30] Craig Calhoun talks of a class of global frequent travellers that endorses a cosmopolitan rhetoric. In this sense, cosmopolitanism is profoundly elitist.[31] And because of its cosmopolitan character, dual citizenship remains largely the prerogative of the world rich. Therefore, dual citizenship as it stands nowadays has the potential to widen global gaps.

B   *Dual Citizens Reside in and Pay Taxes to the Richer of Their Countries*

Dual citizenship increases global inequality also through the working of double taxation agreements that are disadvantageous to the poor. As currently written, those agreements broadly give priority to the state of residence, generally conferring on it an exclusive right to tax even foreign-sourced income.

As argued, the world's very poor are less likely to become dual citizens. But suppose one finds oneself with two citizenships, that of a wealthy state and that of a much less prosperous one. Presumably, such a person will ordinarily want to have her permanent residence in the richer state, where better life conditions prevail. Under double taxation agreements as presently cast, by choosing to reside in the richer state the dual citizen will contribute more to that state and less (or nothing at all) to the poorer state of which she remains a citizen. This is indubitably bad news for global equality.

---

[29] From 2001 information from the World Bank (2001) and the US Office of Personnel Management (2000–1), it can be seen that some of the states with the lowest GDP per capita (in current US dollars) did not recognize dual citizenship. These states include the Democratic Republic of Congo (153 USD), Afghanistan (117 USD), Burundi (133 USD), Malawi (146 USD), Niger (165 USD), Liberia (174 USD), Eritrea (215 USD), Sierra Leone (227 USD), and Rwanda (201 USD).
[30] Falk 1994, pp. 133–5.
[31] Calhoun 2002, pp. 872–3.

Of course, one does not have to be a dual citizen, merely a migrant, to take advantage of double taxation agreements in that way and thus exacerbate global inequalities. But dual citizens, by comparison to migrants, find it easier to relocate to and remain for long periods in the richer state. They have unlimited rights of entry and exit; they cannot under any circumstances be expelled from that state (as legal migrants or even permanent residents can). Their relocation is also less costly, in terms of the paperwork and the money involved. Upon relocating to the richer state, the dual citizen automatically has the right to accept employment there. She may also want to transfer her business and resources to the richer state (this having a more predictable economic environment, a stabler currency, lower interest rates on its sovereign debts, less vulnerability to downgrading of state credit ratings, and so on). This way, the state of residence becomes also a source of income, further undercutting the revenues of the poorer state. With fewer taxpayers, the poorer state has its public revenues diminished for a long time to come, if not permanently.[32] If it is predominately the global poor who have to bear these costs, then global inequality will increase. It is bad enough that the brain drain from poor states boosts the economy of rich receiving states, at the expense of the former.[33] Money drain is just another nail in the poor states' coffins.

In a few cases, the poorer state, as a state of source, might (as discussed) still have an exclusive right to tax a few income streams.[34] But, for example, in the case of dividends and interest, the tax it can impose, even as state of source, is limited. The consequence of such limitations is, as I have said, to reduce the tax take of the poorer state and to increase the financial burden on the rest of the remaining citizens of this state. The non-residing citizen's free riding on contributions to the citizen's compatriots entails additional disadvantages for those already comparatively disadvantaged.

Because dual citizens will, in most cases, be full contributors to their richer state's provision of public goods, their better off fellow citizens in that more prosperous state would not have to contribute more for their being a member of it.[35] There would be no levelling down of the

---

[32] Some states (like Canada and the United States) have adopted 'expatriation taxes on deemed disposition of property to discourage renunciation of citizenship and relocation abroad for tax avoidance'. See, e.g., US Code, title 26, §877, available at www.law.cornell.edu/uscode/text/26/877A.

[33] Bhagwati 1976.

[34] It is far from absurd talking of poor states as sources of income for dual citizens: even the poorest states have plutocratic elites who can afford to relocate while retaining business interests in their state of origin.

[35] The only circumstance in which that might not be the case is where the dual citizen is poorer than the median citizen of this richer state and that state has progressive taxation:

rich involved. On the contrary, it would (as I have pointed out) fall to her co-nationals from her poorer state to contribute more in order to cover her share of the costs of the public goods she is still enjoying there. Insofar as the citizens of this state are already worse off than the citizens of her residence state, the free riding of the dual citizen will leave the former, not the latter, worse off, thus widening the already existing gaps in global equality between the citizens of poorer states and those of richer states.

Some may say that, while the provisions of double taxation agreements generally disadvantage one state (the state of source) to the benefit of the other (the state of residence), this does not necessarily amount to entrenching inequality. Both states can be simultaneously states of source *and* states of residence in relation to their various dual citizens.

True, on the face of it double taxation treaties are utterly symmetrical in their treatment of the contracting states. They seemingly embody a fair division between the two states of the costs and benefits associated with these treaties, making the agreements mutually advantageous. Imagine a double taxation agreement between states A and B, which states also 'share' a group of dual citizens who are members of both. State B loses some tax money to state A when some dual citizens pay the preponderance of their income tax to state A; state B gains at state A's expense when other dual citizens pay the preponderance of their income tax to state B. The contracting states thus swap the role of winner and loser, so in the end all seemingly evens out.

But while *formally* neutral and symmetrical, double taxation treaties are often radically asymmetrical in their *actual impact* on the contracting states. Symmetrical impact would be the rule if and only if both states would be, at the same time and to the same extent, states of source and of residence for their dual nationals. As already stated, there are good grounds for thinking that poorer states have more to lose than to win from double taxation agreements. Poorer states are simply less likely to be states of residence for the dual citizens.[36]

V   Solutions

The existence of citizenship-based claims creates global inequalities, and multiple citizenship has the potential to exacerbate them. What can be done to ameliorate those effects, or perhaps even reverse them?

---

then, despite paying his 'full share' in taxes, the dual citizen might still constitute a 'cost' to the other taxpayers of his richer state of residence.

[36] Or other types of migrants benefitting from such agreements.

A A Levy on Multiple Citizenship

Shachar's solution to global inequality is a birthright levy, a global redistributive mechanism redressing inequalities caused by national citizenship.

As we have seen, multiple citizenship is more damaging to global inequality than simple citizenship. If multiple citizenship redistributes to the advantage of the greedy, not the needy, perhaps (as I have already briefly canvassed) there ought to be imposed a *tax on multiple citizenship* on the particular benefits made available by multiple citizenship, as foreshadowed above. Such a tax could be a function of the sheer number of citizenships one has or (better yet) a function of the particular extra pecuniary benefits afforded by those multiple citizenships through double taxation agreements.[37]

The point of the levy in the present context is not to give any particular state its fair due in terms of taxation, but to counter the unfortunate consequences of multiple citizenship for global inequality. Hence the multiple citizenship tax should be paid to the poorest of the multiple states of which the particular person is a citizen.

Some might worry that the levy would be counterproductive, insofar as it might be imposed accidentally on the global poor. The levy might take, for the sake of argument, from both Malian-Ivorian and Australian-American dual citizens.[38] The universal application of the levy, without further discrimination, might therefore be both unfair and inefficient.

Such worries would be almost completely unfounded, however. By targeting multiple citizens, a levy on multiple citizenship would almost invariably target the global rich, to the benefit of the globally poorer. The global rich are much more often multiple citizens than are the global poor. This is, in part, due to the ban on dual citizenship by most poor African and Asian countries. But even where it is legally allowed, poverty keeps the global poor from acquiring multiple citizenship. As I have argued, poverty prevents relocation, which in turns prevents naturalization, hence eligibility for dual citizenship among the poor. These facts

---

[37] If S1 is the total tax the individual would have to pay to both states normally, and S2 the total tax after the application of the treaties, then we should tax S1−S2, either as a flat tax (say, 5%), or progressively (2% to 7%).

[38] For sure an Australian-American dual citizen would be better off than a Malian-Ivorian one. This, however, is beside the point I am trying to make, concerning the negative externalities of multiple citizenship. What matters is (1) that the Malian-Ivorian citizen is still be better off than his Malian fellow citizens and (2) that his dual citizenship is making his fellow nationals worse off, increasing global inequality (following tax exemptions he gets via double taxation). Thus we should find a way to assist these people even when this involves a reasonable individual cost for the dual citizen who may not be particularly rich.

taken together virtually guarantee that the right people are being taxed: those who can afford being taxed for the benefit of the needier.

So long as the transfer is from those who are richer to those who are poorer, the cause of egalitarianism is well served. If both countries are relatively rich, then the cash flow would be from a rich state to a similarly rich one (as might happen in the case of the Australian-American dual citizen). If both countries are relatively poor, then the cash would flow from a poor state to a similarly poor state (as might happen in the case of a Malian-Ivorian dual citizen). In such cases, the overall redistributive effects of the tax are limited. Yet the tax will also apply to citizens of pairs of countries that are very different in terms of wealth and living conditions. Those cases are the main targets of the levy, as well as of the OECD Model Tax Convention reform I propose.

Insofar as the proposed tax reform also applies to similar countries, the redistributive effects will be more limited. But there is redistribution even there, only less. Certainly, it is true that Australia would pocket more money per Australian-American dual citizen from the levy than Mali would for the Malian-Ivorian one. Still, the cash flows will nonetheless be *egalitarian* because (1) the money would always go from the richer to the poorer of the concerned states and (2) the money would go from dual nationals to mono-nationals, who are on average typically worse off than their dual counterparts. And all that is required for the levy to have egalitarian effects overall is for the *average* multiple citizen to be better off than the global average mono-citizen.

There may be rare cases where such a tax would be levied on already economically disadvantaged individuals. Even so, the levy would not strip the dual citizens of all benefits obtained in virtue of their dual citizenship, but only of *a part* (say 5 per cent of the net benefit they get). After paying the levy, dual citizens would still be better off than their fellow nationals. On balance, making some moderately poor individuals worse off could still pay off for global inequality insofar as even poorer individuals and states benefit in consequence.

B   *Alter Double Taxation Agreements*

Double taxation agreements as currently cast serve as mechanisms of global redistribution in the wrong direction. Recast, they could become more global equality–friendly. Imagine that double taxation agreements were written in such a way that, as between the state of source and the state of residence, one would always have to pay one's income taxes in full to the poorer state (and only pay to the richer state the balance, if any, between what one paid the poorer state and what one would have owed the richer).[39]

This amounts to suggesting the introduction of a *prioritarian clause* in all double taxation agreements. Someone with income in one state but residence in another – a dual citizen or anyone else in that situation – should be obliged to pay her taxes in full in the state with the lowest GDP per capita (or whatever other measure of global living standards is chosen), thus requiring full contributions toward the neediest group of people. Such a person would then be required to pay the balance (if any) to the state with the next lowest GDP, and so on, for citizens with many citizenships. By increasing the tax revenues of the poorer state and decreasing those of the richer state, this would make the dual citizen's fellow citizens from the poorer state better off, while also making the fellow citizens from the richer one worse off. The effect would be one of reducing global inequality, which is what was sought by introducing this prioritarian clause. In this respect, the transfers entailed by the application of this clause would have levelling effects somewhat akin to those that might be obtained through global taxation.

VI Objections to the Proposed Solutions

Public policy often has perverse, unforeseen effects. Those can constitute the basis for serious objections to a policy proposal. What is crucial in decision making, however, is the probability of these effects. What perverse effects can be envisaged for the solutions proposed above, and how likely are they to arise?

A *People Would Renounce Their Additional Citizenships*

Taxes are lucrative for states only if people pay them. It is useless to impose a tax if people avoid being subject to that tax altogether. What use is the French government's 75 per cent income tax on fortunes over 1 million euros, if the potential taxpayers simply 'pull a Depardieu' and avoid the tax by skipping the country? One might fear the same for a multiple citizenship levy. Multiple citizens might simply decide to give up some of their citizenship(s) in order to avoid paying the tax altogether. What then?

Notice that in the context in view here, however, citizenship renunciation would not be a problem, at least not for global equality. On the

---

[39] If the credit method is preferred – or nothing at all (if the exemption method is preferred).

contrary, it would simply eradicate altogether one factor aggravating global inequality, precisely the factor whose effects the tax in question is attempting to ameliorate. The aim of the multiple citizenship levy is not to collect tax money in and of itself; the aim is to reduce the impact of multiple citizenship on global inequality. If people renounce multiple citizenships in response, the levy will have accomplished that goal. Citizenship renunciation would entail a decrease of the benefits rich people get from being multiple citizens.

New taxes are being advocated here not from a love for taxes as such, but as solutions to a problem. One should be undisturbed if the introduction of the tax would go beyond ameliorating the problem to actually eliminating the problem in the long run, which is what would happen if the tax does indeed serve as an incentive to renounce citizenship(s).

B   *Countries Would Close Borders to Immigrants from Poor Countries*

One might also worry that richer states might be deterred from accepting immigration from poorer ones if the tax revenues they receive from those immigrants are reduced. This is a justified worry, and surely we would not want to give states an additional reason for granting individuals differentiated access to their territory on the basis of wealth. If one believes in the global justice mission of open borders, one does not want to close the borders to the neediest. Yet this apocalyptic scenario might well be on its way if tax treaties were revised in such a way as to give tax priority to the poorer countries. Or so the thought would go.

Such scenarios are unlikely, however, for multiple reasons. First, even if poorer states were lexically prioritized in double taxation agreements revised as I have proposed, richer states would still have more to gain than to lose by accepting immigration from poorer states. In respect of most of their revenues there would be no tax conflict, after all. The richer state would have an exclusive claim to tax the immigrant's income, insofar as the richer state would be both the immigrant's state of residence, for tax purposes, while also providing the immigrant's main source of income. In those cases, the richer states would get to tax fully the income of multiple citizens (or immigrants, in the first instance). Hence richer states would not be *so* economically vulnerable to the introduction of a prioritarian clause in double taxation agreements as to take extreme measures like closing borders.

Second, the gains from immigration of richer receiving states go beyond taxation. There is much talk of the many ways in which richer nations depend on qualified migrant labour. This imported labour drives economic growth as well as ensuring the provision of basic public services (like health care) to the populations of the richer states.

C   *The Money Will End Up in the Wrong Hands*

Consider one last objection to both the levy and a reform of double tax agreements. The solutions I propose would treat all poor states alike, irrespective of their political situation or of the causes of their poverty. Some states – more than one would like – are poor largely because of incompetent (or, worse, corrupt and often authoritarian) political elites. Boosting such states' tax revenues may not help their populations. Both solutions I propose assume that the poor states will use the new revenues to benefit their populations. Yet, if corrupt elites are in power, they may use any new revenues merely to consolidate power at the cost of their populations. In such cases, the levy and the prioritarian clause may have the perverse effects of entrenching poverty instead of curing it. A reminder that the road to hell can be paved with good intentions, this is a powerful objection, to be sure. Just note, however, that it is one that applies not only to my solutions but to all international financial aid (or debt relief, for what is worth)[40] that goes to poor, corrupt states.[41]

It is also the case that, while some poor states have corrupt or authoritarian elites in power, *not all* do. There are also poor states led by legitimately elected leaders, with a sincere desire and intention of helping their peoples but who are unable to do so out of a lack of resources. Not supporting my solutions for fear of not supporting corrupt regimes means refusing to help *all* poor states, including all those that might use the resources for a good cause. Provided there are more poor states that would use the money for good causes than poor states that would do otherwise, one should strive to help the former even at the cost of helping the latter as well. One may not succeed in that way in improving the welfare of all poor populations across the globe. Yet it is better to improve the welfare of some rather than none of them.

Might remittances better serve the goal of helping the poor states' populations? Those, after all, go directly to those in need and not into some corrupt leader's pockets. One thought would be that in alleviating

---

[40] Some types of aid, debt relief included, are subject to conditionality arrangements. On the justification of such conditionality, see Barry 2011.
[41] Of course, helping such states may be not only inefficient but also morally wrong (on the grounds of, e.g., enabling a bad regime or political leader and thus harming people in those states).

the tax burden on multiple citizens (which is what double taxation agreements generically do), we encourage the flow of remittances, by leaving more money in their hands to remit. Second, some poor states of emigration (such as Mexico) have also changed their citizenship laws as to allow their emigrants to become dual citizens with the same purpose. If emigrants can keep their birth citizenship upon naturalization elsewhere, then surely they will remit more, supposing that stronger ties (like citizenship) give rise to stronger duties – or so the poor states hope, anyway. In a nutshell, the reasoning here is as follows: multiple citizenship encourages remittances; not taxing multiple citizens means they have more money that they can remit; and money from remittances goes straight to their families. If so, it might look like remittances are doing a better job promoting global equality than a new tax or a tax reform would do.

Remittances may well have all those advantages. But the question remains whether multiple citizens (which are my central concern in this book) actually remit much money in that way. First, since citizenship typically serves as grounds for family reunification, it is less likely for (naturalized) multiple citizens than for migrants at large to have close family abroad to whom to remit. Second, many multiple citizens are second- or third-generation migrants who are born into immigrant families, and thus already living with their close relatives in the richer state. Third, spending more time abroad in virtue of their citizenship, multiple citizens will have fewer incentives to remit to the poor states: fading ties are less likely to be rewarded by remittances.[42]

Finally, while remittances have the advantage of going straight into people's pockets, the question remains whether they go into the *poorest* people's pockets. Remember that the worst off do not migrate in the first instance, or naturalize to become multiple citizens in the second. Poverty or wealth, however, usually runs in families. So, even if multiple citizens remit, it is doubtful the money will go to the worst-off individuals from the poor states. By going to those already relatively well-off members of

---

[42] For example, studies show that skilled workers remit less than unskilled ones, although the former earn more than the latter. This may either (or both) be because their families back home *are not in need of money* or the ties to their families are not so strong as a consequence of their living abroad for a longer time. Evidence shows that the flow of remittances decreases with the time spent by the migrant abroad; see Adams (2008) and Faini (2007, p. 179). What can the above tell us about multiple citizens? Spending time abroad is of course facilitated by their being citizens of another country. So, just like skilled workers, multiple citizens might be less willing to remit (or inclined to remit less) because of their fading ties (as a consequence of spending more time abroad) or because their families are not in urgent need of resources. (See also my discussion above.)

poorer states, remittances might even increase already existing inequalities within those states.[43]

The funds collected through my proposed levy, on the contrary, might be better able to reach the worst off. The state, if not too corrupt, could distribute the resources in a more prioritarian way, whereas such a prioritarian redistribution of resources may not, for the reasons stated above, be possibly achieved through remittances.

VII   An Implementation Strategy

Rewriting double taxation treaties along prioritarian lines might seem wildly unrealistic. But it might actually be easier than it seems, at least in some respects. An international institutional framework for decision making on, and implementation of, such reforms is already in place, in a way that it is not for other global taxation solutions (such as Shachar's birthright levy or Pogge's global resources dividend). That these opportunity structures already exist should not be taken lightly, given the costs and efforts involved in additional institution building.

The mechanism in question is the OECD Model Tax Convention. That forms the basis of more than 3,000 bilateral treaties nowadays. Furthermore, the Convention is revised regularly. Hence a change of the Convention would be the best way to implement the redesign of double taxation agreements in question.

Just how welcoming of these reforms might the decision-making procedures inside the OECD be? Well, procedurally, the Committee on Fiscal Affairs is charged with drafting amendments to the OECD Model Tax Convention. That Committee consists of a team of bureaucrats and experts who make their recommendations to the OECD Council – the political and decisional body of the organization, comprised of delegations from member states. Following the Council's decision, it is then up to the member states to conform to the new model within the limits of their own reservations and the commentaries of the Council.[44]

Prosperous receiving states, the big losers from the proposed solution, might be expected to oppose it. Given that the OECD is *par excellence* a coterie of the wealthiest states, it might be expected they would succeed in burying it. But other features of the OECD might make friendlier to the redesign.

---

[43] Although remittances might promote economic growth of a sort. But it will be consumption induced, not investment induced, and thus unsustainable. Furthermore, this economic growth may not spread throughout society.
[44] OECD 2010, I-1.

154 Consequences

The independence of the bureaucracy and expertise provided by the Committee would help. The OECD employs its own international bureaucracy and expertise. The mission of the Committee on Fiscal Affairs is not to promote the interests of member states specifically. Rather, it is to 'contribute to the shaping of globalization for the benefit of all through the promotion and development of effective and sound tax policies and guidance that will foster growth and allow governments to provide better services to their citizens'.[45] The OECD itself was founded precisely to 'think the unthinkable, because the many existing national and international bodies (universities, ministries, and Cold War organizations) somehow were too enmeshed with the establishment ... In short, the OECD should care about its *independence* and should use it actively *to say some of the things that national politicians did not want to hear.*'[46] OECD civil servants are 'reform entrepreneurs' much more than old-fashioned bureaucrats.[47]

In other words, the OECD officials are not just mouthpieces of state governments, but visionaries setting the agendas of member states.[48] Surprising though that conclusion may seem, it is nonetheless supported by empirical evidence.[49] Noaksson and Jacobsson, comparing the OECD and EU's work on knowledge and policy advice on the labour market, conclude that 'the EU is characterised by a more pragmatic knowledge-use, while the OECD can be characterised as a "truth-seeker" and "truth-teller" with a more dogmatic relationship to knowledge (in the sense of believing firmly in one orthodoxy and attempting to put aside political considerations and values when assessing economic situations, based on that orthodoxy)'.[50] The authors explain this difference partly by the nature of the organizations themselves. While the EU is a *political* organization, the OECD is an *expert* organization. Peer pressure, the social culture of the meetings, and other discursive mechanisms are also more powerful in shaping the actors' choices inside the OECD than inside the EU.[51] The OECD is *par excellence* an epistemic community, successful in ensuring international policy coordination through entrenched patterns of cooperation, but also through the creation of an independent institutional identity.[52] Hence the OECD officials act

---

[45] See http://webnet.oecd.org/OECDGROUPS/Bodies/ListByIndexView.aspx.
[46] Marcussen 2004a, p. 92.
[47] Ibid.
[48] Marcussen 2004b.
[49] The main goal for developing an international civil service is to insulate the international domain from pervasive national interference, which might impede cooperation. See Jonah 1981–2.
[50] Noaksson and Jacobsson 2003.
[51] Ibid., p. 10.
[52] Haas 1992.

independently from particular members states, even to some extent subverting state sovereignty.[53]

The independence and competence of the OECD officials are useful, but will they be enough? Economic experts are not necessarily global justice groupies after all. Interestingly enough, however, the OECD has previously adopted global justice-friendly measures, measures not particularly in the interest of the wealthiest states. For example, the organization participated in the drafting of the Millennium Development Goals, constantly monitored progress toward them, and provided funding for them.[54] Moreover, one of its committees (the Development Assistance Committee) is specifically concerned with global challenges, spearheading the OECD's development strategy.[55] This means that the solution I proposed might find support among the OECD bureaucracy.

Of course, formal decisional power is vested in the OECD Council, consisting of member states' representatives. Would the OECD Council agree with the proposal? According to *Realpolitik* logic, certainly not. But thankfully *Realpolitik* is not the states' only logic of action. There are good chances for an agreement for several reasons having to do with the institutional and collective context of decision making that imposes constraints on the states' capacity to decide purely in a rational, egoistic way.

By comparison to state governments, the legitimacy and the accountability of the state representatives in such intergovernmental settings is fuzzy. They are appointed representatives, not directly elected. The decisions they take are collective ones, which means that individual responsibility is blurred and peer pressure is high. States are not legally bound by the decisions, as there are no sanctioning mechanisms.[56] For all these reasons, agreement of precisely the form that is first secured inside the OECD comes easier among lower-level national representatives. Council delegates would thus be relatively more prone to agree to compromise their national interests at the margins.

Decision-making structures and rules designed to facilitate agreement on thorny issues further cultivate hyperbolic discounting and procrastination by the agents,[57] weak commitments ('keep talking'), and easy exit

---

[53] Libertarians are, for example, baffled by the Congress's acceptance of the OECD's interference with an exclusive right that it has: to tax American citizens. Rahn 2012.
[54] See OECD n.d.
[55] OECD 2012.
[56] Gibson and Goodin 1999.
[57] According to which it is better to agree on an imperfect general solution *now* than to wait for an agreement on a detailed one; details can be worked later on (Gibson and Goodin 1999).

('no strings attached').[58] Issues might clash directly with national interests, often displaying a tragedy of the commons dimension.[59] Progressive implementation of the decisions is another factor facilitating agreement. Present decision makers would be more likely to agree when implementation is a lengthy process that will largely be left to future decision makers. A potential failure to implement would be considered the latter's responsibility.[60] Implementation of a new Model Tax Convention would be a very lengthy process requiring the participation of successive national administrations. All of that means that the present national representatives might be more tempted to accept the prioritarian clause as part of a revised OECD Model Tax Convention.

But what guarantees the actual implementation of a reformed Model Tax Convention, which is itself, of course, merely a soft law instrument?[61] While it is true that the OECD does not have the same enforcement instruments as some other organizations, it nonetheless scores well on implementation. The success of the OECD in implementing decisions in the absence of sanctioning or monitoring mechanisms has been explained in terms of its 'ideational authority'.[62] This form of soft power relying on expert knowledge has, to date, proved very efficient in making unpopular decisions palatable for state governments.[63] But there are other psycho-sociological explanations as well.

Both agreement and implementation might arise simply because they are *appropriate* in the institutional setting of the OECD. Blind, headlong pursuit of national self-interest will simply not do for agents enmeshed in cooperative international institutional settings.[64] Having given their word in the negotiations of the OECD Council, representatives of states will thus have an incentive to pursue and push for actual implementation of the agreement reached. This is how 'in principle' agreements turn into 'in practice' agreements.[65] And this is how the prioritarian clause might come to be included in new or revised double taxation agreements.

Once the revised Convention is accepted by the OECD Council and promulgated to member states, subsequent double taxation agreements

---

[58] Gibson and Goodin 1999.
[59] The ban of chlorofluorocarbons followed this model. Progressive small agreements ultimately lead to important reforms and tight international regulations.
[60] Gibson and Goodin 1999.
[61] Abbott and Snidal 2000. The OECD Council issues a non-binding Recommendation to the member states to conform to the Convention.
[62] Marcussen 2004a, p. 91.
[63] Much to libertarians' chagrin, for example. See posts on the Cato Institute's blog such as Mitchell 2012.
[64] March and Olsen 2009.
[65] Gibson and Goodin 1999.

will almost automatically follow the model, just as they have always done. It is easier to 'copy/paste' the Convention than to engage in drafting a brand-new agreement. When the states are members of the OECD, implementation comes naturally. (This is what the Convention is for, after all: if states would not bother complying, the OECD would not bother drafting every few years a revised Convention; the regular redrafting of the Convention thus serves as a proof, of a sort, of its success.) As for double taxation agreements already in force, these will be accommodated when the treaties come up for renegotiation by the contracting states. That might take a while; hence the implementation of the prioritarian clause would be a gradual process. But that is perhaps a good thing, since the absence of time pressures further incentivizes actors to sign on to the proposal.

VIII   Conclusion

Through double taxation agreements, dual citizens boost their benefits while cutting their costs. Unfortunately, those in greatest need have slim chances of taking advantage of such opportunities. Furthermore, double taxation regimes are detrimental to the poor states' communities. Happily, there is a solution in view – and unlike so many wishful proposals from global egalitarians, there are actually institutional structures in place that might well be willing and able to help implement this proposal.

8 Conclusion

I   The Promises

As pointed out in the first chapter, postnationalists have been among the first to notice the proliferation of multiple citizenship.[1] They have also been among the first to applaud it, on the grounds that multiple citizenship expresses the increasingly *post*national character of citizenship that they have long discussed.[2]

The postnational shift, they say, constitutes 'a profound transformation of the institution of citizenship both in its institutional logic and in the way it is legitimized'.[3] The main aim of this postnational turn is to *erase differences of status* and to promote *equal opportunities* by expanding the rights of non-citizens. Multiple citizenship, in particular, supposedly has an eminently *boundary-dissolving* function: it 'formalizes the fluidity of membership'.[4] '[T]he postnational model ... implies multiplicity of membership', which was previously 'a principal organizational form for empires and city states'.[5] Multiple citizenship 'breaches the traditional notions of political membership and loyalty in a single state'.[6]

These transformations of the citizenship regimes are usually seen as pointing to something bigger: the waning of the nation-state and the erosion of state sovereignty.[7] Increased communication and transmigration, technological advancement, and the human rights revolution all put under stress the states' capacity to control boundaries (in terms of both

---

[1] See Bosniak 2006; Castles and Davidson 2000, p. 24; Jacobson 1996, 1998–9, pp. 444–5; Soysal 1994, 1996.
[2] Cf. Bosniak 2001–2. Note that postnational citizenship does not denote a new citizenship category. It is rather a heuristic used to explain some salient trends like the separation of individual rights from national membership or the blurring of the distinction between nationals and aliens. The concept of 'denizenship' (Hammar 1990) captures the same trend: increasingly, citizenship is no longer the *unique* source of rights.
[3] Soysal 1994, p. 139.
[4] Ibid., p. 141.
[5] Ibid.
[6] Soysal 2004.
[7] Appadurai 1996; Sassen 1996; van Gunsteren 1998.

territory and membership), to allocate goods, and to enforce the law. One symptom of the erosion of state sovereignty is what some postnationalist pessimists call the 'devaluation' or 'debasement' of citizenship brought about by the widespread acceptance of multiple citizenship.[8] To the pessimists' minds, this is obviously bad news. For them the analogy between multiple citizenship and polygamy comes tellingly to mind. Just as the relationship between any two people is somehow devalued inside a polygamous marriage, the relationship between citizen and state or that with one's fellow citizens is devalued when one is a multiple citizen. Exclusivity always adds something to a relationship, whether amorous as between spouses, or social and political as among fellow citizens.

Cosmopolitans, on the other hand, are quite fond of multiple citizenship. Most cosmopolitans champion global governance under the form of a multilevel global polity spanning multiple state jurisdictions, rather than under a unitary world state. As a result, they also favour a type of plural memberships rather than a unitary global citizenship: 'people would come, thus, to enjoy multiple citizenships – political memberships in diverse political communities which significantly affected them'.[9] When cosmopolitans speak of multiple citizenship, they of course have in mind not only multiple national memberships but also forms of multitiered citizenship or nested citizenship, as within a federal state or the European Union.

II   Debunking the Myth: Broken Promises

At the end of this journey, one must wonder to what extent multiple citizenship actually is or does what has been promised above. Does multiple citizenship undermine boundaries? Does it point to a devaluation of state membership today? Does it wipe out global inequalities and differences in status? In a nutshell, does multiple citizenship actually deliver any – much less all – of those goods?

Now, it is true that when multiple citizenship became a widespread reality, national memberships ceased being mutually exclusive. It is also true that states could no longer claim an exclusive, absolute, and perpetual allegiance from their citizens.[10] Yet it would be misleading to think of multiple citizenship as some brandnew type of membership, essentially different from good, old-fashioned citizenship, or to see it as a bastion of global justice. As I have pointed out in the previous chapters, multiple citizenship does not mark a new era; quite the contrary. At best, it is just a

---

[8] Schuck 1998.
[9] Held 1995, p. 233.
[10] Aleinikoff 1986.

reiteration of national membership. It has all its disadvantages. Birth circumstances, for example, play an essential role in the distribution of both dual citizenship and mono-citizenship, with pervasive consequences for global justice (see Chapters 2 and 7).

Multiple citizenship has also some *extra* disadvantages. Citizenship may lose its important 'tagging' function that promotes trust and cooperation among members of the same group where dual citizenship is acquired through pecuniary means (see Chapter 4). Meta-agreement inside a community, which facilitates coherent collective decision making, may also be endangered when people (*qua* dual citizens) join different national communities (*qua* deliberative groups) (see Chapter 5). Not only are the criteria for distribution of multiple citizenship unfair. More to the point of undermining postnationalist claims, its distribution is still fully managed by nation-states: there are no international rules or supranational authorities that intervene in the distribution process of citizenship and hence multiple citizenship.[11]

As for the *boundary-dissolving* function ascribed to multiple citizenship, multiple citizenship reinforces and multiplies the boundaries of belonging instead of dissolving them. The fact that people see a point, indeed an advantage, in accumulating citizenships only serves to show that the boundaries of belonging are as strong as ever.

If people are no longer obliged to make a choice between their citizenship in states *A* and *B*, then it might at first appear that the boundaries between these states are more fluid than before. And indeed it is the case that, for a dual citizen of these states, these boundaries do not make much practical difference. Notice, however, that by letting people become citizens of both *A* and *B*, the boundaries between *A* and *B* are not *actually* erased. Rather, dual *citizenship* implies that there is a good justification for these boundaries, for having two separate political entities, each with its own membership to distribute. Hence, on the face of it, multiple citizenship and open borders are not compatible. Indeed, multiple citizenship is a step back from the cosmopolitan ideal of a borderless world managed through a unitary global state and citizenship. It testifies to the fact that one has come to terms with keeping boundaries in place, and with citizenship serving as the main source of one's rights. This should be a worry for genuine cosmopolitans. As Bosniak says, 'the status of dual or multiple nationals remains anchored to nation-state institutions. The site of nationality may now be multiple, but the status remains nationality nonetheless.'[12] For global cosmopolitans, this surely comes as a disappointment.

---

[11] Bosniak 2001–2, p. 997.
[12] Ibid.

Conclusion 161

Some may say that, on the contrary, multiple citizenship is not necessarily at odds with cosmopolitan ideals. They might argue as follows. Sure, they may say, one way for people to enjoy equal rights and opportunities across the world[13] would be to dismantle territorial and membership boundaries altogether. Another way, however, would be to keep them in place while making everybody a member of every polity, that is, by making everyone a multiple citizen everywhere. That would render boundaries totally innocuous. The problem with boundaries, surely, is not that they exist as such, but that they are so efficient in creating categories of *inclusion* and *exclusion*. And that is precisely where multiple citizenship comes in handy: it is an innovative and feasible way of subverting boundaries by rendering them meaningless. Why continue striving so hard to dismantle what can be easily circumvented?

Yet the situation facing us today is not one where everybody is a multiple citizen everywhere – or even where everybody has an equal opportunity of becoming one. The real world is significantly different from that ideal. The availability of multiple citizenship is determined by one's birth circumstances and one's capacity to migrate and settle elsewhere. It is also a function of the states' willingness to accept multiple citizenship. All this makes multiple citizenship a status that is, in the real world, more accessible to some than others. Furthermore, as I argued in Chapter 7, those to whom it is more accessible will more often be people who are already better off.

Now, one can wonder whether this present situation, where some but not all are multiple citizens, is preferable to the previous one where each is a citizen of a single country. Notice that if our ideal is a world without borders – or its equivalent, a world where *everyone* is a multiple citizen of *every* state, or *universal multiple citizenship* – then it is not clear that a world where at least *some* are multiple citizens (our current situation) should be considered the second-best option. True, a world where some are multiple citizens somewhere is similar to a greater extent to the ideal world of universal multiple citizenship. Yet the second best is not necessarily the option in which most conditions of the ideal are most nearly realized; that is, the second best is not necessarily the option that is most similar in all other respects to the first best. The second-best world may well be one that diverges significantly from the first-best ideal, in our case, the situation where all are citizens of only one state and none is a multiple citizen.[14]

---

[13] Cf. Miller, who makes the point that what matters is that they enjoy equal opportunities inside their own states. See Miller 2005.

[14] For a discussion of the second best in the context of ideal versus non-ideal theory, see Goodin 1995.

Establishing whether that is indeed the case would require a separate, extensive analysis taking into account a multitude of moral considerations that are beyond the remit of this book. Yet in both Chapters 2 and 7 I pointed to some *pro tanto* reasons in favour of an alternative second best, which would at least have to be taken into account in an all-things-considered judgement about what truly is second best.

Finally, does multiple citizenship imply a *devaluation* of national membership, as some authors have argued? I would say, contrary to those claims, that multiple citizenship shows that citizenship is still of *primary importance* for one's welfare today. If citizenship did not make a difference for people's lives, people would not bother collecting citizenships. Citizenship today remains a primary source of rights, and access to dual citizenship actually serves to increase one's capacity to reap a variety of benefits, economic ones included (see Chapter 7). Thus it is no wonder that parents fight for their progeny's right to be dual citizens (see Chapter 2 on the justification of birthright dual citizenship) or that people are reluctant to relinquish one citizenship when acquiring another (see Chapter 3 on dual citizenship by naturalization).

III   A Reprise of Policy Proposals

Over the course of this book, I have offered three broad groups of policy proposals for reforming current practices associated with multiple citizenship. In order of increasing moral importance, and also in order of increasing practical difficulty of implementation, these are the following:

(1) Make multiple citizenship an active rather than a passive choice, requiring people to renew their second (third, and so on) citizenship from time to time (Chapter 2) and to explicitly state their preferences in order to retain their previous citizenship(s) upon acquiring a new one (Chapter 3).

(2) Impose a global tax on multiple citizenship as such or, failing that, at least reform double taxation agreements prioritizing the claims of the poorer of the states with a claim to tax any given income stream (Chapter 7).

(3) In potential cases of multiple citizenship, unbundle the rights currently associated with citizenship, and allocate some categories of rights (especially voting rights) separately from the rest. This would make it possible for people to be citizens of one state without having a say in its national elections, while allowing non-citizens to do so without taking on additional citizenship(s) or acquiring all the other rights associated with that (see Chapter 6).

Conclusion 163

The first of these proposals seems relatively straightforward. Any given state can implement it independently of what any other state does. And the political motivation for doing so is relatively straightforward. After all, each political community presumably would prefer to have members who positively want to be part of it rather than members who just happen to be so – particularly insofar as there is reason to doubt (as citizenship elsewhere gives reason to doubt) whether people are really attached to that community or not.

The second of these proposals is more challenging. Implementing a global tax-transfer system doubtless seems like pie-in-the-sky thinking.[15] But there are already various international norms managing the taxation of income streams where two countries both have a claim to tax it. These norms are embodied in double tax agreements that, although bilateral, are almost invariably based on the OECD Model Tax Convention. As I argued, that provides a natural pressure point within the international system for effecting changes in double tax arrangements for all the countries basing their bilateral arrangements on the Model Tax Convention. In Chapter 7, I have discussed how a reform of the OECD Model Tax Convention might be brought about.

The proposal for *unbundling* the various rights currently wrapped up in citizenship, set out explicitly in Chapter 6 but foreshadowed at various other points as well, is the boldest of all my reform proposals. Being the most novel, it is perhaps also the hardest to understand (much less to implement, perhaps). So let me now elaborate that proposal more detail.

IV   Unbundling Citizenship

In Chapter 6, I explored the relationship between multiple citizenship and various principles for constituting the demos. I argued that multiple citizenship does not get us very far toward implementing any of these principles because it preserves the original features of state membership: it is almost always a *permanent* status (once a citizen, always a citizen),[16] and it is almost always a status that is inextricably tied to the exercise of *political* rights[17] (if a citizen, then entitled to vote).[18] The problem upon which Chapter 6 focuses is that political rights and citizenship are inextricably bundled together. They come as a package. My proposed

---

[15] Although that has not stopped many from floating such proposals, not only Shachar (on whose book my own proposal builds) but also, more famously, Thomas Pogge (2001, 2002).
[16] As I pointed out in Chapter 6, some states reserve the right to revoke the citizenship of naturalized dual citizens in extreme situations (e.g., convictions for state terrorism).
[17] As in Chapter 6, when talking of 'political rights', I refer primarily to the right to vote.
[18] With a few exceptions, as acknowledged in Chapter 6.

solution there was to unbundle citizenship, pluck out political rights, and distribute them on the basis of different criteria. (For example, in some states, residents are already able to vote in regional elections; according to my proposal they could be able to vote in national elections as well, provided residence is considered to be the right criterion for allocating political rights.)

Here I want to come back to this proposal and make an argument for unbundling the rights of citizenship more generally. Not only would the unbundling help us to draw more sharply the boundaries of the demos, as discussed in Chapter 6. It could also provide a solution to various shortcomings of multiple citizenship mentioned in the previous chapters (to which I will return shortly).

Different authors have emphasized the need for new forms of citizenship. Only a few, however, have canvassed the possibility of ceasing to think of citizenship as an all-or-nothing affair.[19] Among them are Blatter and Schlenker, who argue, for example, that 'citizenship can and should come in different degrees'.[20] My proposal of unbundling citizenship rights and distributing them separately goes in the same direction, as it too would result in different *degrees* of citizenship.

Some might worry that these different degrees of citizenship might seem to amount to actual second- or third-class citizenships. My unbundling proposal could be thus conceived as a dreadful *retour en arrière*. This may seem to represent a serious objection to the unbundling – and perhaps it would, if the different bundles of rights were *described* as different 'classes of citizenship'.

Yet there is no reason why these various partial bundles of rights should necessarily amount to different *statuses* – of citizenship or anything else.[21]

---

[19] Exceptions are Bauböck 2009; Blatter and Schlenker 2013; Koenig-Archibugi 2012; Song 2016. For a legal analysis of who would govern the fragmentation of citizenship, see Tratchman 2017.

[20] Blatter and Schlenker 2013, p. 6; Cohen 2009.

[21] Other authors implicitly have something like 'unbundling' in mind when discussing how particular rights should be allocated to long-term immigrants or non-resident citizens. But they do not use the same term and do not discuss the separate allocation of different rights as an overall general policy, rather than as an exceptional policy that targets particular categories of people and that is called for by particular situations (the standard way of allocating rights remaining thus via citizenship). The only author offering any sustained discussion of distributing citizenship rights in a disaggregated fashion is Elizabeth Cohen. She points to the phenomenon of 'semi-citizenship' or 'partial citizenship', by which she means 'different combinations and degrees of citizenship rights' that amount to different citizenship statuses (Cohen 2009, pp. 95). Her study serves to 'identify multiple forms of political membership that are associated with some, but not all, of the democratic rights, responsibilities, activities, and statuses available to citizens of a state, and ... [to] discuss how and why liberal democratic states routinely instantiate such categories of semi-citizenship' (p. 5). She examines historically how these semi-citizenship statuses came to

I am not arguing that states should create new citizenship categories to consecrate different combinations of rights categories to be distributed – for example, 'type 1 citizenship' comprising rights categories (a), (b), and (c) and a lesser 'type 2 citizenship' comprising rights (b) and (c) alone.[22] Indeed, states might even dispense with the category of 'citizenship' altogether when proceeding with the unbundling.[23]

Hence, although states would have different categories of rights up for separate distribution, these need not automatically translate into differences in formal citizenship status.[24] The aim of my unbundling proposal is precisely to sever those important categories of specific rights from omnibus citizenship status. The normative ideal behind my proposal is a world where everybody can standardly enjoy various rights (including political rights) across the globe, irrespective of citizenship status.

A Institutional Design Options

The unbundling proposal could be implemented in various ways. Below I describe, and draw distinctions between, several options:

> Option 1: Rights are distributed only in the bundled form that constitutes citizenship at present. This ensures that, insofar as everyone is a citizen of at least one state, everyone will have all

---

exist and why they are unavoidable. My account differs from Cohen's in three ways, the first two being the most fundamental ones. First, mine is an insistently normative proposal, whereas Cohen's is, by her own account fundamentally descriptive. My argument in favour of unbundling is the logical conclusion, of my normative arguments about multiple citizenship. Cohen, in contrast, explicitly eschews taking any normative stance toward semi-citizenship, saying: 'Although the classifications of semi-citizenship presented in this book invite normative speculation, they are discussed here primarily as analytic tools. As such, they are justified not by the normative judgments to which they point, but rather the degree to which they accurately characterize a set of related political phenomena' (p. 10). Second, my proposal is offered first and foremost as an alternative to multiple citizenship, something that Cohen regards as beyond her book's remit. As she explains in a footnote: 'I have chosen not to include dual nationals in the list. Although dual nationality technically marks an anomalous relationship to nationality, it doesn't place people in a position that alters either nationality radically' (p. 148, n. 20). Third, and less fundamentally, I have argued that it would be preferable to conceive the different combinations of rights *not* as different citizenship statuses, which is how Cohen regards them.

[22] E.g., the UK Nationality Act of 1981 created multiple categories of UK nationality, some with different rights than others.

[23] The question remains as to whether we should prefer having only different categories of rights to be distributed separately without having the whole package (citizenship) available for distribution, or whether we should prefer having both options available (the full citizenship bundle of rights and its various component rights taken separately). I address this in the next sections.

[24] Maine 1977.

those rights somewhere or another. Some can, of course, become multiple citizens and thus acquire multiple bundles of rights.

Option 2: Everyone gets that same full bundle of rights (one such citizenship) at birth, with the possibility of acquiring additional *bits* of the bundle in a different state, that is, instead of a second or third full set of citizenship rights there (as in the current case of multiple citizenships).[25]

Option 3: Everyone gets that same full bundle of rights (one such citizenship) in the birth state (A) and can acquire additional bits of the bundle in a different state (B). But the acquisition of these additional bits in B triggers the loss of the counterpart bits from the initial bundle of rights possessed in A. This option entails thus a trade-off between the newly acquired categories of rights and the corresponding old ones in the person's citizenship of birth, with the latter being automatically cancelled as the former are acquired.

Option 4: A modified version of option 3 where the trade-offs apply only to some but not all categories of rights. Option 4 allows one to accumulate some categories of rights across states, but not others. The trade-off might, for example, be required in the case of political rights; that is, if one acquires political rights in one's residence state B, one loses the political rights one has in virtue of one's birth citizenship in state A. Yet other rights (for example, the right to travel freely and the right of residence) may not be lost in the birth state (A) upon acquiring the same rights in a second state (B).

Option 5: Complete unbundling. Each of the rights currently associated with citizenship is distributed completely independently of

---

[25] Trachtman (2017, p. 609) argues that multiple citizenship inherently requires some unbundling on the grounds that multiple citizens cannot bear military and taxation duties in multiple states and cannot hold rights to health or pension in multiple states. This is simply not true. Pension and healthcare rights are typically not based on citizenship at all, but rather on residence or a history of contributions. Thus someone who has worked in and made contributions to the pension schemes of multiple countries, no matter whether as a multiple citizen or a mere immigrant, may draw a pension from all the states in question. In my view, option 2 – where one is a full citizen of one state (enjoying the complete set of rights subsumed by that citizenship) and also able to enjoy discrete rights in another state without being citizen there – is superior to the form of multiple citizenship Trachtman envisages, where one is a full citizen of one state and also a *partial* citizen of another (in the sense that despite holding the formal status of citizen, one is not entitled to the full suite of rights normally associated with it). That makes that person literally a 'second-class citizen' in the latter state, in a way unbundling of the sort described in option 2 would not.

one another and never bundled up in the form of citizenship. The category of citizenship disappears.

B   Advantages and Disadvantages

What are the pros and cons of the alternatives mentioned above, and which one should be preferred?

Imagine that states would proceed to a *complete unbundling* of citizenship rights (option 5). We would no longer distribute an *identical package* of rights *once and for all* (that is, citizenship) on the basis of birth circumstances or on a basis of mixed criteria in naturalization (residence, civic competence, economic sustainability). Instead, states would distribute *separately* each category of rights – civic, political, social, economic – on the basis of whatever criteria[26] they deem most appropriate for each category of rights. These might include residence, civic competence, affected interests, subjection to law, financial capital, financial contribution, affective ties, and so on. Furthermore, states might deem it appropriate to allocate a person such rights only for as long as the corresponding criteria are fulfilled (that is, *not* necessarily for life). Broadly the same pattern of distribution could occur within options 2, 3, and 4 as well – with the only difference being that citizenship, as a legal category, would still exist in all of those cases. However, all three options would make the allocation of rights associated with it more fluid and flexible.

Suppose, for example, subjection to law is deemed to be the most appropriate criterion for distributing political rights.[27] If so, long-term immigrants would be enfranchised in the receiving state and disenfranchised in the sending state (assuming they are no longer subject to the laws there) – which is possible under options 3 and 4 (and of course 5).[28]

---

[26] Of course, there are some rights that states may want to distribute (largely) unconditionally to everyone. The right to a fair trial might be one, for example. Or the right to enter and stay for a short period of time on the states' territory. I come back to this below.

[27] I do not defend the legally subjected principle here, but merely use it as one example of principle that might be used for the allocation of political rights.

[28] There is, of course, the special case of those forced (i.e., coerced) into exile. According to Bauböck (2007b, p. 2438) they should keep their voting rights on the grounds that they would have been residing citizens had they not been unjustly driven away by their state. Perhaps. Yet notice several things. First, exiles constitute a tiny subset of multiple citizens. Second, even if we grant Bauböck that first-generation expats (those who were actually driven away) should retain their political rights, we cannot say the same about their progeny. That would mean that a great number of people (distant descendants of those forced into exile during WWII, WWI, etc.) should hold political rights in countries with which they have only faint historical connection. Third, and most important, it is morally dubious to distribute political rights on the basis of counterfactuals alone, unless

As argued in Chapter 6, their disenfranchisement is not currently possible insofar as, *qua* citizens of the sending state, they enjoy political rights there for life (regardless their actual residence, regardless of whether or not their interests are affected by the policies of the state, or regardless of their civic competence).[29] Currently, their disenfranchisement[30] is not possible outside their complete denationalization (withdrawal of *all* the rights currently associated with citizenship).[31] At the same time, their enfranchisement in the receiving states is not possible without them becoming citizens, under the current rules prescribing that all and only citizens can vote in national elections. But the problem would disappear if states could conceive of distributing to some people political rights in the absence of full citizenship (what in Chapter 6 I called *political rights-sine-citizenship* in the receiving state) and other people other of the current rights of citizenship without political rights

that is being done as a form of compensation. But notice that would itself be problematic; surely, the best restitution measure would be to *undo* the harm done to them (forced exile) by granting them the right of return with all its benefits, political rights included, rather than giving them the right to vote there without actually returning. Saying that exiles should have a vote in their state of origin because, had they not been forced into exile they would have been subjected to the laws of the state, is akin to saying that their state of origin should tax their income because, had they not been forced into exile, they would have had their income sourced on that state's territory. If we find the latter claim absurd, we should doubt the former claim as well.

[29] Indeed, it is usually taken for granted that political rights cannot be distributed in the absence of citizenship. Bauböck (2007b, p. 2439) for example starts his analysis by saying: 'whether such minorities [external kin minorities] should have external voting rights ... presupposes that *they must also* be granted external citizenship status'. More discussed is the possibility of granting external citizenship without external voting rights (notice that a few states already are not allowing their citizens living abroad to vote in national elections). This is the solution Bauböck (2007b, p. 2409) advocates for those non-resident citizens who do not satisfy his proposed stakeholder criterion for the allocation of political rights.

[30] Bauböck (2007b, p. 2402) argues, for example, that it would be unfair if 'external voting rights are first extended and then curtailed', and expats 'will lose a fundamental right they have been previously granted'. There are two points we can discuss here: the first concerns the fundamental nature of political rights and the second *taking away* rights once granted. Indeed, political rights are fundamental but that does not constitute in itself an argument in favour of voting in *any particular* state, nor can it be an argument for exercising political rights in *more* states rather than just one. We generally consider political rights fundamental because they serve individual self-determination by allowing people to influence the laws that govern them, and because they allow people to further the interests they have there. Furthermore, *taking away* some rights is not *prima facie* wrong in itself, if one should not have been granted them to begin with. Thus whether the loss of political rights is *prima facie* unfair or not depends on what we take to be the fair criteria for the distribution of political rights.

[31] With some exceptions: for example, citizens of a state may lose their voting rights after residing for a period of time abroad, irrespective of other considerations. At the time of writing, this is the case for Germany, Canada, and the United Kingdom where citizens would lose their voting rights after, respectively, 25, 5, and 15 years.

(in the terminology of Chapter 6, *citizenship-sine-political rights* in the sending state).

The unbundling would be equally useful if one believes (as I do) that affected interests rather than residence or citizenship status should entitle one to voting rights in the national elections of a state. That is typically seen as a response to the numerous ways, in a globalized world, in which one's life can be affected by a distant state's elections. But I also believe that the loose and flexible allocation of political rights allowed by the unbundling has an additional advantage; it is a better political solution to the increasing *uncertainty* that people face in their lives than is multiple citizenship as it is presently cast. Let me explain.

One important purpose of political rights is giving people, *collectively*, some control over the events affecting their lives, some control over their environment, thereby enabling them to make and pursue life plans and further their interests.[32] Voting is not only a way of expressing one's political preferences; more importantly, it is a means to promote one's autonomy and self-determination. Now increasingly one's life plans depend on environments that extend beyond one state's borders. We live in a word that has made possible a nomadic life, with global labour markets and fairly permeable borders. Of course, some people (professionals) freely choose such a life, while for others (refugees) it is a matter of necessity. For numerous others the driver is a mixture of choice and necessity. Yet as a characteristic of the global risk society, uncertainty plays a central role in all these people's lives. They don't know where their next move will take them, or where they will settle. And while much of that migration is internal, within the state's borders, much of it crosses state borders.

If exercising political rights helps us to make and pursue life plans, then it is harder to say in which states exactly all these people should have a say, politically and for good. They might take up work in any of many states; or in the case of refugees, they might be transferred to just about any state. Irrespective of their situation, however, they would all benefit from a more flexible allocation of political rights.

Notice that this possibility of distributing and enjoying political rights in the absence of the other rights of citizenship could undermine multiple citizenship by rendering it superfluous, as noted in Chapter 6.[33] Those

---

[32] Of course, individually, one person's vote will be inconsequential. However, the proposal in view here would enfranchise whole groups of people. Together their votes could well make a difference for their welfare.

[33] Authors like Weinstock (2010) have defended the exercise of political rights by multiple citizens. For a critique of such arguments, see Goodin and Tanasoca (2014). Here, however, I limit my case to pointing out that political rights should be distributed

who want to become citizens of a state only to enjoy political rights, for example, would lose their reason to seek citizenship if they could have political rights without it.

The same goes for residence and entrance rights. Another important advantage of being a citizen is, of course, that it allows one to freely enter and reside in a state's territory. The various unbundling options would allow states to detach these rights of entry and residence and distribute them separately on other grounds, independently of whether one is or is not a fellow citizen. Perhaps everybody should enjoy the right to enter any state's territory irrespective of other circumstances, solely on the ground that free movement is an essential component of personal autonomy.[34] Or perhaps not. Perhaps social ties – having family[35] and friends in one country – should entitle one to free entrance and residence (on a short-term, if not permanent, basis) in that country. (Indeed, one major argument in favour of multiple birthright citizenship is that this status ensures that parents and children would not be cut off from one another, as discussed in Chapter 2.) So, too, perhaps should the need for urgent medical treatment there (provided the individuals themselves or their states are willing and able to pay for it, so that they would not be a burden on the host community). Unbundling citizenship rights and distributing them separately (irrespective of the status of citizenship) would open the door to numerous ways in which the quality of people's lives could be improved and their legal entitlements be made to follow more closely their moral entitlements.

Many people today naturalize as a way of getting something extra that is not available to them as temporary migrants or permanent residents. They might do so reluctantly, insofar as naturalization comes with various costs to them. One advantage of the unbundling would be to decrease the costs these people have to bear for the enjoyment of particular categories of rights. And in addition to that, the unbundling along the lines of option (5) would, by eliminating the status of citizen altogether, finally break the nefarious dichotomy between citizens and non-citizens that can so poison social relationships.[36] Following the

---

separately according to whatever freestanding principles we see fit (being subjected to that state's law is one example among many, as discussed in Chapter 6) and that distributing them via the grant of citizenship (which gives rise to instances of multiple citizenship) is problematic insofar as it enables overinclusiveness with respect to these principles.

[34] For this view, see Oberman 2016.
[35] 'Family ties' because with the advance of assisted reproductive technology (for both heterosexual and queer couples) and the possibility for adoption, families are no longer based exclusively on 'blood ties'.
[36] Again, the debate in the United Kingdom over the immigrants' access to social benefits is a good example.

Conclusion

unbundling, and with the consequent disappearance of the status of 'citizenship', the differences between people would be so many and varied that nobody would bother making a big issue of them.

Presently, people already sometimes enjoy certain rights irrespective of citizenship status. Some social rights are already (and increasingly) allocated on the basis of individual contributions or residence. And more globally integrated labour markets mean that people can increasingly carry some social credits and entitlements with them when moving from a state to another (think of portable pension schemes).[37] On the other hand, at least in Europe (recall the UK debate on the benefits enjoyed there by other non-British EU citizens during the Brexit referendum campaign), certain political discourses strongly favour restricting social rights to citizens only. Also, in many states, residing non-citizens are already allowed to vote in local and regional elections and in a few states even in national elections.[38] At the same time there are many social rights that are conditional upon residence that citizens who are not actually resident there cannot enjoy in their 'home' state. The unbundling proposal would make such instances the rule rather than the exception. Unbundling means that not just some rights, but *all* rights, would come to be systematically distributed on grounds other than citizenship. Instead of granting some people a full second or third citizenship (and with it, perhaps some categories of rights people should not be entitled to), the unbundling proposal would allow states to distribute to those who otherwise would have been dual or triple citizens only those categories of rights to which they are entitled to according to the proper allocation criteria governing those particular rights. The unbundling proposal represents a 'targeted approach' to rights allocation, whereas the allocation of rights via citizenship is significantly rougher and thus more likely to cause overinclusiveness or underinclusiveness.

How would dismembering citizenship solve the problems of multiple citizenship presented in the previous chapters? Consider, for example, the problems associated with dual citizenship acquired via investment. While buying citizenship is problematic in all sorts of different ways, investors have a good reason for wanting to do so. Certain economic rights and opportunities may be available only to citizens, or the exercise of those rights and access to those opportunities might come more easily to citizens than to foreigners. (For example, foreigners often need to complete more paperwork.) At the time of this writing, for example, France allowed only citizens to sell alcohol, and many Central and

---

[37] For discussions, see Hansen and Weil 2002; Schuck 1998; and especially Cohen 2009.
[38] For an overview of voting rights provisions for non-citizens, see Bauböck 2005.

Eastern European states still restricted foreigners' right to buy farmland despite objections from the EU. As pointed out in Chapter 4, the depth of a person's pocket might make a good criterion for the distribution of economic rights, but not so also for the distribution of other rights bundled up with citizenship, most especially political rights. Unbundling citizenship rights would thus be a good solution insofar as it would allow investors to acquire economic rights – but nothing more – according to the size of their purses. And, of course, states would thereby secure the freedom of distributing the other traditional rights of citizenship (political rights included) according to other criteria that they may find more appropriate.

It is important, however, for people to enjoy all the component parts of the citizenship bundle – all the rights presently comprised by citizenship – somewhere or another in the world. That is why a universal right to citizenship exists in the first place today. Only by ensuring that all people are citizens of one state can we be sure that all will have access to that full suite of rights. Yet although it is vitally important that all people should enjoy all the rights comprised by the citizenship bundle somewhere, they do not have to enjoy all of them necessarily inside the *same* state and in the form of citizenship as we now know it. This is the point of my unbundling proposal.

Might the unbundling risk leaving some people without some of the rights? If it does, that would be a serious criticism of it as compared with protecting those rights through citizenship, be it single or multiple, in its currently bundled-up form. Maybe multiple citizenship does not guarantee that our desired criteria (whichever these might be) for the distribution of each category of rights will be *perfectly* satisfied.[39] But at least when conferring it, states are always erring on the side of caution, which is *over*inclusiveness rather than *under*inclusiveness.[40] That is to say, multiple citizenship errs on the side of bestowing rights on people who, according to each right-specific distribution criterion, should not hold these rights, rather than withholding rights from those who should hold them according to those same criteria.

---

[39] I take no stance on what the distribution criteria should be for each category of rights; that would require a lengthy separate discussion. But there are good reasons to believe that different rights should be distributed on different grounds insofar as they serve different purposes; thus they should not be distributed all bundled together as they currently are on condition of being a citizen.

[40] But as Bauböck (2015) properly notices, theorists need to find new ways of defining the demos that can avoid both over- and underinclusion and thus 'be compatible with long-term stability of the demos and vary with the type of polity to which they apply' – that is, forms of citizenship that are highly malleable (p. 821).

Conclusion   173

Notice that the risk of leaving some people altogether bereft of some categories of rights currently composing the citizenship bundle is only really a danger for one of the unbundling options, namely, option 5 (complete unbundling). Completely unbundling all of the component rights that currently constitute citizenship and letting states allocate them separately would indeed require a serious bureaucratic effort on the part of these states. They would have to monitor individuals to figure out what their proper entitlements are, on a regular basis. One can easily imagine how, in such scenario, it could be entirely possible for some individuals to miss out on some (or indeed all) of the bits of the current citizenship bundle somewhere along the line.

At the beginning of this chapter I bemoaned the fact that the distribution of multiple citizenship is controlled uniquely by states. At least some forms of the unbundling proposal (specifically, options 3, 4, and 5) could call for a *global* mechanism of coordination between states as a way of tracking and establishing people's rights entitlements. Even in the complete unbundling scenario (option 5), states would still be sovereign to establish whatever criteria they see fit to govern the allocation of each of the different categories of rights. Insofar as states have not perfectly synchronized their registries and databases in relevant ways with one another's, or in the absence of a global coordination mechanism, some individuals may fall between the cracks and be left without one bit or another of the bundle. Beyond that, one can surely expect some states to be incapable of rising to such a complex and burdensome bureaucratic task. While multiple citizenship of the traditional sort might err on the side of *over*inclusiveness, at least it does not involve depriving some individuals of their rights by accident. Just as it is better to risk letting some guilty people go unpunished rather than to risk jailing innocent ones, it is better to risk allocating excess rights to people who are not entitled to them than to risk withholding rights from those who are entitled to them.

In the case of a complete unbundling (option 5) there are thus two risks:

(a) states would not be able to cope with the complex bureaucratic task, and thus some individuals would be left without some categories of rights to which they would be entitled according to the relevant distribution criteria for those category of rights, and
(b) even if states could allocate all categories of rights perfectly according to their own selected distribution criteria, owing to mismatches of those criteria between states it would be entirely possible for some individuals to be left with fewer rights than they would have under

the current citizenship regime, that is, as citizens of one or more states.

That is why it would be wise to keep available both options: both the allocation of the full package of rights that currently travel under the label 'citizenship' and the separate additional allocation – in other states beyond that of an individual's citizenship – of different 'unbundled' categories of rights. That would be possible, in one form or another, according to all three options 2, 3, and 4. However, it seems that option 2 would be the safest in this respect, permitting the allocation of one citizenship (of one full package of rights) at birth, and in *addition* to that the separate allocation of distinct rights in an unbundled fashion *only* in cases of what would – under current arrangements – be claims for a second (third and so on) citizenship.

Depending on the principles for allocating the various component rights, this compromise may not solve overinclusiveness with respect to *all* categories of rights. Take the example of political rights. If being legally subjected is the relevant principle for allocating these rights, then according to the compromise sketched above, where both citizenship and unbundled rights are a possibility, someone could acquire political rights in one state (*B*) in virtue of his residence there, and still hold political rights in another state (*A*) in virtue of his birth citizenship. Hence there would be overinclusiveness with respect to the distribution of political rights in state *A*, by the standards of the legally subjected principle.[41]

Even so, there is still a real advantage to allocating *K* one full bundle of citizenship rights in *A* plus the enjoyment of separate categories of rights in state *B*, compared with letting *K* be a dual citizen of both *A* and *B*. The unbundling might still avoid overinclusiveness with respect to some categories of rights in state *B*, even if it does not solve potential overinclusiveness in state *A*. But as said, such overinclusiveness would be the result of the compromise: upholding the institution of citizenship as we currently know it alongside the allocation of unbundled rights, out of fear that complete unbundling (option 5) might leave some people without some of the rights that comprise the current full citizenship bundle anywhere in the world. Because of that it may seem that option 2 would constitute a better solution than multiple citizenship: while multiple

---

[41] Note that I refer here to overinclusiveness in relationship to the criteria established by a particular state for the allocation of a particular category of rights. Yet the situation described above is a case of overinclusiveness also by reference to a (global egalitarian) standard, which is external to states' policies, i.e., that nobody should enjoy the same bit of the bundle in more than one state.

citizenship may cause overinclusiveness in several states, the overinclusiveness caused by option 2 would be limited to one state only (the birth state).

By contrast, option 3 would always impose trade-offs between the same rights in the state of one's birth and the rights one may acquire in a second or third state. Option 3 would ensure that a person *cannot* acquire some category of rights in a second state *B* without at the same time losing that identical category of rights in state *A*. This means that option 3 involves some degree of unbundling of rights in a person's birth state as well as the person's second or third state, whereas option 2 would preserve the old model of citizenship, as we currently know it, in the person's birth state. The distinctive feature of option 3 is that one would enjoy the same number of rights as comprised by *one* citizenship bundle and no more, although in option 3 those rights are distributed across different states. One obvious problem with this option would, of course, be that its application may prevent people from enjoying the same category of rights in different states, even though they may be justly entitled to them according to the various principles of distribution of these rights.

Options 2 and 3 clearly represent solutions to different problems, and they speak to different values. The aim of option 2 is to ensure that nobody would be deprived of one or another category of rights comprising his or her current citizenship rights in the process of unbundling (which is logically possible in options 4 and 5). Option 2 might therefore be considered a *sufficientarian* version of the unbundling proposal; in keeping the full bundle of citizenship rights intact in the first-acquired citizenship, states are just ensuring that *everyone* will enjoy *all* the bits of the citizenship bundle somewhere in the world. States do so, even at the risk of creating (a) *overinclusiveness* by reference to the preferred distribution criteria for some bits of the bundle, in some states, and (b) *inequality* among citizens of the world (some will enjoy the same category of rights in multiple countries).

Option 3, on the other hand, is primarily concerned with keeping a tight rein on *inequality* among world citizens, by forcing trade-offs between existing and newly acquired rights. Its aim is to prevent some individuals from exercising the same category of rights in two or more countries. However, option 3 is deficient in one important respect. According to the differing distribution criteria we consider legitimate for those particular categories of rights, some people could easily be properly entitled to the same category of rights in several countries. If so, then option 3 would, for the sake of formal global equality among people, deprive some individuals of their just entitlements, thereby creating underinclusiveness with respect to these criteria in particular countries. Hence, in comparison to option 3, option 2 once again proves to be a better solution: it gives people formal access to their entitlements (to different rights categories) in different states, while being able to correct for global inequalities by adjusting the exact *substantive* entitlements provided by these rights, formally.[42]

Option 4 would also constitute a good solution in this respect, insofar as trade-offs between a person's rights in one state and in another would be required only for *particular* rights categories, not *all* rights categories. For example, state A may insist that its birth citizens lose their political rights upon acquiring these same rights in a second state (B), but it may allow them to keep their rights to reside and enter freely state A if they wish to do so. Both options 2 and 4 would allow individuals to accumulate some categories of rights, if not full bundles of rights, as multiple citizenship presently allows them to do. This means that some individuals would still enjoy more rights across the globe than others – and the advantages they bring – and that some individuals could also exercise more political power across the world than others. The same objection applies to multiple citizenship, of course. Yet from a global egalitarian perspective, unbundling citizenship rights, as in options 2 and 4, would perhaps be superior to multiple citizenship insofar as at least *some* bits of the package would not be automatically duplicated (or triplicated), as would necessarily be the case with multiple citizenship.

If our worry about options 2 and 4 is mainly that some people, enjoying the franchise in multiple states, would thereby exercise *more political power* globally than others, then there is a simple solution to the problem. All states would have to do is *control the actual amount* of political power vested in such people's exercise of political rights in those different places. This could be achieved through weighted voting, for example: if someone has a vote in two states' national elections, her vote would be weighted one-half as much as the vote of a person having a vote in each of those states alone; if she has a vote in three states' national elections, her vote would be weighted one-third; and so on.[43]

Notice there already are, in other realms, mechanisms in place to ensure that those holding more formal rights than others do not get a better treatment than others. For example, dual citizens formally have the right to diplomatic protection from two states. Logically, this could translate into dual citizens enjoying more diplomatic protection than mono-nationals. Yet there are international rules preventing dual nationals

---

[42] See the discussion on weighted voting in Goodin and Tanasoca 2014.
[43] For a discussion, see Goodin and Tanasoca 2014.

from benefitting from both of their states' protection (couched in terms of notions pertaining to the establishment of 'effective citizenship').[44] Or, again, international rules prevent dual citizens from appealing to the protection of one of their states of citizenship against their other state of citizenship.[45]

V   Conclusion to the Conclusion

The bottom line would seem to be that a full unbundling of all the rights that currently comprise citizenship would be an ambitious (perhaps overly ambitious) project. Yet even the most modest form of partial unbundling, along the lines of option 2, would go a long way toward solving the problems of multiple citizenship revealed in the previous chapters.

For those who see the naturalization of the world poor in rich states as a matter of global justice, the partial unbundling I propose should be particularly appealing. Rich states are likely to be more amenable to granting the world poor separate categories of rights – progressively, one category of rights at a time – than to granting them the full package of citizenship rights at once. As a solution to global injustice, therefore, the partial unbundling is thus perhaps more feasible than multiple citizenship.

To be sure, more theoretical work needs to be done on the unbundling proposal sketched in this Conclusion. Much more needs to be done in exploring the desirability and feasibility of new ways of envisaging the exercise of constituent citizenship rights, *across* states and not just inside them. Much more needs to be done to elaborate the most appropriate principles for the distribution of each category of rights, from both a moral and a practical perspective. Nevertheless, revealing what might be problematic about multiple citizenship as currently practiced – having exposed the problem to which such unbundling of citizenship might be a desirable solution – is an important first step.

---

[44] Oeter 2003.
[45] This longstanding rule has been broken, however, in the case of claims addressed to the Iranian-American Claims Tribunal where, for the first time, dual nationals used the protection of one of their states of citizenship against the other. Since this precedent, such cases have multiplied. See Aghahosseini 2007.

Bibliography

Abbott, Kenneth W., and Duncan Snidal. 2000. Hard and soft law in international governance. *International Organization*, 54, 421–56.
Abizadeh, Arash. 2008. Democratic theory and border coercion: no right to unilaterally control your own borders. *Political Theory*, 36, 37–65.
  2012. On the demos and its kin: nationalism, democracy, and the boundary problem. *American Political Science Review*, 106, 867–82.
Adams, Richard H. Jr. 2008. The demographic, economic and financial determinants of international remittances in developing countries. World Bank Development Economics Department. Policy Research Working Paper, 4583. Available at http://elibrary.worldbank.org/doi/book/10.1596/1813-9450-4583.
Aghahosseini, Mohsen. 2007. *Claims of Dual Nationals and the Development of Customary International Law*. Leiden: Martinus Nijhoff.
Aleinikoff, T. Alexander. 1986. Theories of loss of citizenship. *Michigan Law Review*, 87, 1471–503.
Aleinikoff, T. Alexander, and Douglas Klusmeyer, eds. 2001. *Citizenship: Comparison and Perspectives*. Washington, DC: Carnegie Endowment for International Peace.
Aleinikoff, T. Alexander, and Rubén G. Rumbaut. 1998–9. Terms of belonging: are models of membership self-fulfilling prophecies? *Georgetown Immigration Law Journal*, 13, 1–24.
Alter, Jean. 1970. *Les Origines de la Satyre Anti-Bourgeoise en France*. Droz: Geneva.
Anderson, Elizabeth. 1990. The ethical limitations of the market. *Economics and Philosophy*, 6, 179–295.
Anonymous. 1963. State reciprocity statutes and the inheritance rights of nonresident aliens. *Duke Law Journal*, 12, 315–26.
  1969. Alien inheritance statutes and foreign relations power. *Duke Law Journal*, 18, 153–71.
  2011. Developments in the law: extraterritoriality. *Harvard Law Review*, 124, 1226–304.
Appadurai, Arjun. 1996. *Modernity at Large: Cultural Dimensions of Globalization*. Minneapolis, MN: University of Minnesota Press.
Arendt, Hannah. 1968. *The Origins of Totalitarianism*. New York, NY: Harcourt, Brace and Jovanovich.
  2004. *The Origins of Totalitarianism*. New York, NY: Schocken.

Bibliography

Ariely, Dan, Joel Huber, and Klaus Wertenbroch. 2005. When do losses loom larger than gains? *Journal of Marketing Research*, 42, 134–8.

Arneson, Richard. 1989. Equality and equal opportunity for welfare. *Philosophical Studies*, 56, 77–93.

  2001. Luck and equality. *Proceedings of the Aristotelian Society*, 75, 73–90.

Arrhenius, Gustaf. 2005. The boundary problem in democratic theory. Pp. 14–29 in Folke Tersman (ed.), *Democracy Unbound: Basic Explorations I*. Stockholm: Filosofiska Institutionen, Stockholm Universitet.

Arrow, Kenneth J., and Anthony C. Fisher. 1974. Environmental preservation, uncertainty and irreversibility. *Quarterly Journal of Economics*, 88, 312–19.

Arundell, Thomas. 1603. Letter to Lord Cecil. *The Cecil Papers*, CP. 187/93. Available at http://cecilpapers.chadwyck.com/search/displayItem.do?QueryType=articles&ResultsID=141BCB39F4F11CC27F&filterSequence=0&ItemNumber=1&ItemID=15_0480.

Asch, Solomon. [1955] 2011. Opinions and social pressure. Pp. 17–26 in Elliott Aronson (ed.), *Readings about the Social Animal*. New York, NY: Worth.

Australian Government. Department of Immigration and Border Protection. Character requirements. Available at www.immi.gov.au/allforms/character-requirements/.

Axelrod, Robert, and William D. Hamilton. 1981. The evolution of cooperation. *Science*, 211, 1390–6.

Balzan, Jurgen. 2013. Contentious citizenship scheme approved. *Malta Today*, November 12. Available at www.maltatoday.com.mt/en/newsdetails/news/national/Contentious-citizenship-scheme-approved-20131112.

Bancroft Naturalization Treaties with the German States. 1868. Edited by Charles Munde. New York: W. Radde. Available at https://archive.org/details/cu31924005227503.

Banerjee, Abhijit. 1992. A simple model of herd behaviour. *Quarterly Journal of Economics*, 107, 797–817.

Barry, Christian. 2011. Sovereign debt, human rights, and policy conditionality. *Journal of Political Philosophy*, 19, 282–305.

Barry, Christian, and Luara Ferracioli. 2016. Can withdrawing citizenship be justified?. *Political Studies*, 64, 1055–70.

Bauböck, Rainer. 1994. *Transnational Citizenship: Membership and Rights in International Migration*. Aldershot: Edward Elgar.

  2005. Expansive citizenship: voting beyond territory and membership. *PS: Political Science and Politics*, 38, 683–7.

  2007a. Political boundaries in a multilevel democracy. Pp. 85–109 in S. Benhabib and I. Shapiro (eds.), *Identities, Affiliations and Allegiances*. Cambridge: Cambridge University Press.

  2007b. Stakeholder citizenship and transnational political participation: a normative evaluation of external voting. *Fordham Law Review*, 75, 2393–447.

  2009. The rights and duties of external citizenship. *Citizenship Studies*, 13, 475–99.

  ed. 2010. Dual citizenship for transborder minorities? How to respond to the Hungarian-Slovak tit-for-tat. EUI Working Papers. Robert Schuman Centre for Advanced Studies, 75.

2015. Morphing the demos into the right shape: normative principles for enfranchising resident aliens and expatriate citizens. *Democratization*, 22, 820–39.

Bauböck, Rainer, and Christian Joppke, eds. 2010. How liberal are citizenship tests? EUI Working Papers, Robert Schuman Centre for Advanced Studies, 41.

Beckman, Ludvig. 2014. The subjects of collectively binding decisions: democratic inclusion and extraterritorial law. *Ratio Juris*, 27, 252–70.

Benhabib, Seyla. 2005. The right to have rights in contemporary Europe. Draft paper. Available at www.georgetown.edu/centers/cdacs/benhabibpaper.pdf.

Bentham, Jeremy. 2002. *The Collected Works of Jeremy Bentham: Rights, Representation, and Reform*, ed. Philip Schofield et al. Oxford: Clarendon Press.

Berger, Peter. 1970. On the obsolescence of the concept of honor. *European Journal of Sociology*, 11, 338–47.

Bertossi, Christophe, and Abdellali Hajjat. 2013. Country report: France. EUDO Citizenship Observatory, RSCAS/EUDO-CIT-CR 2013/4. San Domenico di Fiesole: European University Institute.

Bhagwati, Jagdish N. 1976. Taxing the brain drain. *Challenge*, 19, 34–8.

Bikhchandani, Sushil, et al. 1998. Learning from the behaviour of others: conformity, fads and informational cascades. *Journal of Economic Perspectives*, 12, 151–70.

Bitton, David. 1969. *The French Nobility in Crisis*. Stanford, CA: Stanford University Press.

Black, Duncan. 1948. On the rationale of group decision-making. *Journal of Political Economy*, 56, 23–34.

1998. *The Theory of Committees and Elections*. Boston, MA: Kluwer.

Blackstone, William. [1753] 1893. *Commentaries on the Laws of England in Four Books*, vol. 1. Philadelphia, PA: J. B. Lippincott.

Blais, André, Louis Massicotte, and Antoine Yoshinaka. 2001. Deciding who has the right to vote: a comparative analysis of election laws. *Electoral Studies*, 20, 41–62.

Blake, Michael. 2013. Immigration, jurisdiction, and exclusion. *Philosophy & Public Affairs*, 41, 103–30.

Blatter, Joachim. 2011. Dual citizenship and theories of democracy. *Citizenship Studies*, 15, 769–98.

2013. Dual citizenship and political participation. Paper presented at the Expert Seminar on Minorities and Migrants: Citizenship Policies and Political Participation. European University Institute in Florence. May 2–3. Available at http://eudo-citizenship.eu/images/docs/joachim%20blatter%20eui-hcnm.pdf.

Blatter, Joachim, and Andrea Schlenker. 2013. Between nationalism and globalism: spaces and forms of democratic citizenship in and for a post-Westphalian world. Working paper 6, Department of Political Science, University of Lucerne. Available at www.unilu.ch/fileadmin/shared/Publikationen/WP_Spaces-and-Forms-of-Democratic-Citizenship_Post-Westphalian-World.pdf.

Bibliography

Bloch, Jean-Richard. 1934. *L'Anoblissement en France au temps du François I: Essai d'une définition de la condition juridique et sociale de la noblesse au début du XVIe siècle*. Paris: Felix Alcan.

Bloemraad, Irene. 2004. Who claims dual citizenship? The limits of postnationalism, the possibilities of transnationalism and the persistence of traditional citizenship. *International Migration Review*, 38, 389–426.

Boll, Alfred M. 2007. *Multiple Nationality and International Law*. Leiden: Martinus Nijhoff.

Borjas, George J. 1995. The economic benefits from immigration. *Journal of Economic Perspectives*, 9, 3–22.

Bosniak, Linda S. 2001–2. Multiple nationality and the postnational transformation of citizenship. *Virginia Journal of International Law*, 42, 979–1004.

  2006. *The Citizen and the Alien: Dilemmas of Contemporary Membership*. Princeton, NJ: Princeton University Press.

Bostrom, Nick, and Julian Savulescu. 2009. *Human Enhancement*. Oxford: Oxford University Press.

Bowles, Samuel, and Herbert Gintis. 2011. *A Cooperative Species: Human Reciprocity and Its Evolution*. Princeton, NJ: Princeton University Press.

Brand, Laurie A. 2013. Arab uprising and the changing frontiers of transnational citizenship: voting from abroad in political transitions. *Political Geography*, 30, 1–10.

Brighouse, Harry, and Adam Swift. 2009. Legitimate parental partiality. *Philosophy & Public Affairs*, 37, 43–80.

Brochmann, Grete. 2013. Country report: Norway. EUDO Citizenship Observatory, RSCAS/EUDO-CIT-CR 2013/21. San Domenico di Fiesole: European University Institute.

Brock, Michael. 1973. *The Great Reform Act*. London: Hutchinson University Library.

Brown, Roger. 1986. *Social Psychology*. New York, NY: Free Press.

Brubaker, Rogers. 1992. *Citizenship and Nationhood in France and Germany*. Cambridge, MA: Harvard University Press.

Buchanan, Allen. 1995. Equal opportunity and genetic intervention. *Social Philosophy and Policy*, 12, 105–35.

Buchanan, James M. 1965. An economic theory of clubs. *Economica*, 32, 1–14.

Cain, Bruce E., and Brendan J. Doherty. 2006. The impact of dual nationality on political participation. Pp. 89–105 in Taeku Lee, S. Karthick Ramakrishnan, and Ricardo Ramirez (eds.), *Transforming Politics, Transforming America: The Political and Civic Incorporation of Immigrants in the United States*. Charlottesville, VA: University of Virginia Press.

Calhoun, Craig J. 2002. The class consciousness of frequent travellers: toward a critique of actually existing cosmopolitanism. *South Atlantic Quarterly*, 101, 869–97.

Canada Revenue Agency. Dispositions of property. Available at www.cra-arc.gc.ca/tx/nnrsdnts/ndvdls/dspstn-eng.html.

Caney, Simon. 2001. Cosmopolitan justice and equalizing opportunities. *Metaphilosophy*, 32, 113–34.

2006. *Justice beyond Borders: A Global Political Theory*. Oxford: Oxford University Press.
Carens, Joseph H. 1987. Aliens and citizens: the case for open borders. *Review of Politics*, 49, 251–73.
  1998. Why naturalization should be easy: a response to Noah Pickus. Pp. 141–6 in Noah Pickus (ed.), *Immigration and Citizenship in the Twenty-first Century*. Totowa, NJ: Rowman and Littlefield.
  2008. Rights of irregular migrants. *Ethics and International Affairs*, 22, 163–86.
  2010. *Immigrants and the Right to Stay*. Cambridge, MA: MIT Press.
  2013. *The Ethics of Immigration*. Oxford: Oxford University Press.
  2016. In defense of birthright citizenship. In Sarah Fine and Lea Ypi (eds.), *Migration in Political Theory: The Ethics of Movement and Membership*. Oxford: Oxford University Press.
Castles, Stephen, and Alastair Davidson. 2000. *Citizenship and Migration. Globalization and the Politics of Belonging*. Hampshire: Macmillan.
Cohen, Elizabeth F. 2009. *Semi-Citizenship in Democratic Politics*. Cambridge: Cambridge University Press.
Cohen, G. A. 1989. On the currency of egalitarian justice. *Ethics*, 99, 906–44.
  2009. *Why Not Socialism?* Princeton, NJ: Princeton University Press.
Cohen, Joshua. 1989. Deliberation and democratic legitimacy. Pp. 17–34 in Alan Hamlin and Philip Pettit (eds.), *The Good Polity*. Oxford: Blackwell.
Collier, Paul. 2013. *Exodus: How Migration Is Changing the World*. Oxford: Oxford University Press.
Collier, Paul, and Anke Hoeffler. 2000. Greed and grievances in Civil War. Policy Research Working Paper 2355. Washington, DC: World Bank.
Conrad, Naomi. 2014. Dual citizenship law takes effect in Germany. *Deutsche Welle*, December 19. Available at www.dw.com/en/dual-citizenship-law-takes-effect-in-germany/a-18143002.
Cook-Martin, David. 2013. *The Scramble for Citizens: Dual Nationality and State Competition for Immigrants*. Stanford, CA: Stanford University Press.
Cordelli, Chiara. 2015. Justice as fairness and relational resources. *Journal of Political Philosophy*, 23, 86–110.
Dawes, Robyn M., Jeanne McTavish, and Harriet Shaklee. 1977. Behavior, communication, and assumptions about other people's behavior in a commons dilemma situation. *Journal of Personality and Social Psychology*, 35, 1–11.
de Groot, Gerard-René. 2002. Conditions for acquisition of nationality by operation of law or by lodging a declaration of option. *Maastricht Journal of European and Comparative Law*, 9, 121–60.
  2003. The background of the changed attitude of Western European states with respect to multiple nationality. Pp. 99–119 in Atsushi Kondo and Charles Westin (eds.), *New Concepts of Citizenship: Residential/Regional Citizenship and Dual Nationality*. Stockholm: CEIFO.
de Groot, Gerard-René, and Marteen Vink. 2010. Loss of citizenship: trends and regulations in Europe. EUDO Citizenship Observatory, 4.
de Groot, Gerard-René, Maarten Vink, and Iseult Honohan. 2010. Loss of citizenship. EUDO Citizenship Policy Brief, 3. Available at http://eudo-citizenship.eu/docs/policy_brief_loss.pdf.

Bibliography

de Schutter, Helder, and Lea Ypi. 2015. Mandatory citizenship for immigrants. *British Journal of Political Science*, 45, 235–51.

Der Spiegel. 2013. Hit by the levy: Cyprus mulls citizenship offer for Russians. April 15. Available at www.spiegel.de/international/europe/cyprus-mulls-giving-russian-investors-citizenship-a-894409.html.

Dickinson, Edwin D. [1932] 1935. Jurisdiction with respect to crime. Reprinted in *American Journal of International Law*, 29 (Supplement), 439–651.

Doyle, Charles. 2012. *Extraterritorial Application of American Criminal Law, CRS Report for Congress 94–116*. Washington, DC: Congressional Research Service.

Dryzek, John S., and Christian List. 2003. Social choice theory and deliberative democracy: a reconciliation. *British Journal of Political Science*, 33, 1–28.

Dryzek, John S., and Simon Niemeyer. 2006. Reconciling pluralism and consensus as political ideals. *American Journal of Political Science*, 50, 634–49.

Dworkin, Ronald. 1981. What is equality? Part 1: Equality of welfare. *Philosophy and Public Affairs*, 10, 185–246.

  2000. *Sovereign Virtue*. Cambridge, MA: Harvard University Press.

  2003. Equality, luck and hierarchy. *Philosophy and Public Affairs*, 31, 190–8.

Dzankic, Jelena. 2012a. Citizenship by investment: can money buy citizenship? *EUDO Citizenship News*. February 15. Available at http://globalcit.eu/citizenship-by-investment-can-money-buy-citizenship/.

  2012b. The pros and cons of ius pecuniae: investor citizenship in comparative perspective. European University Institute working paper, Robert Schuman Centre for Advanced Studies, no. 14. San Domenico di Fiesole: European University Institute.

  2015. Investment-based citizenship and residence programmes in the EU. European University Institute working paper, Robert Schuman Centre for Advanced Studies, no. 8, January. San Domenico di Fiesole: European University Institute. Available at http://cadmus.eui.eu/bitstream/handle/1814/34484/RSCAS_2015_08.pdf.

Elster, Jon. 1986. The market and the forum. Pp. 103–32 in Jon Elster and Aanund Hylland (eds.), *Foundations of Social Choice Theory*. Cambridge: Cambridge University Press.

  2007. *Explaining Social Behaviour: More Nuts and Bolts for the Social Sciences*. Cambridge: Cambridge University Press.

Epstein, Richard. 1985. Why restrain alienation? *Columbia Law Review*, 85, 970–90.

Escobar, Cristina. 2004. Dual nationality and political participation: migrants in the interplay of United States and Colombian politics. *Latino Studies*, 2, 45–69.

Eslund, David. 2009. *Democratic Authority*. Princeton, NJ: Princeton University Press.

Etzioni, Amitai. 2007. Citizenship tests: a comparative, communitarian perspective. *Political Quarterly*, 78, 353–63.

EUDO Glossary on Citizenship and Nationality. N.d. Automatic loss of nationality. Available at http://globalcit.eu/glossary_citizenship_nationality/.

European Commission. 2008. Review of the transitional measures for the acquisition of agricultural real estate set out. Available at http://ec.europa.eu/internal_market/capital/docs/2008_0461_en.pdf.

European Commission for Democracy through Law (Venice Commission). 2011. Draft Report on Out-of-country Voting. No. 580/2010.
Faini, Riccardo. 2007. Remittances and the brain drain: do more skilled migrants remit more? *World Bank Economic Review*, 21, 177–91.
Faist, Thomas. 2001. Dual citizenship as overlapping membership. Willy Brandt Series of Working Papers in International Migration and Ethnic Relations, 3.
Faist, Thomas, and Jurgen Gerdes. 2008. Dual citizenship in an age of mobility. Migration Policy Institute. Available at www.migrationpolicy.org/research/dual-citizenship-age-mobility.
Faist, Thomas, and Peter Kivisto, eds. 2008. *Dual Citizenship in Global Perspective*. London: Palgrave Macmillan.
Falk, Richard. 1994. The making of global citizenship. Pp. 127–40 in Bart van Steenbergen (ed.), *The Condition of Citizenship*. London: Sage.
Farrar, C., J. S. Fishkin, D. P. Green, C. List, R. C. Luskin, and E. L. Paluck. 2010. Disaggregating deliberation's effects: an experiment within a Deliberative Poll. *British Journal of Political Science*, 40, 333–47.
Feldblum, Miriam. 2000. Managing membership: new trends in citizenship and nationality policy. Pp. 475–99 in T. A. Aleinikoff and D. Klusmeyer (eds.), *From Migrants to Citizens: Membership in a Changing World*. Washington, DC: Carnegie Endowment for International Peace.
Fishkin, James. 1983. *Justice, Equal Opportunity and the Family*. New Haven, CT: Yale University Press.
Frazer, Michael. 2014. Including the unaffected. *Journal of Political Philosophy*, 22, 377–95.
Frey, Bruno S., and Reiner Eichberger. 1999. *The New Democratic Federalism for Europe: Functional, Overlapping, and Competing Jurisdictions*. Cheltenham: Edward Elgar.
Friedrich, Daniel. 2013. A duty to adopt? *Journal of Applied Philosophy*, 30, 25–39.
Fuerstein, Michael. 2014. Democratic consensus as an essential byproduct. *Journal of Political Philosophy*, 22, 282–301.
Geyer, Georgie Anne. 1996. *American No More: The Death of Nationality*. New York, NY: Atlantic Monthly Press.
Gibney, Matthew J. 2013a. 'A very transcendental power': denaturalisation and the liberalisation of citizenship in the United Kingdom. *Political Studies*, 61, 637–55.
  2013b. Should citizenship be conditional? The ethics of denationalization. *Journal of Politics*, 75, 646–58.
Gibson, Diane, and Robert E. Goodin. 1999. The veil of vagueness: a model of institutional design. Pp. 357–85 in Morten Egeberg and Per Lægreid (eds.), *Organizing Political Institutions: Essays for Johan P. Olsen*. Oslo: Scandinavian University Press.
Gintis, Herbert, Eric Alden Smith, and Samuel Bowles. 2001. Costly signalling and cooperation. *Journal of Theoretical Biology*, 213, 103–19.
Glaeser, Edward. 2006. Paternalism and psychology. *University of Chicago Law Review*, 73, 133–56.

GLOBALCIT. 2016. Global database on modes of loss of citizenship: L05: acquisition of foreign citizenship. San Domenico di Fiesole: Global Citizenship Observatory, Robert Schuman Centre for Advanced Studies, European University Institute. Available at http://globalcit.eu/loss-of-citizenship/.

Goodin, Robert E. 1986. Laundering preferences. Pp. 75–102 in Jon Elster and Aanund Hylland (eds.), *Foundations of Social Choice Theory*. Cambridge: Cambridge University Press.

  1990. Property rights and preservationist duties. *Inquiry*, 33, 401–32.

  1992. *Motivating Political Morality*. Cambridge, MA: Blackwell.

  1993. Structures of political order: the relational feminist alternative. Pp. 498–522 in Ian Shapiro and Russell Hardin (eds.), *Political Order*. New York, NY: New York University Press.

  1995. Political ideals and political practice. *British Journal of Political Science*, 25, 37–56.

  1996. Inclusion and exclusion. *European Journal of Sociology*, 37, 343–71.

  1998. Communities of enlightenment. *British Journal of Political Science*, 28, 531–58.

  2004. Support with strings: workfare as an 'impermissible condition'. *Journal of Applied Philosophy*, 21, 297–308.

  2006. Liberal multiculturalism: protective and polyglot. *Political Theory*, 34, 289–303.

  2007. Enfranchising all affected interests, and its alternatives. *Philosophy & Public Affairs*, 35, 40–68.

  2016. Enfranchising all subjected, worldwide. *International Theory*, 8, 365–89.

Goodin, Robert E., and Michael Saward. 2005. Dog whistles and democratic mandates. *Political Quarterly*, 76, 471–6.

Goodin, Robert E., and Kai Spiekermann. 2018. *An Epistemic Theory of Democracy*. Oxford: Oxford University Press.

Goodin, Robert E., and Ana Tanasoca. 2014. Double voting. *Australasian Journal of Philosophy*, 92, 743–58.

Grace, Jeremy. 2004. Challenging the norms and standards of absentee voting. IFES, Working Paper. Available at www.ifes.org/files/Graceabsenteestandardsfinal.pdf.

Grofman, Bernard, and Scott L. Feld. 1988. Rousseau's general will: a Condorcetian perspective. *American Political Science Review*, 82, 567–76.

Grotius, Hugo. [1625] 2012. *On the Law of War and Peace*, ed. Steven Neff. Cambridge: Cambridge University Press.

Guardian. 2007. 'Cash-for-honours' timeline. October 11. Available at www.theguardian.com/politics/2007/oct/11/partyfunding.uk.

Guarnizo, Luis Eduardo, Alejandro Portes, and William Haller. 2003. Assimilation and transnationalism: determinants of transnational political action among contemporary migrants. *American Journal of Sociology*, 108, 1211–48.

Gutmann, Amy, and Denis Thompson. 1996. *Democracy and Disagreement*. Cambridge, MA: Belknap Press.

Haas, Peter M. 1992. Introduction: epistemic communities and international policy coordination. *International Organization*, 46, 1–35.
Habermas, Jürgen. 1995. Reconciliation through the public use of reason. *Journal of Philosophy*, 92, 109–31.
  1996. *Between Facts and Norms*. Cambridge, MA: MIT Press.
Halliday, Daniel. 2013. Is inheritance morally distinctive? *Journal of Law and Philosophy*, 32, 619–44.
Hammar, Tomas. 1985. Dual citizenship and political integration. *International Migration Review*, 19, 438–50.
  1990. *Democracy and the Nation State: Aliens, Denizens and Citizens in a World of International Migration*. Aldershot: Avebury.
Hansen, Randall. 2008. A new citizenship bargain for the age of mobility? Citizenship requirements in Europe and North America. Migration Policy Institute. Available at www.migrationpolicy.org/research/new-citizenship-bargain-age-mobility-citizenship-requirements-europe-and-north-america.
Hansen, Randall, and Patrick Weil, eds. 2002. *Dual Nationality, Social Rights and Federal Citizenship in the US and Europe*. New York, NY: Berghahn.
Hardin, Garrett. 1968. The tragedy of the commons. *Science*, 162, 1243–8.
Heath, Joseph. 2005. Rawls on global distributive justice: a defence. Pp. 193–26 in Daniel Weinstock (ed.), *Global Justice, Global Institutions*. Calgary: University of Calgary Press.
Held, David. 1995. *Democracy and the Global Order*. Cambridge: Polity Press.
Hill, William. 1915. My wife and my mother-in-law. *Puck*, 78, 11.
Hirsch, Fred. 1977. *Social Limits to Growth*. London: Routledge and Kegan Paul.
Hirschman, Albert O. 1970. *Exit, Voice, and Loyalty*. Cambridge, MA: Harvard University Press.
Honoré, Anthony M. 1961. Ownership. Pp. 107–47 in A. G. Guest (ed.), *Oxford Essays in Jurisprudence*. Oxford: Oxford University Press.
Huntington, Samuel. 2004. *Who Are We? The Challenges to America's National Identity*. New York, NY: Simon and Schuster.
International Institute for Democracy and Electoral Assistance (IDEA). 2007. Voting from Abroad Handbook. Available at www.idea.int/publications/voting_from_abroad/.
Jacobson, David. 1996. *Rights across Borders: Immigration and the Decline of Citizenship*. Baltimore, MD: Johns Hopkins University Press.
  1998–9. New border customs: migration and the changing role of the state. *UCLA Journal of International Law and Foreign Affairs*, 3, 443–53.
Jastrow, Joseph. 1899. The mind's eye. *Popular Science Monthly*, 54, 299–312.
Jonah, James O. C. 1981–2. Independence and integrity of the international civil service: the role of executive heads and the role of states. *NYU Journal of International Law and Politics*, 14, 841–59.
Jones-Correa, Michael. 2001. Under two flags: dual nationality in Latin America and its consequences for naturalization in the United States. *International Migration Review*, 35, 997–1029.
Joppke, Christian. 2010a. *Citizenship and Immigration*. Cambridge: Polity.
  2010b. The inevitable lightening of citizenship. *European Journal of Sociology*, 51, 9–32.

Bibliography

Just, Aida, and Christopher J. Anderson. 2011. Immigrants, citizenship and political action in Europe. *British Journal of Political Science*, 42, 481–509.

Kahneman, Daniel, and Amos Tversky. 1984. Choices, values, and frames. *American Psychologist*, 39, 341–50.

Kahneman, Daniel, Jack L. Knetsch, and Richard H. Thaler. 2000. Anomalies: the endowment effect, loss aversion, and status quo bias. Pp. 159–70 in Daniel Kahneman and Amos Tversky (eds.), *Choices, Values, and Frames*. Cambridge: Cambridge University Press.

Kalekin-Fishman, Devorah, and Pirkko Pitkänen, eds. 2007. *Multiple Citizenship as a Challenge to European Nation-States*. Rotterdam: Sense.

Kant, Immanuel. 2012. *Groundwork of the Metaphysics of Morals*, trans. and ed. Mary Gregor. New York, NY: Cambridge University Press.

Kantorowicz, Ernst. 1997. *The King's Two Bodies: A Study in Medieval Political Theology*. Princeton, NJ: Princeton University Press.

Kennedy, Maev. 2016. From Lloyd George to the lavender list: the history of honours scandals. *Guardian*, August 1. Available at www.theguardian.com/politics/2016/aug/01/from-lloyd-george-to-the-lavender-list-the-history-of-honours-scandals.

Kihlstrom, John. 2006. A new reversible figure and an old one. Paper presented at the annual meeting of the Society of Experimental Psychologists, La Jolla, CA.

Koenig-Archibugi, Mathias. 2012. Fuzzy citizenship in a global society. *Journal of Political Philosophy*, 20, 456–80.

Koinova, Maria. 2009. Diasporas and democratization in the post-communist world. *Communist and Post-Communist Studies*, 42, 41–64.

Kolodny, Niko. 2010. Which relationships justify partiality? The case of parents and children. *Philosophy & Public Affairs*, 38, 37–75.

Kornhauser, Lewis A., and Lewis G. Sager. 1993. The one and the many: adjudication in collegial courts. *California Law Review*, 81, 1–59.

2004. The many as one: integrity and group choice in paradoxical choice. *Philosophy and Public Affairs*, 32, 249–76.

Kovatch, William J. Jr. 2000. Recognizing foreign tax judgments: an argument for the revocation of the revenue rule. *Houston Journal of International Law*, 22, 265–86.

Kruger, Thalia, and Jinske Verhellen. 2011. Dual nationality=double trouble? *Journal of Private International Law*, 7, 601–26.

Kuran, Timur. 1998. Ethnic norms and their transformation through reputational cascades. *Journal of Legal Studies*, 27, 623–59.

Kuran, Timur, and Cass Sunstein.1999. Availability cascades and risk regulation. *Stanford Law Review*, 51, 683–768.

Lafleur, Jean-Michel. 2015. The enfranchisement of citizens abroad: variations and explanations. *Democratization*, 22, 840–60.

Landemore, Hélène. 2013. *Democratic Reason*. Princeton, NJ: Princeton University Press.

Lazar, Seth. 2010. A liberal defence of (some) duties to compatriots. *Journal of Applied Philosophy*, 27, 246–57.

Le Roux, Nicolas. 2011. L'épreuve de la vertu. Condition nobiliaire et légitimation de l'honorabilité au XVIe siècle. Paper presented at the Conference on Les vecteurs de l'idéel. La Légitimité implicite, organized by Laboratoire de Médiévistique Occidentale Paris, Rome, December 14–17.

League of Nations. 1930. *Convention on Certain Questions Related to the Conflict of Nationality Law*, April 13, League of Nations, Treaty Series, vol. 179, p. 89, no. 4137. Available at www.refworld.org/docid/3ae6b3b00.html%3E.

Legal Information Institute. US Code. Title 26, Internal revenue code. §877, Expatriation to avoid tax. Available at www.law.cornell.edu/uscode/text/26/877.

US Code. Title 26, Internal revenue code. §877A. Tax responsibilities of expatriation. Available at www.law.cornell.edu/uscode/text/26/877A.

Lenard, Patti. 2018. Democratic citizenship and denationalization. *American Political Science Review*, 112, 99–111.

Letter of Thomas Arundell to Lord Cecil. 1603. *The Cecil Papers*, CP. 187/93. Available at http://cecilpapers.chadwyck.com/search/displayItem.do?QueryType=articles&ResultsID=141BCB39F4F11CC27F&filterSequence=0&ItemNumber=1&ItemID=15_0480.

Lewis, David K. 1969. *Convention*. Cambridge, MA: Harvard University Press.

Lipset, Seymour Martin, and Stein Rokkan, eds. 1967. *Party Systems and Voter Alignments*. New York: Free Press.

List, Christian. 2002. Two concepts of agreement. *The Good Society*, 11, 72–9.

2011a. Group deliberation and the revision of judgments: an impossibility result. *Journal of Political Philosophy*, 19, 1–27.

2011b. The logical space of democracy. *Philosophy and Public Affairs*, 39, 262–97.

2012. The theory of judgment aggregation: an introductory review. *Synthese*, 187, 179–207.

List, Christian, and Robert E. Goodin. 2001. Epistemic democracy: generalizing the Condorcet Jury Theorem. *Journal of Political Philosophy*, 3, 277–306.

List, Christian, and Philip Pettit. 2004. Aggregating sets of judgments: two impossibility results compared. *Synthese*, 140, 207–35.

List, Christian, Robert C. Luskin, James S. Fishkin, and Ian McLean. 2013. Deliberation, single-peakedness, and the possibility of meaningful democracy: evidence from deliberative polls. *Journal of Politics*, 75, 80–95.

Lister, Andrew. 2013. Reciprocity, relationships and distributive justice. *Social Theory and Practice*, 39, 70–94.

Locke, John. [1690]1764. *Two Treatises of Government*, ed. Thomas Hollis. London: A. Millar et al.

Long, Gerald M., and Thomas C. Toppino. 2003. Enduring interest in perceptual ambiguity: alternating views of reversible figures. *Psychological Bulletin*, 130, 748–68.

López-Guerra, Claudio. 2005. Should expatriates vote? *Journal of Political Philosophy*, 13, 216–34.

Luskin, Robert C., and James S. Fishkin. 2002. Deliberation and 'better citizens'. Center for Deliberative Democracy, Stanford University. Available at http://cdd.stanford.edu/research/papers/2002/bettercitizens.pdf.

Machiavelli, Niccolò. [1532] 1882. *The Prince*. In *The Historical, Political, and Diplomatic Writings of Niccolò Machiavelli*, trans. Christian E. Detmold, vol. II. Boston, MA: J. R. Osgood and Co.

Mahncke, Julia, and Christian Ignatzi. 2013. European citizenship sold to the super wealthy. *Deutsche Welle*, November 15. Available at www.dw.de/european-citizenship-sold-to-the-super-wealthy/a-16756198.

Maine, Henry Sumner. 1901. *Ancient Law*, 17th ed. London: John Murray.
  1977. *Ancient Law*. New York: E. P. Dutton & Co.

March, James G., and Johan O. Olsen. 2009. The logic of appropriateness. Pp. 478–97 in Robert E. Goodin (ed.), *Oxford Handbook of Political Science*. Oxford: Oxford University Press.

Marcussen, Martin. 2004a. The Organization for Economic Cooperation and Development as ideational artist and arbitrator. Pp. 90–106 in Bob Reinalda and Bertjan Verbeek (eds.), *Decision Making Within International Organizations*. London: Routledge.
  2004b. OECD governance through soft law. Pp. 103–28 in Ulrika Mörth (ed.), *Soft Law in Governance and Regulation*. Cheltenham: Edward Elgar.

Martin, David A. 1999. New rules on dual nationality for a democratizing globe: between rejection and embrace. *Georgetown Immigration Law Journal*, 14, 1–34.
  2002. New rules for dual nationality. Pp. 36–60 in Randall Hansen and Patrick Weil (eds.), *Dual Nationality, Social Rights, and Federal Citizenship in the US and Europe*. New York: Berghahn.
  2014. Dual citizenship: reflections on Theodore Roosevelt's 'self-evident absurdity'. *Virginia Public Law and Legal Theory Research Paper*, 58. Available at http://papers.ssrn.com/sol3/papers.cfm?abstract_id=2500463.

Martin, David A., and Kay Hailbronner, eds. 2003. *Right and Duties of Dual Nationals*. New York, NY: Kluwer Law International.

Marx, Karl. 1973. *Grundrisse*, trans. Martin Nicolaus. Harmondsworth: Penguin.

Mathias, Albert, David Jacobson, and Yosef Lapid, eds. 2001. *Identities, Borders, Orders*. Minneapolis, MN: University of Minnesota Press.

Mayes, Charles R. 1957. The sale of peerages in early Stuart England. *Journal of Modern History*, 29, 21–37.

McGraw, Peter, Jeff T. Larsen, Daniel Kahneman, and David Schkade. 2010. Comparing gains and losses. *Psychological Science*, 21, 1438–45.

Mill, John Stuart. [1861] 1975. *Considerations on Representative Government*. In *Three Essays on Liberty*. Oxford: Oxford University Press.

Millbank, Adrienne. 2000–1. Dual citizenship in Australia. Canberra Parliamentary Library, *Current Issues Brief*, 5. Available at www.aph.gov.au/About_Parliament/Parliamentary_Departments/Parliamentary_Library/Publications_Archive/CIB/cib0001/01CIB05.

Miller, David. 1995. *On Nationality*. Oxford: Clarendon Press.
  2005. Against global egalitarianism. *Journal of Ethics*, 9, 55–79.
  2009. Democracy's dominion. *Philosophy & Public Affairs*, 37, 201–28.
  2010. Why immigration controls are not coercive: a reply to Arash Abizadeh. *Political Theory*, 38, 111–20.

Mitchell, Daniel J. 2012. Acting as the Typhoid Mary of the global economy, the OECD urges higher taxes in Latin America. Cato Institute. February 7.

Available at www.cato.org/blog/acting-typhoid-mary-global-economy-oecd-urges-higher-taxes-latin-america.
Mitroff, Stephen, David Sobel, and Alison Gopnik. 2006. Reversing how to think about ambiguous figure reversals: spontaneous alternating by uninformed observers. *Perception*, 35, 709–15.
Morton, Jennifer. 2014. Cultural code-switching: straddling the achievement gap. *Journal of Political Philosophy*, 22, 259–81.
Murphy, Daniel. 1967. Statutory regulation of inheritance by nonresident aliens. *Villanova Law Review*, 13, 148–69.
Nicolaas, Han. 2009. New statistical data on dual citizens in the Netherlands. European Union Democracy Observatory on Citizenship. Available at http://eudo-citizenship.eu/index.php?option=com_content&view=article&id=197:new-statistical-data-on-dual-citizens-in-the-netherlands&catid=5:news&Itemid=7.
Niemeyer, Simon, and John S. Dryzek. 2007. The ends of deliberation: meta-consensus and inter-subjective rationality as ideal outcomes. *Swiss Political Science Review*, 13, 497–526.
Niemi, Richard. 1969. Majority decision-making with partial unidimensionality. *American Political Science Review*, 63, 488–97.
Noaksson, Niklas, and Kerstin Jacobsson. 2003. The production of ideas and expert knowledge in OECD. The OECD jobs strategy in contrast with the EU employment strategy. SCORE Reports, 7. Available at http://eucenter.wisc.edu/OMC/Papers/EES/noakssonJacobsson.pdf.
Oberman, Kieran. 2016. Immigration as a human right. Pp. 32–56 in Sarah Fine and Lea Ypi (eds.), *Migration in Political Theory*. Oxford: Oxford University Press.
OECD. 2010. Model Tax Convention. Available at www.keepeek.com/Digital-Asset-Management/oecd/taxation/model-tax-convention-on-income-and-on-capital-2010_9789264175181-en.
  2012. OECD Strategy on Development. Meeting of the OECD Council at Ministerial Level, Paris, May 23–24. Available at www.oecd.org/development/50452316.pdf.
  n.d. The OECD and the Millennium Development Goals. Available at www.oecd.org/dac/theoecdandthemillenniumdevelopmentgoals.htm.
Oeter, Stefan. 2003. Effect of nationality and dual nationality on judicial cooperation, including treaty regimes such as extradition. Pp. 55–77 in D. Martin and K. Hailbronner (eds.), *Rights and Duties of Dual Nationals*. The Hague: Kluwer.
Okun, Arthur M. 1975. *Equality and Efficiency, the Big Tradeoff*. Washington, DC: Brookings Institution.
Oltermann, Philip. 2016. Austria rejects far-right candidate Norbert Hofer in presidential election. *Guardian*, December 4, available at www.theguardian.com/world/2016/dec/04/far-right-party-concedes-defeat-in-austrian-presidential-election.
Orbell, John M., Alphonse J. C. van de Kragt, and Robyn M. Dawes. 1988. Explaining discussion-induced cooperation in social dilemmas. *Journal of Personality and Social Psychology*, 54, 811–19.

Orfield, Lester B. 1949. The legal effects of dual nationality. *George Washington Law Review*, 17, 427–45.
Orgad, Liav. 2010. Illiberal liberalism: cultural restrictions on migration and access to citizenship in Europe. *American Journal of Comparative Law*, 58, 53–106.
Østergaard-Nielsen, Eva. 2008. Dual citizenship: policy trends and political participation in EU member states. Directorate-General Internal Policies Policy Department C Citizens' Rights and Constitutional Affairs. European Parliament. PE 408.299.
Owen, David. 2010. Resident aliens, non-resident citizens and voting rights. Pp. 52–73 in Gideon Calder et al. (eds.), *Citizenship Acquisition and National Belonging*. Basingstoke: Palgrave.
  2011. Transnational citizenship and the democratic state. *Critical Review of International Social and Political Philosophy*, 14, 641–63.
Parfit, Derek. 1997. Equality and priority. *Ratio*, 10, 202–21.
Perez v. Brownell. 1958. 356 U.S. 44 (1958). Available at https://supreme.justia.com/cases/federal/us/356/44/case.html.
Peter, Laurence. 2013. EU shrugs off European race to woo rich foreigners. *BBC News*, November 18. Available at www.bbc.co.uk/news/world-europe-24940012.
Pettit, Philip. 1997. *Republicanism: A Theory of Freedom and Government*. Oxford: Clarendon Press.
  2001. Deliberative democracy and the discursive dilemma. *Philosophical Issues*, 11, 268–99.
Pitkänen, Pirkko, and Devorah Kalekin-Fishman, eds. 2007. *Multiple State Membership and Citizenship in the Era of Transnational Migration*. Rotterdam: Sense.
Pocock, J. G. A. 1987. *The Ancient Constitution and the Feudal Law*. Cambridge: Cambridge University Press.
Pogge, Thomas. 2001. Eradicating systematic poverty: brief for a global resources dividend. *Journal of Human Development*, 2, 59–77.
  2002. *World Poverty and Human Rights*. Cambridge: Polity.
Prak, Maarten. 1997. Burghers into citizens: urban and national citizenship in the Netherlands during the revolution era (c. 1800). *Theory and Society*, 26, 403–20.
Prokic, Tijana, Maarten Vink, Derek Hutcheson, and Kristin Jeffers. 2013. Citizenship acquisition and political participation of immigrants in Europe. Paper presented at the HCNM-EUI conference on Minorities and Migrants: Citizenship Policies and Political Participation, May 2–3, European University Institute in Florence.
Quong, Jonathan. 2011. *Liberalism Without Perfection*. Oxford: Oxford University Press.
  2013a. On the idea of public reason. Pp. 265–80 in Jon Mandle and David A. Reidy (eds.), *A Companion to Rawls*. Hoboken, NJ: John Wiley and Sons.
  2013b. Public reason. In Edward Zalta (ed.), *Stanford Encyclopedia of Philosophy*. Available at http://plato.stanford.edu/archives/sum2013/entries/public-reason/.

Radin, Margaret Jane. 1987. Market inalienability. *Harvard Law Review*, 100, 1849–937.
  1996. *Contested Commodities*. Cambridge, MA: Harvard University Press.
Rahn, Richard. 2012. Rise of the global tax collectors: Congress is giving international bureaucrats the power to intrude. *Washington Times*, July 9. Available at www.washingtontimes.com/news/2012/jul/9/rise-of-the-global-tax-collectors/.
Ramakrishnan, S. Karthick. 2005. *Democracy in Immigrant America: Changing Demographics and Political Participation*. Stanford, CA: Stanford University Press.
Rawls, John. 1971. *A Theory of Justice*. Cambridge, MA: Harvard University Press.
  1993. *Political Liberalism*. New York, NY: Columbia University Press.
  1997. The idea of public reason revisited. *University of Chicago Law Review*, 64, 765–807.
  2000. *A Theory of Justice*, rev. ed. Oxford: Oxford University Press.
Renshon, Stanley. 2001. *Dual Citizenship and American National Identity*. Washington, DC: Center for Immigration Studies.
Revlin, Russell. 2012. *Cognition Theory and Practice*. New York, NY: Worth.
Riker, William H. 1982. *Liberalism against Populism*. Prospect Heights, IL: Waveland Press.
Roche, John P. 1951. Loss of American nationality: the year of confusion. *Western Political Quarterly*, 4, 268–94.
Roemer, John E. 1996. *Theories of Distributive Justice*. Cambridge, MA: Harvard University Press.
Roikanen, Juusi Kasperi. 2011. Mononationals, hyphenationals, and shadow-nationals: multiple citizenship as practice. *Citizenship Studies*, 15, 247–63.
Rokkan, Stein. 1999. *State Formation, Nation-Building, and Mass Politics in Europe: The Theory of Stein Rokkan*, ed. Peter Flora with Stein Kunhle and Derek Urwin. Oxford: Oxford University Press.
Rose-Ackerman, Susan. 1985. Inalienability and the theory of property rights. *Columbia Law Review*, 85, 931–69.
Ross, Lee, and Richard Nisbett. 2011. *The Person and the Situation: Perspectives of Social Psychology*. London: Pinter and Martin.
Rubio-Marin, Ruth. 2000. *Immigration as a Democratic Challenge*. Cambridge: Cambridge University Press.
Rumbaut, Ruben. 1994. The crucible within: ethnic identity, self-esteem and segmented assimilation among children of immigrants. *International Migration Review*, 28, 748–94.
Sandel, Michael J. 2009. *The Case against Perfection*. Cambridge, MA: Harvard University Press.
  2012. *What Money Can't Buy: The Moral Limits of Markets*. New York, NY: Farrar, Straus and Giroux.
Sandelson, Michael. 2013. Australian-Norwegian couple fight officialdom for children's dual nationality right. *The Foreigner*, July 29. Available at http://theforeigner.no/pages/news/australian-norwegian-couple-fight-officialdom-for-childrens-dual-nationality-right/.

Sangiovanni, Andrea. 2011. Global justice and the moral arbitrariness of birth. *The Monist*, 94, 571–83.
Sassen, Saskia. 1996. *Losing Control? Sovereignty in the Age of Globalization.* New York, NY: Columbia University Press.
  1999. *Globalization and Its Discontents.* New York, NY: New Press.
  2002a. The repositioning of citizenship: emergent subjects and spaces for politics. *Berkeley Journal of Sociology*, 46, 4–25.
  2002b. Toward post-national and denationalized citizenship. Pp. 277–92 in Engin F. Isin and Bryan S. Turner (eds.), *Handbook of Citizenship Studies.* London: Sage.
Satz, Debra. 2010. *Why Some Things Should Not Be for Sale: The Moral Limits of Markets.* New York, NY: Oxford University Press.
Scharpf, Fritz H. 1999. *Governing in Europe: Effective and Democratic?* Oxford: Oxford University Press.
Scheffler, Samuel. 1997. Relationships and responsibilities. *Philosophy and Public Affairs*, 26, 189–209.
Schmidt, Vivien A. 2013. Democracy and legitimacy in the European Union revisited: input, output and 'throughput'. *Political Studies*, 61, 2–22.
Schmitter, Philippe. 1997. Exploring the problematic triumph of liberal democracy and concluding with a modest proposal for improving its international impact. Pp. 297–307 in Axel Hadenius (ed.), *Democracy's Victory and Crisis.* Nobel Symposium no. 93. Cambridge: Cambridge University Press.
Schofield, Philip. 2004. Jeremy Bentham, the French Revolution and political radicalism. *History of European Ideas*, 30, 381–401.
Schuck, Peter H. 1998. *Citizens, Strangers, and In-Betweens: Essays on Immigration and Citizenship.* Boulder, CO: Westview Press.
Schuck, Peter H., and Roger Smith. 1985. *Citizenship Without Consent: Illegal Aliens in the American Polity.* New Haven, CT: Yale University Press.
Sears, D. O., and S. Levy. 2003. Childhood and adult political development. Pp. 60–109 in D. O. Sears, L. Huddy, and R. Jervis (eds.), *Oxford Handbook of Political Psychology.* New York, NY: Oxford University Press.
Sejersen, Tanja. 2008. 'I vow to thee my countries': the expansion of dual citizenship in the twenty-first century. *International Migration Review*, 42, 523–49.
Shachar, Ayelet. 2009. *The Birthright Lottery: Citizenship and Global Inequality.* Cambridge, MA: Harvard University Press.
Shachar, Ayelet, and Ran Hirschl. 2014. On citizenship, states, and markets. *Journal of Political Philosophy*, 22, 231 57.
Shain, Yossy. 1999. *Marketing the American Creed Abroad.* Cambridge: Cambridge University Press.
Singer, Peter. 1972. Famine, affluence and morality. *Philosophy and Public Affairs*, 1, 229–43.
Smith, Jay M. 1996. *The Culture of Merit.* Ann Arbor, MI: University of Michigan Press.
Somin, Ilya. 2017. The case for keeping DACA. *Washington Post*, September 4. Available at www.washingtonpost.com/news/volokh-conspiracy/wp/2017/09/04/the-case-for-daca/?utm_term=.71bd4e77046a.

Song, Sarah. 2016. The significance of territorial presence and the rights of immigrants. In Sarah Fine and Lea Ypi (eds.), *Migration in Legal and Political Theory*. Oxford: Oxford University Press.

Soysal, Yasemin Nuhoglu. 1994. *Limits of Citizenship: Migrants and Postnational Membership in Europe*. Chicago, IL: University of Chicago Press.

  1996. Changing citizenship in Europe: remarks on postnational membership and the national state. Pp. 17–29 in David Cesarani and Mary Fulbrook (eds.), *Citizenship, Nationality and Migration in Europe*. London: Routledge.

  2004. Postnational citizenship: reconfiguring the familiar terrain. Pp. 333–42 in Kate Nash and Alan Scott (eds.), *The Blackwell Companion to Political Sociology*. Malden, MA: Blackwell.

  2011. Postnational citizenship: rights and obligations of individuality. *Heirich Böll Stiftung Migrationspolitisches Portal*. Available at http://heimatkunde.boell.de/2011/05/18/postnational-citizenship-rights-and-obligations-individuality.

Spiro, Peter J. 1997. Dual nationality and the meaning of citizenship. *Emory Law Journal*, 46, 1411–85.

  1998–9. Questioning barriers to naturalization. *Georgetown Immigration Law Journal*, 13, 479–520.

  2008a. *Beyond Citizenship: American Identity after Globalization*. New York, NY: Oxford University Press.

  2008b. Dual citizenship: a postnational view. Pp. 189–202 in Thomas Faist and Peter Kivisto (eds.), *Dual Citizenship in Global Perspective*. London: Palgrave Macmillan.

  2010. Dual citizenship as human right. *International Journal of Constitutional Law*, 8, 111–30.

  2016. *At Home in Two Countries: The Past and Future of Dual Citizenship*. New York, NY: New York University Press.

Spiro, Peter J., and Peter H. Schuck. 1998. Dual citizens, good Americans. *Wall Street Journal*, March 18.

Staton, Jeffrey K., Robert A. Jackson, and Damarys Canache. 2007a. Costly citizenship? Dual nationality, institutions, naturalization, and political connectedness. Available at http://ssrn.com/abstract=995569 or http://dx.doi.org/10.2139/ssrn.995569.

  2007b. Dual nationality among Latinos: what are the implications for political-connectedness? *Journal of Politics*, 69, 470–82.

Stone, Lawrence, 1958. The inflation of honours 1558–1641. *Past and Present*, 14, 45–70.

Sunstein, Cass R. 1995. Incompletely theorized agreements. *Harvard Law Review*, 108, 1733–72.

  2000. Deliberative trouble? Why groups go to extremes. *Yale Law Journal*, 110, 71–119.

  2001. Switching the default rule. Working paper no. 114, John M. Olin Program in Law and Economics.

  2002. The law of group polarization. *Journal of Political Philosophy*, 10, 175–95.

  2013a. Deciding by default. *University of Pennsylvania Law Review*, 162, 1–57.

2013b. *Simpler: The Future of Government*. New York, NY: Simon and Schuster.

Swinnen, Johan, and Liesbet Vranken. 2008. Review of the transitional restrictions maintained by new member states on the acquisition of agricultural real estates. Centre for European Policy Studies. Available at http://ec.europa.eu/internal_market/capital/docs/study_en.pdf.

Tan, Kok-Chor. 2011. Luck, institutions, and global distributive justice: a defence of global luck egalitarianism. *European Journal of Political Theory*, 10, 1394–421.

Tanasoca, Ana. 2014. Double taxation, multiple citizenship and global inequality. *Moral Philosophy and Politics*, 1, 147–69.

  n.d. Enfranchising unaffected interests and the quest for impartiality. Unpublished manuscript.

Thaler, Richard H., and Cass R. Sunstein. 2009. *Nudge: Improving Decisions about Health, Health, and Happiness*. London: Penguin.

Tobin, James. 1970. On limiting the domain of inequality. *Journal of Law and Economics*, 13, 263–77.

  1974. *The New Economics, One Decade Older*. Princeton, NJ: Princeton University Press.

Toppino, Thomas C. 2003. Reversible-figure perception: mechanisms of intentional control. *Perception and Psychophysics*, 65, 1285–95.

Toppino, Thomas C., and Gerald M. Long. 2005. Top-down and bottom-up processes in the perception of reversible figures: toward a hybrid model. Pp. 37–58 in N. Ohta, C. M. Macleod, and B. Uttl (eds.), *Dynamic Cognitive Processes*. Tokyo: Springer-Verlag.

Trachtman, Joel P. 2017. Fragmentation of citizenship governance. Pp. 500–620 in A. Shachar, R. Bauböck, I. Bloemraad, and M. Vink (eds.), *The Oxford Handbook of Citizenship*. Oxford: Oxford University Press.

Tribe, Laurence H. 1985. The abortion funding conundrum: inalienable rights, affirmative duties, and the dilemma of dependence. *Harvard Law Review*, 99, 330–43.

Trivers, Robert L. 1971. The evolution of reciprocal altruism. *Quarterly Review of Biology*, 46, 35–57.

Tversky, Amos, and Daniel Kahneman. 1981. The framing of decisions and the psychology of choice. *Science*, 211, 453–8.

UN Refugee Agency. N.d. Stateless people. Available at www.unhcr.org/pages/49c3646c155.html.

United Nations. 1948. Universal Declaration of Human Rights. Adopted in Paris, 10 December 1948. Available at www.un.org/en/universal-declaration-human-rights/.

US Office of Personnel Management. 2001. Citizenship laws of the world survey. Available at www.multiplecitizenship.com/worldsummary.html.

US Code. Title 26: Internal Revenue Code. Available at www.law.cornell.edu/uscode/text/26.

Vallier, Kevin. 2011. Convergence and consensus in public reason. *Public Affairs Quarterly*, 25, 261–79.

Vallier, Kevin, and Fred D'Agostino. 2013. Public justification. In Edward Zalta (ed.), *Stanford Encyclopedia of Philosophy*. Available at http://plato.stanford.edu/archives/spr2014/entries/justification-public/.

van Gunsteren, Herman. 1998. *A Theory of Citizenship: Organizing Plurality in Contemporary Democracies*. Boulder, CO: Westview Press.

Velleman, David. 1992. The guise of Good. *Noûs*, 26, 3–36.

Vink, Maarten P. 2013. Immigrant integration and access to citizenship in the European Union: the role of origin countries. INTERACT Research Report, Robert Schuman Centre for Advanced Studies. San Domenico di Fiesole (FI): European University Institute.

Vink, Maarten P., and Gerard-René de Groot. 2010. Birthright citizenship: trends and regulations in Europe. EUDO Citizenship Observatory, no. 8. Robert Schuman Centre for Advanced Studies. San Domenico di Fiesole (FI): European University Institute.

Vonk, Olivier W. 2012. *Dual Nationality in the European Union*. Leiden: Brill.

Vrousalis, Nicholas. 2012. Jazz bands, camping trips and decommodification: G. A. Cohen on community. *Socialist Studies*, 8, 141–63.

Waldron, Jeremy. 1985. What is private property? *Oxford Journal of Legal Studies*, 5, 313–49.

2000. What is cosmopolitan? *Journal of Political Philosophy*, 8, 227–43.

Wall, Steven. 2010. On justificatory liberalism. *Politics, Philosophy and Economics*, 9, 123–49.

Walzer, Michael. 1983. *Spheres of Justice: A Defense of Pluralism and Equality*. Oxford: M. Robertson.

Weil, Patrick. 2002. L'accès à la citoyenneté: Une comparaison de vingt-cinq lois sur la nationalité. Pp. 9–28 in Travaux du Centre d'Études et de Prévision du Ministère de l'Intérieur, Nationalité et Citoyenneté. *Nouvelle donne d'un espace européen*, 5.

Weinstock, Daniel M. 2010. On voting ethics for dual nationals. Pp. 177–95 in Keith Breen and Shane O'Neill (eds.), *After the Nation? Critical Reflections on Nationalism and Postnationalism*. Basingstoke: Palgrave.

Wellman, Christopher. 2008. Immigration and the freedom of association. *Ethics*, 119, 109–41.

Whelan, Frederick G. 1983. Prologue: democratic theory and the boundary problem. Pp. 13–47 in J. R. Pennock and J. W. Chapman (eds.), *Nomos: Liberal Democracy*. New York, NY: New York University Press.

Willis, Lauren E. 2013. When nudges fail: slippery defaults. *University of Chicago Law Review*, 80, 1155–229.

World Bank. 2001. GDP per capita (current US$). Available at https://data.worldbank.org/indicator/NY.GDP.PCAP.CD?end=2001&page=2%3E.&start=1960.

Yang, Phillip Q. 1994. Explaining immigrant naturalization. *International Migration Review*, 28, 449–77.

Index

adaptive preferences. *See* multiple citizenship, adaptive preferences and
adoption, 31
affected interests. *See also* unaffected interests
  birthright multiple citizenship and, 120–1
  boundary problem and, 12, 83, 113–16
  citizenship renunciation and, 121
  dead or dying, 121–2
  direction of fit and, 122–3
  expensive tastes and, 122
  Goodin on, 130
  multiple citizenship and, 119–24, 129
  possible and potential, 121
  strategically cultivated, 122–4, 134
  unbundling citizenship rights and, 131–2, 169
Australia, 18–19, 23, 25, 28–9
Australian Bureau of Statistics, 1
Austria
  investor citizenship in, 57, 127
  2016 presidential election in, 104–5

Bancroft treaties, 2–3
Bauböck, Rainer, 28, 52–3, 114
  on citizenship rights, 131, 168
  on instrumental interests, 123
  on overinclusion, underinclusion, 172
  on voting, 167–8
Bentham, Jeremy, 119, 126–7
birthright citizenship, 10, 17–18, 28, 80. *See also jus sanguinis; jus soli*
  affected interests and, 120–1
  boundary problem and, 112–13
  Carens on, 23–4
  democracy conflicting with, 33
  efficiency principle and, 20–2, 24–5
  as entitlement, 22–3
  identity, right to, and, 31–2
  inequality and, 31, 33–4
  minimal global equality guaranteed by, 22

  moral justification of, 20, 26–8
  reforming, 34–5
  residence and, 27, 35
  as self-fulfilling prophecy, 25–7, 34
  statelessness and, 20–1
  tribalism of, 33
Black, Duncan, 90
Blackstone, William, 2, 24, 139
Blatter, Joachim, 164
Bosniak, Linda S., 158, 160
boundary problem, 112, 131
  affected interests principle and, 12, 83, 113–16
  birthright citizenship and, 112–13
  legally subjected principle and, 12, 83, 113–14, 116–17
  multiple citizenship and, 112–13, 116, 129–30, 163
  political overinclusiveness and, 113
  political rights-sine-citizenship and, 130–1
  unaffected interests principle and, 12, 83, 113–14, 117–19
  unbundling citizenship rights and, 12, 131–3, 163–4, 172
  voting rights and, 12
Brexit, 104–5, 171
bystander effect, 24

Calhoun, Craig, 144
Carens, Joseph, 23
  on birthright citizenship, 23–4
  on citizenship and feudal privilege, 23, 30, 79
  on citizenship and justice, 22–3
  on common identity, citizenship and, 30–1
  on *jus soli*, 25–6
  on naturalization, entitlement to, 43
  opting in and, 50
  on renunciation, 38
Cato Institute, 156

Index

citizenship, 63, 164. *See also* global citizenship; mono-nationality
 acquisition (*See* birthright citizenship; investor citizenship; naturalization)
 allocation of, 20–1, 26, 32, 35, 74–5
 character and, 69–70
 of choice, 37–8, 43, 50–4, 162–3
 common identity and, 30–1
 common reference frames and, 98–9
 of convenience, 38, 53–4
 debasement, devaluation of, 72–5, 159, 162
 deliberation and, 97–9
 as democratically deficient institution, 23
 distributive justice and, 12, 29–30
 effective, 176–7
 egalitarianism of, 71
 as entitlement, 22–3
 external, 86–7
 feudal privilege and, 23, 30, 79–80
 global, 7, 52
 honorary, 56–7, 126–7
 as human right, 20–2, 72–4, 172
 ideal of, 80
 inheritance rights and, 39
 loss of, 38, 40
 as lottery, 28, 135
 meaning of, 33, 72–5
 non-resident, 117, 124–6, 132
 political basis of, 33
 as property, 30, 32
 renewal of, 34–5, 129, 162
 restoration of, 15
 rigidity of, 129–30
 signalling and, 68–72
 as social construction, 15, 23
 social value of, 72–5
citizenship, withdrawal of, 32, 38, 121
citizenship renunciation, 38–9, 43–4, 52
 affected interests and, 121
 consistency of, 41–3
 equality and, 41–2
 harmfulness of, 39
 immigrant interests and, 45
 legally subjected principle and, 125–6
 legitimate state powers and, 44
 loss aversion bias and, 46–7, 51–2
 other naturalization requirements, compared to, 43
 political rights and, 39
 unbundling citizenship rights and, 40–1
citizenship-by-investment. *See* investor citizenship
citizenship-sine-political rights.
 See unbundling citizenship rights
code-switching, 105

Cohen, Elizabeth F., 164–5
Cohen, G. A., 64–5
collective decision-making, 4, 8–9.
 See also public reason theories
 aggregating judgments in, 90–2
 aggregating preferences in, 90
 aggregating reasons in, 90–2
 bounded disagreement and, 86, 93
 collective rationality and, 11–12, 85–6, 89, 91, 93, 97, 99–106, 109–11
 common reference frames and, 11–12, 85–6, 93, 96–9, 104–10
 Condorcet, Jury Theorem of, 89
 Condorcet, paradox of, 89–90
 consistency of, 92–4, 97
 deliberation and, 83, 96–101, 104–5
 democratic legitimacy and, 89
 discursive dilemma and, 90–2
 framing effects and, 108, 110
 legitimacy of, 89
 majority rule and, 94, 105–6
 meta-agreement and, 39, 94–6, 98–106
 optical illusions and, 106–11
 pluralism in, 92–3
 single-peakedness and, 93–4, 96–8, 100–6
 social choice theory on, 11–12
 unidimensionally-aligned judgments and, 93–5
Collier, Paul, 86–7
Commentaries on the Laws of England in Four Books (Blackstone), 2
commodification. *See* investor citizenship
Condorcet, Marquis de, 89
Condorcet Jury Theorem, 89
Condorcet paradox, 89–90
conventions, 74
cosmopolitanism, 144, 159, 161
Cyprus, 57

DACA. *See* Deferred Action for Childhood Arrivals
De Schutter, Helder, 37, 86
default rules, 48–51
 choice modes and, 49
 loss aversion and, 48–9, 51–2
 naturalization and, 37–8, 47–8, 137–8
 nudging and, 49
 opting out and, 48–9
 stickiness of, 48–9
 Sunstein on, 48–9
Deferred Action for Childhood Arrivals (DACA), 27
degrees of citizenship. *See* unbundling citizenship rights

Index

deliberation. *See also* voting
  bounded, 100
  citizenship and, 97–9
  collective decision-making and, 83, 96–101, 104–5
  conflicting groups of, 100–1, 104–5
  immigration and, 98
deliberative theorists, 96
democracy
  birthright dual citizenship conflicting with, 33
  citizenship institution and, 23
  immigrant political rights under, 40
  immigration and, 39
  multiple citizenship and, 8, 46, 83
democratic legitimacy, 89
demos. *See* boundary problem; collective decision-making; political rights; voting
denaturalization, denationalization, 38, 168
  conditioned naturalization compared with, 38
  partial, 132–3
denizenship, 4–5, 158
diplomatic protection, 176–7
discursive dilemma, 90–2
distributive justice, citizenship and
  global, 12
  jus sanguinis and, 29–30
  parental partiality and, 30
Dominica, Commonwealth of, 57
duration
  reciprocity and, 62
  rights and, 62

economic rights, separate allocation of. *See* unbundling citizenship rights
egalitarianism. *See also* luck egalitarianism
  of citizenship, 71
  global, 83, 176
  left, 135–6, 138
1812, war of, 2
Elster, Jon, 96
England, 58–9, 61
equality. *See also* global equality
  citizenship renunciation requirement and, 41–2
  domestic, naturalization and, 33–4, 66–7
  of gender, 3
European Arrest Warrant, 116
European Convention on Nationality (1997), 3
ex lege loss of citizenship, 37
exiles, 167–8

expatriation, voluntary. *See also* citizenship renunciation
  recognition of, 2
  right to, 2
Expatriation Act, US (1868), 2

Falk, Richard, 144
Fenian Brotherhood, 2
feudalism
  citizenship and, 23, 30, 79–80
  jus sanguinis and, 79
  jus soli and, 24
Fishkin, James S., 96–7
framing effects. *See* collective decision-making
France, 52–3, 60–1, 126–7
Frazer, Michael, 118–19
freedom of association, 43
French Revolution, 55

Germany, 19
  dual citizenship policy of, 42, 128
  2017 parliamentary elections in, 104–5
global citizenship, 7, 52
global egalitarianism. *See* egalitarianism
global equality, 22
  birthright citizenship conflicting with, 31, 33–4
  birthright citizenship guaranteeing minimal, 22
global inequality, 11, 135–6. *See also* equality; inequality
  multiple citizenship exacerbating, 12–13, 22, 33, 136, 138, 142–7, 161
  objections to, 135–6
  redistributive taxation for, 135–6, 147
  taxation and, 12–13, 136, 138, 148–51
  taxing multiple citizenship and, 134–6
  unbundling citizenship rights and, 175–6
global justice, 11
globalization, 6–7
Goodin, Robert E., 44, 113, 115, 130, 155–6, 169–70
Grotius, Hugo, 44

Hague Convention on Certain Questions Relating to Conflicts of Nationality Laws (1930), 2–3
Heath, Joseph, 135–6
human rights
  of citizenship, 20–2, 72–3, 172
  citizenship guaranteeing, 26
  Universal Declaration of, 20–1, 73

illegal migrants, 125
immigration
  deliberation and, 98
  democracy and, 39–40
  naturalization and, 36–7
  political duties and, 86
  political rights and, 40, 117
impartiality. *See* Frazer, Michael; multiple citizenship, impartiality and; unaffected interests
inclusiveness, 173. *See also* political overinclusiveness
  Bauböck on, 172
  boundary problem and, 113
  legally subjected principle and, 124–6, 129
  unbundling citizenship rights and, 8, 171–2, 174–6
inequality
  birthright citizenship and, 31, 33–4
  jus sanguinis and, 135, 143
  jus soli and, 135
inheritance
  citizenship and rights of, 39
  citizenship as, 30–3
instrumental interests, 123
international law
  extraterritorial enforcement and, 116
  multiple citizenship and, 2–3, 9, 52, 116, 176–7
Interpol, 116
investor citizenship, 11, 55–7, 143
  in Austria, 57, 127
  character and, 69–70
  commodification and, 55–6, 63–5, 72–7, 79–80
  corruption and, 57–8, 75–7
  in Cyprus, 57
  economic benefits of, 56–8
  fairness and, 66–8
  honorary citizenship and, 127
  in Malta, 57
  in Montenegro, 57
  multiple citizenship and, 81, 137
  political consequences of, 62–4, 80
  public scrutiny of, 57
  reciprocity and, 62–5
  sale of honours and, 11, 56, 58–65, 68–72, 75–7, 79–80
  selling political rights and, 77–9, 81
  signalling and, 68–72
  in St. Kitts and Nevis, Commonwealth of Dominica, 57

statelessness and, 73
unbundling citizenship rights and, 80–1, 171–2
voting rights and, 78
Iran. *See* US-Iran claims tribunal

Jacobsson, Kerstin, 154
Jastrow, Joseph, 106–7
jurisdiction shopping, 9
jurisdictional conflict, 9
  military service and, 9, 39
  persistence of, 39
jus domicili (urban citizenship), 17
jus sanguinis, 17, 28. *See also* birthright citizenship
  adoption of, 17
  boundary problem and, 112–13
  distributive justice and, 29–30
  efficiency principle and, 20
  feudal privilege and, 79
  identity, right to, and, 31–2
  inequality and, 135, 143
  inheriting citizenship and, 30–3
  jus soli a patre et a matre, 3, 29
  moral justification of, 28–30
  Norway and, 28–9
  parental partiality and, 30
  political relationships and, 32–3
  property and, 30, 32
  reforming, 34–5
  restrictions on, 10
  special relationships and, 29–30
jus soli, 10, 17, 28. *See also* birthright citizenship; *jus sanguinis*
  adoption of, 17
  boundary problem and, 112–13
  Carens on, 25–6
  efficiency principle and, 20, 24–5
  feudal system of, 24
  inequality and, 135
  proximity and, 25
  restrictions on, 18
  as self-fulfilling prophecy, 25–7
  state territory, birth on, and, 23–4

Kahneman, Daniel, 110
Kant, Immanuel, 75

Latino immigrants, in US, 88
League of Nations, 2–3
left egalitarianism. *See* egalitarianism
legally subjected principle, 124
  boundary problem and, 12, 83, 113–14, 116–17

Index

inclusiveness and, 124–6, 129
multiple citizenship and, 124–6, 129
non-citizen residents and, 124–5
renunciation requirement and, 125–6
unbundling citizenship rights and, 131–2, 167–9, 174
List, Christian, 93–4, 96–7
Locke, John, 44
López-Guerra, Claudio, 124, 132
loss aversion bias, 46–9, 51–2
loss of citizenship. *See* citizenship, loss of; denaturalization, denationalization; *ex lege* loss of citizenship
Louis XIV, 71
luck egalitarianism, 28, 135–6
  multiple citizenship via birthright, and, 136–7
  multiple citizenship via naturalization and, 137–8
Luskin, Robert C., 96–7

Machiavelli, Niccolò, 63
Malta, 57
Mansfield (lord), 139
Martin, David A., 7, 53
Marx, Karl, 64
McLean, Ian, 96–7
merit
  modern citizenship and, 61–2
  noble conception of, 60–1
meta-agreement (meta-consensus). *See* collective decision-making
military service, 3, 9, 39, 77
Mill, John Stuart, 85, 93, 98
Miller, David, 161
Molière, 69
mono-nationality
  Blackstone on, 2, 139
  perpetual allegiance doctrine and, 2, 139
  revised default rule and, 51
Montenegro, 57
Morton, Jennifer, 105
multiple citizenship, 5–6, 159–60, 162. *See also* birthright citizenship; investor citizenship; *jus sanguinis*; *jus soli*; naturalization
  acquisition of, grounds for, 10, 15
  adaptive preferences and, 46–7
  additional conditionality for, 28
  affected interests and, 119–24, 129
  Australian-Norwegian case of, 18–19, 23, 25, 28–9
  ban on, 3
  boundaries reinforced by, 160
  boundary problem and, 112–13, 116, 129–30, 163
  cognitive dissonance of, 109
  collective rationality undermined by, 99–106, 110–11
  consistency in granting, 41–2
  cosmopolitanism and, 161
  default, 11, 37–8, 47–54, 137–8
  democracy and, 8, 46, 83
  diplomatic protection and, 176–7
  estimates of, 1
  gender equality and, 3
  German policy on, 42, 128
  global inequality exacerbated by, 12–13, 22, 33, 136, 138, 142–7, 161
  human rights and (*See* human rights)
  impartiality and, 117–19, 126–30
  increasing, 1–2
  international law and, 2–3, 9, 52, 116, 176–7
  investor citizenship and, 81, 137
  left egalitarianism and, 138
  legal history of, 2–3
  legal theorists on, 7–8
  legally subjected principle and, 124–6, 129
  limitation of birthright, 18–22, 27–8, 33, 35
  luck egalitarianism and, 136–8
  meta-agreement disrupted by, 99–106
  military service and, 3
  moral justification of, 15, 18–19, 22–3, 35
  naturalization and default, 11, 37–8, 47–54, 137–8
  Norway granting, 28
  optical illusions and, 106–11
  political participation and, 8–9, 87–8
  political rights and, 39, 87, 112, 169–70
  poorest countries not recognizing, 144
  postnationalism and, 6–8, 136, 158–9
  as privilege, 22
  real-existing, 15
  right of return and, 28
  second best and, 161–2
  spillovers and, 104–5, 128
  tax on, 12–13, 134–7, 147–53, 162
  unaffected interests and, 119, 126–9
  unbundling citizenship rights, consequences for, 132–3
  voting and, 83, 88, 119–24
  (*See also* boundary problem)

naturalization, 8, 36–7. *See also* citizenship renunciation; denaturalization, denationalization; *ex lege* loss of citizenship; immigration; investor citizenship
   active choice and, 11, 37–8, 43, 47–8, 50–4
   character and, 69–70
   citizenship renunciation requirement and, 37–47
   conditioned, 38
   default dual citizenship and, 11, 37–8, 47–54, 137–8
   default rules and, 37–8, 47–8, 137–8
   domestic equality and, 33–4, 66–7
   expatriation-conditioned, 38
   fast-tracked, 57
   as immigrant duty, 37
   loss aversion bias and, 46–7, 51–2
   luck egalitarianism and, 137–8
   opting out and, 49–50, 53
   political rights and, 40
   receiving states and, 36–8, 45–6
   reciprocity and, 65
   requirements for, 43
   sending states and, 37–8
   state advantages of, 36–7
   state duties and, 36
   state powers and, 44
   structure of choice and, 47–54
Netherlands, 17
Noaksson, Niklas, 154
Norway, 18
   birthright citizenship case of, 18–19, 23, 25, 28–9
   jus sanguinis and, 28–9
   multiple citizenship granted by, 28
nudging, 11, 25, 49

OECD. *See* Organisation for Economic Co-operation and Development
Okun, Arthur M., 73
opting in, 50, 52–3
opting out, 48–50, 53
Organisation for Economic Co-operation and Development (OECD), 153, 155–6
   Committee on Fiscal Affairs of, 153–4
   Council of, 153, 155–6
   Development Assistance Committee of, 155
   Millennium Development Goals of, 155
   Model Tax Convention of, 13, 83, 139–40, 148, 153–7, 163
   officials of, 153–5
overinclusiveness. *See* inclusiveness

Paine, Thomas, 55, 126–7
Parfit, Derek, 135
perpetual allegiance doctrine, 2, 139
pluralism, 92–3
Pogge, Thomas, 134, 153, 163
political inequality. *See* political rights
political overinclusiveness, 4, 8, 113, 171–2
political participation. *See* multiple citizenship
political rights
   allocation of, 4–5, 8, 12, 40–1, 62, 123, 131, 162–4, 167–9, 171, 173–6
   citizenship based on, 33
   of immigrants, democracy and, 40
   multiple citizenship and, 39, 87, 112, 169–70
   naturalization and, 40
   renunciation requirement and, 39
   of residents, 40–1, 117, 132, 163–4
   sale of, 77–9, 81
political rights-sine-citizenship
   boundary problem and, 130–1
   unbundling citizenship rights and, 40–1, 130–2, 164–5, 168–9
political underinclusiveness. *See* inclusiveness
postnationalism, 6
   globalization and, 6–7
   multiple citizenship and, 6–8, 136, 158–9
Priestley, Joseph, 126
psychology of perception, 12
public justification. *See* public reason theories
public reason theories, 91, 95–6

Radin, Margaret Jane, 74
Rawls, John, 31, 33
   on overlapping consensus, 95
   public reason and, 91
   on substantive agreement, 95–6
reciprocity, 65
   investor citizenship and, 62–5
   naturalization and, 65
remittances, 126, 151–3
renunciation. *See* citizenship renunciation
residents
   birthright citizenship and, 27, 35
   legally subjected principle and, 124–5
   political rights of, 40–1, 117, 132, 163–4
   voting rights of, 40, 130, 163–4, 171
rights. *See also* unbundling citizenship rights
   dollars distinguished from, 73
   duration and, 62
   economic (*See* unbundling citizenship rights, investor citizenship and)

Index

as inalienable, relational, 78–9
of inheritance, 39
Riker, William H., 90, 94

sale of citizenship. *See* investor citizenship
sale of honours, 60–1
  corruption and, 59, 75
  investor citizenship and, 11, 56, 58–65, 68–72, 75–7, 79–80
  merit and, 60–1
Schlenker, Andrea, 164
Schmitter, Philippe, 119
Schofield, Philip, 126–7
Schuck, Peter H., 23, 53
Shachar, Ayelet
  birthright levy, 134, 136, 147, 153, 163
  luck egalitarianism and, 28, 135–6
Shinawatra, Thaksin, 57
signalling
  investor citizenship and, 68–72
  membership distribution and, 70–2
Singer, Peter, 24
single-peakedness. *See* collective decision-making
Smith, Roger, 23, 53
social choice theory. *See* collective decision-making
Song, Sarah, 131
spillovers. *See* multiple citizenship, spillovers and
Spiro, Peter J., 7, 38
St. Kitts and Nevis, 57
stakeholder principle, 114
Stanhope, Philip, 68–9
statelessness, 21, 53
  birthright citizenship preventing, 20–1
  birthright dual citizenship restrictions and, 20
  investor citizenship and, 73
states of residence. *See* taxation
states of source. *See* taxation
Strasbourg Convention on the Reduction of Cases of Multiple Nationality and Military Obligations in Cases of Multiple Nationality (1963), 3
subjection to law. *See* legally subjected principle
Sunstein, Cass, 48–9, 95–6

taxation, 139, 145. *See also* international law
  double, 13, 83, 134–5, 138–9
  double, agreements on, 138–40, 142–3, 148–51, 153, 156–7, 162–3
  double, multiple citizens and, 140–6
  global, 134–5, 149, 163
  global inequality and, 12–13, 134–6, 138, 147–51
  interactive effects of, 138–40
  of multiple citizenship, 12–13, 134–7, 147–53, 162
  OECD Model Tax Convention on, 13, 83, 139–40, 148, 153–7, 163
  redistributive, 135–6, 147
  reform proposals for, 13, 83, 147–9, 153–7
Tobin, James, 134
Trachtman, Joel P., 166
tragedy of the commons, 78, 142
transnationalism, 7
Tribe, Laurence H., 78
Trump, Donald, 104–5
Tversky, Amos, 110

UK. *See* United Kingdom
UK Nationality Act (1981), 165
unaffected interests, 118, 129–30
  boundary problem and, 12, 83, 113–14, 117–19
  honorary citizenship and, 126–7
  multiple citizenship and, 119, 126–9
  unbundling citizenship rights and, 131–2
unbundling citizenship rights, 13, 133, 162–4. *See also* boundary problem; human rights; political rights; rights; voting rights
  affected interests and, 131–2, 169
  boundary problem and, 12, 131–3, 163–4, 172
  citizenship renunciation and, 40–1
  citizenship-sine-political rights and, 41, 130–2, 168–9
  Cohen, E., on, 164–5
  complete, 166–7, 170–1, 173–4, 177
  degrees of, 164
  family ties and, 170
  global inequality and, 175–6
  implementation of, 165–77
  inclusiveness and, 8, 171–2, 174–6
  investor citizenship and, 80–1, 171–2
  legally subjected principle and, 131–2, 167–9, 174
  multiple citizenship, consequences for, 132–3
  partial, 13, 133, 166, 174–7
  political overinclusiveness and, 8, 171–2
  political rights-sine-citizenship and, 40–1, 130–2, 164–5, 168–9
  sufficientarian version of, 175
  Trachtman on, 166

unbundling citizenship rights (cont.)
  unaffected interests and, 131–2
  voting rights and, 167–9, 176
underinclusiveness. *See* inclusiveness
unidimensionally-aligned judgments. *See* collective decision-making
United Kingdom (UK), 165, 170–1. *See also* England
United States (US), 2, 9, 88, 177
Universal Declaration of Human Rights, 20–1, 73
urban citizenship. *See jus domicili*
US. *See* United States
US-Iran claims tribunal, 9, 177

voting. *See also* boundary problem; collective decision-making; political rights; unbundling citizenship rights
  double, 127–8
  external, 86–7, 117, 168
  multiple citizenship and, 83, 88
  weighted, 142, 176
voting rights, 59. *See also* boundary problem; collective decision-making; political rights; unbundling citizenship rights
  boundary problem and, 12
  of exiles, 167–8
  investor citizenship and, 78
  in states of residence, 40, 130, 163–4, 171
  unbundling citizenship rights and, 167–9, 176

Walzer, Michael, 74
Weinstock, Daniel M., 169–70
Whelan, Frederick G., 115, 130–1

Ypi, Lea, 37, 86